LOST
BATTLEFIELDS
OF WALES

LOST
BATTLEFIELDS
OF WALES

MARTIN HACKETT

AMBERLEY

First published 2014
This edition 2016

Amberley Publishing
The Hill, Stroud
Gloucestershire, GL5 4EP

www.amberleybooks.com

British Library Cataloguing in Publication Data.
A catalogue record for this book is available from the British Library.

ISBN 978 1 4456 5522 2 (print)
ISBN 978 1 4456 3703 7 (ebook)

Typesetting and Origination by Amberley Publishing.
Printed in Great Britain.

Contents

Foreword

My earliest memory of Wales is as quite a young child; I was probably no more than six or seven years old and I was playing with my four special toy lorries that accompanied me everywhere at that time, under the careful chaperoning of my Nan and Granddad at the small guest-house in Barmouth where they always stayed. The narrow but many floored house clung to a narrow ledge of rock high above the valley floor, which meant that there was a panoramic view out over the Irish Sea. At the rear the ever-present mountains, which march so determinedly down almost to the water's edge, formed a slate-grey wall blocking out almost all of the light. While there, I remember being fascinated by two things, apart from my four metal toy lorries that is! The first of these were the massive jellyfish; being so small these gelatinous blobs, which were as big as upturned soup terrines, seemed to me to be some kind of alien creatures from the world of *Stingray* (my favourite television programme at the time) as they lay on the sandy surface splattered all over the place; now termed a bloom, they were a blooming nuisance to me as I couldn't kick my football about on the beach! The second thing was Harlech castle, which we visited as a treat. I was familiar with castles as I had a toy castle of my own, lovingly scratch-built by my father to accommodate the Airfix 20mm figures. I had never seen anything so enormous as the stone battlements of this fortification; as I knew what a castle was, this was a brilliant one!

Over the next twenty years, I experienced several more holidays at the sea on the west coast of Wales and got to know many of her magnificent castles and isolated hillforts, which dominated the landscape then as many of them still do today, just as they dominated the people who they were built to suppress. In fact, it was the castles that would finally put an end to the resistance of the Welsh people as they struggled to remain independent from English rule. It would take a lot longer for the Normans and their Anglo-French successors to subdue Wales, but eventually, after centuries of conflict, Wales and her people would finally be subdued. Just as the Normans' motte and bailey castles had allowed them to subdue the Saxons, the castles of Edward and his imposed

'English' lords would allow them to rule over the land of rock and water with an iron grip. This English tyranny would at times drive the Welsh to rise in open rebellion, as death on the battlefield for them was better than being next to worthless under English tyranny. These rebellions are just a part of the reasons for the many battlefields of Wales, and we will examine more than a score of these key battles which decided the fate of the Welsh people as we move chronologically through this book.

Rhuddlan Castle in Denbighshire.

Acknowledgements

I am eternally grateful to those people that have accompanied me and helped me interpret the many varied sites I have visited over the years, not least on my recent circular trips across Wales. Alan Hewitt has accompanied me on many expeditions and our friendship extends as far back as our first attempts at wargaming back at KEGS in the early 1970s. Alan's approach as a questioning academic who is always ready to challenge any written source as well as my own interpretations is always welcome and will always be so. Similar comments apply to my good friend Derek Crawford, my companion on many a long journey to a remote landscape, and his help in interpretation is just as challenging as Alan's and his knowledge of the different types of wood is particularly useful when examining old weapons and looking at castle fortifications. Both Alan and Derek have once again accompanied me while researching this book, Alan across most of south and mid Wales and Derek in the north. Thank you both my friends, for all the map reading and battlefield interpretations: we certainly came upon a few mysteries to solve for this work. Derek also helped with the cross referencing while we worked through the *Archaeologia Cambrensis* in the local library.

My thanks to my son in law Ed and my daughter Sabrina, who are now established as photographers in their own right and who now help me with each of my book projects with both advice on photography in general and help with individual shots; they also take responsibility for the close-ups when we have a specialist photo shoot. Imogen, my youngest daughter, is the ancient historian of the family and her knowledge of the way army lists function and her ability with maths make her the perfect foil for checking all my army calculations; also, a big thank you for helping with the Roman research and my personal tour of the Dolaucothi Gold Mines, where she worked as a guide in the summer and autumn of 2013. Imogen also helped when my car decided it had had enough of battlefield visits for a while and had to visit the garage for considerably longer than I expected, so thanks for playing taxi.

My sincere thanks to my dear friends Louise and her daughter Emma, both of whom take a keen interest in history and who gave me tremendous

Sabrina, Ed and Imogen at Pilleth, the site of Owain Glyndŵr's great victory.

Derek on the steep slope of the motte of Oswestry Castle.

Alan studies the OS map that shows Orewin Bridge, ready for the afternoon's detective work.

support as we researched our way around Lake Vyrnwy, working out where the conference of the different rivers might have been. This was followed by further research along the Dee Valley looking for the Alleluia Victory and the settlements connected with Owain Glyndŵr. Louise's sister and brother-in-law, Anne and Sam Armstrong, were also able to help with this book as their house backs into the side of a small motte, a mound high up on the hills along the valley from Llangollen. It is recorded to be a former watchtower of Owain Glyndŵr's and given its position it is easy to see why. However, it is likely to have been a watchtower since the very earliest of times as no commander would overlook such a vantage point as it overlooks the stunning upper Dee Valley, giving general advance warning of any approach. While travelling the length and breadth of Wales, I have been given many small but invaluable snippets of local information which have allowed me to drive up the correct lane, spot the relevant monument, or find a convenient place to park in order to get the best photograph of a site. As regards the latter, I owe a big thank you to Janet Lewis and her father, who allowed me to take a vital photograph from their back garden, the only way I could capture the picture I required of a bridge spanning the River Cothi near Carmarthen.

I was fortunate to be able to help in a small way with the establishment of the 1403 Visitor Centre at Shrewsbury and I am most grateful that they have allowed me to use photographs of some of their exhibits from their excellent exhibition, so my thanks to Joyce and Chris for their permission. The 1403 Visitor Centre exemplifies what a great visitor centre should be. There is a museum which is free to enter, an excellent licensed café and a shop selling a huge selection of local produce as well as books and souvenirs related to the battle. There are plenty of parking spaces and marked walks across the battlefield and down to the Church of St Mary Magdalene, built by Henry IV to commemorate his victory over Hotspur. Serendipity, that beloved luck of life, once more came to my aid just two weeks ago. I was struggling to find some images to compare chain mail and plate mail as armour, my own photographs being a little old now; but fate kicked in and I was fortunate enough to come across the Ty Mawr medieval hall, not far from Welshpool, Powys. There, Gary Ball, who is the project manager for History Matters, was able to supply me with two images which appear in the book, clearly showing the difference between the two types of armour. History Matters is a group which aims to encourage and promote a greater understanding of history, from the age of the timber and earth castle and 'llys', which was a native Welsh hall or palace, right through to the beginning of the Tudor dynasty and beyond. History Matters encourages and promotes an appreciation and understanding of heritage through the practice of traditional agricultural skills and the buildings that were lived in as well as using early forms of crafts, arts and technology so that this knowledge can be preserved.

My sincere thanks to Gary and the society; more information can be found at www.historymattersonline.com.

A big thank you to all the team at Amberley Publishing, who ensure that all those vital elements of a modern book are met to provide the reader with a complete and 'typo' free guide to not just Welsh but also British military history, so my sincere thanks to Louis, Emily, Sarah, Eleri and Campbell. The maps have been drawn by User Design. Finally, a big thank you to my mum, who in her own career (which was now long before the advent of a PC or laptop) was an accomplished RSA3 shorthand typist; I only wish I was that quick across the keys! When the chips are down and the deadline looms, I am grateful for the hot meals and drinks provided at regular intervals to keep me going, while every available flat surface in the house seems to have a detailed map of a different part of Wales spread out upon it with a rainbow of sticky notelets attached.

If there is anyone else who I have forgotten, I sincerely apologise and an extra big thank you to you.

Martin Hackett 2014

CHAPTER 1

Lost Battlefields

I expect that some people will take issue with the word 'lost' being used in the title of this book on Welsh battlefields, maintaining that some of the battles in this work are well known to military enthusiasts, some having display boards and perhaps even a small exhibition. For a variety of reasons, the vast majority of the battlefields included in this book are lost, and lost because one of the following reasons applies to the battlesite. Firstly, the vast majority of people in Wales, and certainly in the rest of the United Kingdom, do not know anything about Welsh battles. Secondly, even for those battlesites that are well known in terms of their history, for the most part no-one really knows where the battlesites are. Finally, very few of the Welsh battlesites have the relevant direction signs, parking facilities and information boards to warrant those sites being visited.

To complete the time-line of Welsh history, the well-known battlesites of Pilleth and Fishguard have been included, yet clearly even these battles are not known to the vast majority of people outside of their own immediate vicinity. So when settling on the title and realising that it would be questioned, I decided to conduct my own unofficial survey while I travelled around Wales researching and photographing the battlesites which follow. I have deliberately asked those people I have seen in the street, in inns, in hotels, those sitting by the sea or walking in the mountains and even some who have been sitting and fishing on a battlesite the same question: 'Do you know anything about the battle which was supposed to have been fought here?' I have spoken with everyone who has presented me with an opportunity to do so, walkers, joggers, college students, retired people and office workers, and the overwhelming majority have never heard of any of the battles in their area and very, very few people have heard of sites like Pilleth or Montgomery, arguably two of the most important battles in Wales in the last 1,000 years, both of which had an effect far beyond the borders of Wales.

Having just completed a book on the Jacobite Rebellions called *Raise the Clans*, it is interesting to note the different approaches taken by the two respective governments and their associated historical bodies to the way that they promote the history of their country and the battles that were the stepping stones along their historical journey. Travelling in Scotland, the first thing one will notice is the abundant signage, indicating to the traveller where a particular battlesite is located and the distance to it. On arrival at the nearest location to a battlefield, there are normally some spaces provided to allow you to park your vehicle in safety, with arrows pointing the relevant walkways to take. The vast majority of battlesites have at least one sign-board, often more, telling the visitor briefly what happened and why it was important and this information is often located near an appropriate cairn that had been raised to commemorate the fallen. Some of the most important sites, Bannockburn and Culloden for example, have comprehensive visitor centres which are busy with visitors even on cold winter days.

In Wales it is a very different story: Buttington, near Welshpool, which is one of the most important Dark-Age battlesites in Europe, does not even have a plaque, or sign, to commemorate the battle. Pilleth, one of the greatest of Welsh victories and one which united the Welsh people against the English in 1402, has a small amount of information but many other battlesites have nothing at all. Fishguard is the only place I have visited where information and reference points were clearly signposted around the town, the beach and headland to allow visitors to absorb a complete picture of what happened, the information being complemented by a museum as part of the local library. Elsewhere, there are no inspiring visitor centres, and very little undercover to put before either local people or visitors; surely some history of the Welsh nation should be portrayed, telling the story of how it stood up for itself time and again against invaders. Most sadly of all, with the exception of Fishguard, there is nowhere to take an educational visit to so as to allow children to learn the history of their own country and relate it to the topics of the Romans and Vikings which are covered on the school curriculum. While at the 1403 visitor centre in May 2014, I encountered a school trip which was visiting the Battlefield of Shrewsbury site, yet many of the Welsh battlesites connected with those time periods do not have the facilities to allow such visits to even be considered. This is not about the glorification of war or making a theme park for tourists to hurtle about on 'torture train-rides' and 'rebellion roller-coasters'. This is about preservation, which can be funded, hopefully profitably, by explanation and education to both schools and the general public. Many of the castles of Wales are well served with excellent shops and museums, but with the exception of Fishguard, no battlesite has any such facility. The sites of Bosworth and Culloden are packed with visitors from all over the world who go to see the milestones in the history of Britain and the cafés and shops at these sites provide income to support the maintenance and ongoing archaeological investigation of the site and its facilities.

It is fitting that the first battle to be examined in this book on 'lost' Welsh battles is Cefn Carnedd, where Caratacus, the great Celtic chieftain, fought, as far as we know, his one and only full-scale engagement against the might of a Roman army. This site typifies the challenges that the battlefield investigator encounters. This was a large battle, possibly the largest ever fought in Wales, but the source information is brief and the archaeological evidence scant. Even though I am confident to within a few miles as to where the battle was fought, exactly which part of the hills was defended or which crossing of the river was forced remains unknown. Cefn Carnedd has more site candidates than any other battle, and exemplifies the theme of alternative sites that is repeated throughout the battlefield investigations I have undertaken, as the reader will see as we work through this military history of Wales. Fortunately there are some Welsh battlesites where the location can be pinned down to somewhere within a square mile; Buttington, Pilleth, Maes Gwenllian and Monmouth are all examples. Equally, there is the Alleluia Victory and Coleshill, where the site could be in a number of different valleys. The information that follows clearly indicates the type of issues that the battlefield historian encounters, because for the majority of battles there are possible sites, plausible sites, even totally improbable sites, and places that have their own champions, who support their respective theory as to why they believe the battle was fought at their certain location. This difficulty not only relates to Welsh battlefields but extends to many battlesites throughout the world, and where there are few sources then the interpretation and speculation will be all the more extensive. In addition, the older a battle is, the more susceptible the possible sites have been to alteration. Whether such change is due to natural erosion, from the forces of the wind, rain and flooded rivers, or through human intervention, they further cloud the

Lake Vyrnwy covers not only a lost village but a lost battlefield too.

picture and hinder the historian's ground research. The generally accepted site for Coleshill, near Flint, which is marked on the Ordnance Survey map, is actually buried beneath an industrial estate; while the most likely site for the Battle of Vyrnwy is now completely buried beneath a huge lake created by the construction of a reservoir to store and supply water to homes in the city of Liverpool in the north-west of England.

The reasons outlined above are why I consider the majority of battlefields of Wales to be lost and I have only included twenty-four of the most important. There are many more battles mentioned in the various Welsh annals, but each one would require an enormous amount of research without any guarantee of ever finding where some of them were fought. For my part, the battles that I have included cover the length and breadth of modern Wales and cover over 1,700 years of Welsh history, ranging from the Celtic struggles against the Romans to playing a small part in the titanic European struggle that eventually became known under the umbrella title of the Napoleonic Wars.

This lack of information drives one of my aims in producing this work; I am looking to bring some fresh light into some of the most important battles of Welsh history, with photographs current to the time of publication, so that the reader can see for themselves what the battlefield location looks like. Perhaps it will encourage readers to visit, walk, explore and draw their own conclusions on some of these battlesites and compare my own vision of what happened with other scholarly interpretations, all of which should help to bring the fascinating history of Wales to the attention of more people. It would be most rewarding if this work stimulated some local people to visit the battlesites close to them and so understand how their local history relates to the rest of the country they live in and to the wider world. Maybe this could be a catalyst to encourage new care and consideration to be shown to these sites and so allow new life to be breathed into them, with if not an actual visitor centre then some information boards so that the inquisitive visitor can understand what they are seeing from where they are standing and appreciate what took place there.

The detailed research for the battles in the first half of this book is made all the harder by the lack of Welsh archaeological evidence before the twelfth century; there are, for instance, very few remains of any weapons from the early period of Welsh history and, as the Welsh were Christians, they did not normally bury any weapons with their dead, so any discovered burials reveal nothing of military life. We do not even know what these Welsh people wore and can only assume it was a shirt and a woollen plaid (not dissimilar to the Highland Jacobites in the eighteenth century), based on the observations of Gerald of Wales from his tour in 1188. A few spearheads have been found, but these cannot be dated to any particular period, including one close to the site of the Battle of Hyddgen, which we will examine in detail later. Unlike the Picts, there are no depictions of their fighting men on any stone sculptures and the few Welsh manuscripts that survive do not depict fighting men apart from some brief references, until we come to Gerald's history. From Gerald's time several hundred small household items and objects of daily life have been discovered, but of these only six are military; so while we have many different rings, some chess pieces, a few coins, varied musical instruments, even locks and keys, we have just one spearhead and a couple of arrowheads and crossbow bolts. There is no doubt that a flourishing Welsh culture and a successful armed force existed, but there are huge gaps in its history that still remain to be filled. Despite the number of battlesites, particularly for medieval battles (1066–1421), to the author's knowledge, none have yet had any kind of modern archaeological survey done; there is still so much of Welsh history to be uncovered.

Battles and Skirmishes

The largest battle ever fought in Wales would have been very early in the history of the country and long before the name of Wales was born. This was an attempt by the Romans to subdue the Welsh tribes and their inspirational leader Caradoc (Caradog, or Caratacus). When the two distinct cultures, Celtic and Roman, clashed at Cefn Carnedd in 51 AD there were at least 40,000 men on the battlefield and maybe many more. We will examine this battle in detail in the next chapter, but it is important to show that this size of battle was the exception. When Cefn Carnedd is compared with Montgomery in 1644, one of the most important battles of the English Civil war, there were only around 9,000 men present. When we look at Buttington and other Dark Age battles, the numbers involved were even smaller, only perhaps 500 to 1,000 per side, so in that time a battle involving armies of 1,000 men a side would be a significant one. For the most part, the armies that fought in all of these Welsh battles were small in terms of the numbers of men involved, and certainly when compared to the enormous numbers of men that took part in the battles across Europe and the Middle East in comparative time periods. The importance, however, comes not from the size of the armies involved, but from the lasting effect that the battle had in the wider political sphere of the time, and, as the reader will observe, the conflicts within the borders of Wales were made all the more complicated as at times Welsh people from one princedom were fighting against their neighbours. When they were not disputing who should be Prince of Wales, they were fighting as mercenaries for the French, English and Scottish armies, sometimes appearing on both sides within a battle as at Agincourt in 1415.

Battlesites

If the towns and villages have changed dramatically with expansion over the last few hundred years, then it is refreshing that the majority of Welsh battlesites have not changed and would still be recognisable if the soldiers were to return to re-fight the battle today. Most routes have had their drovers' tracks or Roman roads replaced by modern tarmac roads or railway lines, but others have continued being tilled for agriculture or left for animals to graze, so that while the vegetation may have changed, much of the actual shape of the land remains unchanged. Naturally, with the passing of time some battlesites, notably those close to early settlements or castles, have been built upon as the town or village has expanded and there is now very little chance of ever doing an accurate archaeological excavation. The natural features that have seen the biggest changes are the rivers. The dams of the Elan Valley and the enormous Clywedog and Vyrnwy dams have resulted in the regulation of the flows for the River Severn and Vyrnwy respectively. This, coupled with advances in drainage within the valley bottoms, has further reduced the width of these great rivers and shepherded them into more regular but deeper courses. Pre drainage, these rivers would have covered much of a valley floor, if not in flowing water then in pools and marshy ground alongside the main flow of the river. Drainage has allowed the water to be collected in a more consistent channel and so the flow of the river concentrates at the deepest point of the valley. This provides the farmer with dry riverside pasture for most of the year, except in times of flood. In most cases this means that in the past the river, although much wider, was much easier to cross if a way through the reed beds and across the marshes could be traced; this is because the water was not so concentrated and therefore not so deep. To an advancing army, the river crossing was always the most dangerous part of a day's march, a time when they were at their most vulnerable to a surprise attack. With their hands needed to try and keep both themselves and their equipment dry and upright while wading through the water, it was extremely difficult to use weapons or to defend themselves and keep their footing if under attack.

Battlefield Walks

When one walks upon a battlefield for the first time, one feels a range of emotions: sadness, sometimes an air of foreboding, a sort of oppressiveness that seems to push down upon you. Conversely, there is sometimes an air of lightness and euphoria; if so, then I always question if I am actually standing where people were slain and I revisit my notes and references just to be sure. I have found some of the battlesites in Wales to be particularly atmospheric, others quite airy and light, and clearly (as I am neither agoraphobic nor claustrophobic) it is the narrowness of the valleys and the height of the hills that can rise steeply on either side of you which create the heavy atmosphere. As we shall see, the style of fighting that the Welsh armies employed means that time and again they looked to fight the invading force on similar terrain: the Alleluia Victory and the battle of Crogen were fought over an almost identical landscape, perhaps in the same valley.

For almost forty years now I have walked and studied military sites, castles, hillforts, bays and battlefields; around half of those places, I have visited alone, though that has not always been through choice but through current circumstances. I would rather have company for many reasons and so I am immensely grateful to both my family and my many friends who have accompanied me at times on my many expeditions over the last thirty-nine years of my research. It is comforting to have someone with you, not only because you can discuss the evidence as to where a battle might have been fought, but because you can share your feelings and see if those people with you are similarly affected. The ability to refer to and to debate what is documented on a battle while standing on the actual location allows a stimulated discussion to develop as to where the battle would have been fought. This is especially important if trying to work out if an army could see the other army from a certain point: the ability to have two people stand in the relevant locations and converse through the wonders of the mobile telephone as to what each can see is a tremendous benefit. This can lead to an idea as to whether a battle was fought east–west or north–south; such simple contrasts can make a huge difference to the interpretation of a battle. For any of you that may have read any of my previous works, for which I thank you, you will know that I always start my battlefield analysis from what knowledge we have of where the armies ended up after the battle. Then, using that premise, while standing upon the different parts of the battlefield, one can work out from the topography how the armies were most likely to have deployed, and from that one can then work out how the course of the battle itself would have developed and unfolded, until eventually one reaches the point where the troops left the field, thus completing the circle of interpretation. At each critical point within the battle, the movements of the troops is rechecked to make sure they are still logical. This may read as rather a lot of guesswork, and to a certain extent it is, but it is based upon the logical interpretation of known military troops, their weapons, style of fighting, normal dispositions and tactics; this is not simply obscure speculation and such work can only be done when on site. The choice of where to fight is dependent upon the type of troops that are fighting and so, armed with knowledge of the composition of an army for a given period, one can surmise as to the terrain that a general would have picked for his troops. So no matter whether one is examining a battle from the Ancient period, the Dark Ages, Medieval times or from more recent wars (a time when the horse and the musket combined to be the twin masters of the battlefield), there are certain elements that are fundamental to all military conflict, and these elements are common to all pre-mechanised warfare. One must understand that for the most part (even though, of course, there are exceptions which prove the rule) the military commanders of their time knew the capabilities of their troops, they knew the type of terrain that their men would perform best upon and they knew where not to deploy so as to put their army at risk of defeat. These ancient and medieval generals were not stupid; the ones that were so inept did not last very long.

This practical knowledge can be brought into play when examining potential battlesites, always making allowances in case the terrain may have been altered by mining, quarrying, erosion or construction. Generals would always look to find terrain where the infantry (for almost without exception it was the infantry that made up the majority of the troops within an army) could deploy with room to fight, but with their flanks and rear protected. Cavalry do not deploy on the steep sides of hills or behind deep rivers that they cannot ford at need; this is because horsemen need open and fairly flat terrain, so as to be able to move smoothly and charge at need into their enemy. Most cavalry are used to support the infantry, to exploit a weakness in the enemy's lines to turn an enemy flank, or to get behind the enemy's lines to attack from the rear. If they achieve this latter manoeuvre the cavalry can turn a retreat into a rout and ensure a victory for their general. Heavy cavalry are effective in a charge against infantry, but only if those infantry are lightly armed and armoured and in a loose formation. An infantry unit formed with long spears and shields tightly packed together would not be threatened by a heavy cavalry charge; the horsemen would be kept away by the hedgehog-like spines of the infantry unit. Light infantry need rough and broken terrain to operate in as they try to get close enough to harass their enemy without getting into a direct fire-fight or melee where they would come off worse. Instead, they are looking to weaken the enemy so as to allow their army's heavier troops to exploit the falling numbers of their enemy with a direct charge. Light troops would therefore use their missile weapons to snipe at their opponents and then withdraw. When examining Welsh battles, one looks for this kind of rough, broken terrain, steep hills and narrow valleys, rocky outcrops, misty marshes and patches of natural woodland, all of which would be uncomfortable terrain for heavily armoured men marching into hostile territory but was perfect for a Welsh army to ambush its unsuspecting enemy from. We will examine these opposing armies that fought in this unforgiving terrain and look at the weapons and the tactics they employed.

General Touring Information

The author has personally visited and photographed each battlesite listed within this book, many of them within the last six months, so the information read and the photographs you see should be as accurate and as up to date as possible; all those photographs without a specific credit were taken by the author. The majority of the photographs were taken during the winter months, so be prepared for some fields to look different if they are rich with abundant crops where once bare soil lay; similarly with hedges and trees, their natural spring and summer growth may now obscure some landmarks that were clearly visible before. Also the land use, infrastructure, road systems and rights of way can all change, sometimes at very short notice. If you encounter difficulties in following any tour then we would very much like to hear about it, so that we can incorporate changes in future additions; your comments should be sent to the publisher at the address provided at the front of this book. To derive maximum value and enjoyment from your exploration of these battlesites, we would suggest that you equip yourself with the following items:

- Appropriate maps: a general road map to navigate to the appropriate location and, if more detail is required, either the Landranger or Explorer series of maps from the Ordnance Survey, which are available from all good book sellers in most high streets of the UK.
- Lightweight waterproof clothing and robust footwear are essential, especially if one leaves the footpaths of built-up areas.
- A compass is always a useful tool, and it allows the reader to verify the locations of troops and their movements upon the battlefield. This is particularly important if visiting sites high up in the hills such as Hyddgen or Mount Badon. The countryside is very rough if you step off a recognised track and the rapid descent of a hill-fog can rapidly disorientate someone.
- A camera and spare films. The author always carries a cheap disposable camera as emergency cover for his more expensive equipment and they have saved the day on more than one occasion.
- A notebook to record details of any photograph taken and to jot down any changes that have occurred with the information about which you feel it would be useful to notify the publishers.
- Food, drink and fuel. Although in Britain you are in theory never far from a retail outlet, there are roads in Wales and Scotland where even in the twenty-first century passing another car can be a rarity, especially in winter. It is therefore sensible to always ensure that the fuel tank is full, and that you have drinking water and some light refreshments, particularly if you are planning to do some full-length walks or circular tours.
- Binoculars. An excellent aid, especially when verifying the location and interpreting how much each army could have seen of the other when they were deploying for battle.

The author has visited all of the sites by vehicle as very few of them are accessible by rail; some, like Hyddgen, require a planned walk in addition to the initial drive, while others, like Vyrnwy, can be enjoyed without even leaving a vehicle. Within each chapter, details are given as appropriate on other sites that relate to the campaign, but this is not a definitive list of places or attractions and, as the reader will appreciate, whole brochures are available on some towns and cities and it would be impossible to include every attraction or indeed cater for every taste. The author would advise anyone planning to visit any of these sites to contact the local tourist office as they can provide news of any special events and are generally happy to post out information, including maps and places with accommodation. The author has contacted or visited over twenty tourist offices in the last year and has received excellent service from all of them. For those disabled visitors wishing to visit a battlesite who may not be able to walk far and perhaps require wheelchair access, please take note of the routes and location points detailed and while it may not be possible to explore a complete site due to the nature of the terrain, many of the salient viewpoints mentioned here can be seen from a layby or convenient access track and some of the sites are clearly visible without having to leave a vehicle.

Some Dos and Don'ts

Touring a battlefield can be an interesting, a rewarding and sometimes a most emotional experience, especially if you have studied the battle beforehand or are related to people that were involved in it. However, it is clear from my tours that although there are some locals familiar with the battle having been fought within their vicinity, there will also be people who are totally unaware that there was any kind of military action in their area, so be patient if you are quizzed and simply explain the reason for your interest in their domain. Few sites have routes clearly marked that are either on the public highway, along public footpaths and bridleways or across other recognised footpaths; but, a long-distance footpath may cross a battlesite. Therefore, when walking please keep to these designated rights of way, but if you do stray and you are asked to leave the land you are on then please do so immediately by the quickest and safest way possible. Particularly in Wales, keep to the designated paths: there are bogs and ditches that lie unseen, covered by layers of moss and heather, which can cause injury if one is unlucky enough to step down into one. Always be aware, especially in rural areas, of not blocking gates or drives to farms when choosing a place to park. If you take a dog with you, and Rosie in the past accompanied the author on all of his walks without any problem, remember that there are times when the dog must be on the lead both in the town and the country; this is both for the dog's safety and that of wildlife and farm animals. If there is no clear parking place, choose an open stretch of road where vehicles coming from both directions can clearly see your position. If you have to use a gate to continue your walk then please ensure that the gate is closed behind you before you move on. Do not feed animals that you find on the walks: it is dangerous to the animal and potentially dangerous to the person providing the food, as these are wild animals not domesticated pets. The owner of one estate upon which a Jacobite battlesite encroaches was fortunate enough to see and stop a woman feeding crisps to one of her Highland cows; the woman was pleased that the cow appreciated the crisps sufficiently to nuzzle the 24-inch pointed horns up the side of her head and face, unaware that a sudden move could have led to her being gored or blinded. Many country estates have shoots or equestrian events and although the author is unaware of any battlesites in this book being near such an estate, as stated above, things change. Therefore, if you hear gunshots, or there are signs indicating that there is a shoot or a cross-country event in progress, make sure that you are on the correct route and if unsure try and verify with the local farmer or landowner where the event is taking place and what walks will be affected.

A word of caution in relation to battlefields in general, but particularly to those found in the more remote parts of Scotland and, in the case of this book, Wales: take care and wear appropriate clothing and footwear when exploring these sites. Some of these battles were fought over very rough terrain, with bogs, streams, waterfalls, water-cut ravines and hidden drops in what looks like a flat moor or hillside. If travelling alone it is worth advising someone where you are going and when you are likely to be back. Mobile phone signals are not strong in all places and should the unthinkable happen and the walker incur an injury or a sudden illness then at least there will be someone with knowledge of where you were intending to be.

Finally, one sometimes reads in the press about someone finding a small artefact, a ring, a coin or perhaps a cannon ball. If you find any artefacts upon the battlesite, if possible leave them where they are and mark their location with a stone or stick and then photograph a landmark in relation to the object so that the post can be found; use a Global Satellite Positioning instrument if you have one. Then contact the landowner and the local police, who will be able to put you in touch with the relevant archaeological department. If it is likely that the artefact could be damaged or taken by someone else then, before removing it, mark it in some way and record its location as above, and then report the matter to the local landowner; if this cannot be determined then inform the local police, who will take all the necessary details. As regards stone structures such as castles, walls and buildings or memorials and cairns that have been placed there to remember the dead, these should not be damaged or marked in any way, and none of the items placed upon these monuments should be removed. If you wish then please place your own flowers at the site, as your own mark of remembrance. I find that I when I visit a site myself it is rare if a recent floral tribute has not been left.

Wales

When within the text reference is made to 'Wales', it will refer to those lands that exist today within the borders of the modern country. The land that we now know as Wales only came into being in the middle of the Dark Ages, when people occupying that land were left isolated to the west of the boundary between them and Saxon England known as Offa's Dyke. The land area within that ditch and dyke border has not changed greatly since that time and it is the military campaigns within the land of Wales, west of that great border rampart, and which affected the peoples within that land that we will be examining in this book.

Chronology of the Battles Covered in Detail in This Book

All of the battles that are described in detail within this book were fought within the last 2,000 years and therefore after the acknowledged birth of Christ, which has been taken as the year zero. They are documented without the need of any time period reference and they can all be taken as being Anno Domini (AD) or Common Era (CE). Occasionally within the text there will be need to refer to events which happened before the birth of Christ and these will be referred to as BC (or Before Common Era, BCE).

Ref	Year	Battle
A	51	Cefn Carnedd, Llandinam, Powys
B	60	Menai Straits, Gwynedd
C	429	Alleluia Victory, Denbighshire
D	516	Mount Badon, Mid-Glamorgan
E	537	Camlann, Gwynedd
F	893	Buttington, Powys
G	1022	Abergwyli, Carmarthenshire
H	1039	Rhyd-Y-Groes, Powys
I	1098	Priestholm (Anglesey Sound), Isle of Anglesey
J	1116	Aberystwyth, Ceredigion
K	1136	Maes Gwenllian, Carmarthenshire
L	1136	Crug Maer, Ceredigion
M	1157	Ewloe (Coleshill), Flintshire
N	1165	Crogen, County Borough of Wrexham
O	1231	Abermule, Powys
P	1233	Monmouth, Gwent
Q	1257	Cymerau (Coed Llathen), Carmarthenshire
R	1282	Irfon Bride (Orwein Bridge), Powys

Lost battlefields of
Wales site locations

S	1295	Maes Moydog, Powys
T	1400	Vyrnwy, Powys
U	1401	Hyddgen, Ceredigion
V	1402	Pilleth, Powys
W	1644	Montgomery, Powys
X	1797	Fishguard, Pembrokeshire

CHAPTER 2

Wales – An Historical Background

Ancient Times and the Welsh People

In the days before basic industry and technology, all indigenous peoples were shaped by the land they lived upon so that the two were intertwined, the human 'animal' in tune with 'Mother' nature. In the recent past, and to give the reader an indication of this bond, the cultures of the native North American Indian tribes and the Aborigine people of Australia are prime examples of where the survival of the humans and the development of their culture and beliefs go hand in hand, first simply existing long enough to produce the next generation and then thriving in an extremely hostile environment, using only what nature provided within that environment. So it was with the original people of Wales, who first used the natural resources of wood, water and stone to construct their defences based upon the densely wooded valleys which provided hunting grounds for meat and, where tamed, a secure shelter. Then, as the people discovered metal deposits in the streams that emanated from the mountains, they were eventually able to extract the metals, which they could then trade for the commodities that they did not have immediately to hand.

Archaeological remains have been found that show that early humanoids, the Neanderthals, lived in Wales over 200,000 years ago. The oldest human skeleton to be found in Wales is that of man whose bones were painted in red ochre, incorrectly named the Red Lady of Paviland (following 'her' discovery in 1823 in the Paviland Caves on the Gower Peninsula), considered to be the oldest known ceremonial burial in Western Europe to date. Sometime between 12,000 and 10,000 years ago, the last Ice Age began to retreat and in doing so carved and shaped the mountains that form the central spine of Wales today and the river arteries that cut through the mountains. The water escaping from the ice only strove to better its mother's scraping and cut deeper channels while the richly laden waters deposited great fertile estuaries between the high mountains, perfect for wildlife, for fish and for human occupation. Little wonder then that as the ice retreated north, hunter-gatherers moved in to occupy the empty and fertile lands along the coastline, where today remains of their megalithic tombs span the country from Anglesey in the north to Pentre Ifan in Pembrokeshire. These humans gathered in small settlements, civilisation gradually developed and the Stone Age slowly evolved into the metal ages, the first of which were the three distinct Bronze Ages, which, when time-lined together, ran from 2,500 until 700 BCE. The mountains of Wales bore some very rich fruits for its small population: copper, gold, lead and silver; the only key metal of ancient times that was not present in Wales was tin, but as this was found in nearby Cornwall it could be obtained through trade with other tribes across what we now call the Severn Estuary.

Then, sometime around 1,000 BCE, a new people arrived in Britain, if the legends and early chroniclers are to be believed, and the knowledge of those metals may well have been the lure that bought them here. There is, of course, no surety as to which wandering peoples settled these green and fertile lands in those centuries before the Celts and Romans. According to legend, documented by Nennius in his *Historia Brittonum*, Britain derives its name from one 'Brutus.' who was a direct descendent of Aeneas, who had fled from the ruins of Troy after the destruction of the city by the Greeks. Aeneas and his army of now homeless Trojans had been invited to settle in Latium by Latinus before, in time, becoming the king of the Latin lands. Latium was a rich, flat and fertile land that extended around the Tiber basin and south to the Pontine Marshes, an area within which Rome would eventually become the dominant city. It may well be that the name Latinus simply refers to the title of the ruler for the Latin people, but it was the Greek cities that ruled much of the coastal fringes of modern day Italy and Sicily at this time so it would not be unreasonable to invite a like-minded people to settle if those people were warriors and could be used for defence of the land; Rome would pursue a similar policy within its empire. Brutus was either the grandson or great-grandson of Aeneas and would, after a series of adventures, eventually arrive and establish a settlement with his followers in the islands of Brutus, or British Isles. This legend of Nennius appears to be either based upon, or perhaps entwined with, a seventh-century work by the Spanish chronicler Isidore of Seville, entitled *Etymologiae*, in which it was speculated that Britain was named after the Roman general Decimus Junius Brutus Callaicus, who pacified Spain in 138 BC by defeating the Celts, but there is no evidence that this Roman Brutus ever came to Britain. However, it is possible that he forced Celtic peoples to flee the Iberian Peninsula, who then headed north to escape the advancing Romans. But at that time the British Isles were already populated with Celts who had arrived there after crossing Gaul, so this would not have been an invasion or have led to a renaming of the land. It cannot have been easy for any chroniclers to try and piece together a history of Britain when they were compiling information from a series of oral histories carried from generation to generation by learning alone and many hundreds of years after the events. The name of Brutus is a common one and occurs repeatedly in the Roman hierarchy, so little wonder there is confusion and misinterpretation. It is also very possible that neither of these men may have had any part in the naming of Britain.

To return to the earlier theory, it is not impossible that fleeing Trojans heading west sometime around 1,200 BCE would take stepping stones across the Mediterranean Sea until they found a new country in which they could properly settle. The fall of Troy, which some archaeologists have put at 1184 BCE, was right in the middle of the Bronze Age and bronze relies upon two metals, copper and tin, both of which were mined in Britain. Herodotus, around 430 BCE, writes in his work *The Histories* of the Cassiterides, which translates as the Tin Islands, and where they were located. Britain had been an important source of tin and copper for the Greeks and the rest of the Eastern Mediterranean for many centuries and it is not impossible that the Trojans knew of the wealth in those far-flung islands that even to the Romans were seen as at the edge of the world. Michael Wood has shown in his 'In Search of' series that tales such as Jason and the Golden Fleece were not simply fables but a series of coded, verbal instructions, which, when learned and if followed, would prove to be directions to a given location. So by learning a fable a merchant, or a sea captain, would be able to find his way without the need to draw a map or write things down on parchments which other people might then steal, allowing them to become a rival to a potential source of wealth. This may seem an incredibly far-fetched claim, but no stranger than the fact that Joseph of Arimathea himself travelled to Britain when Christ was a child to trade for tin and that the Christian Messiah may have indeed accompanied him on his travels to this 'sceptred Isle'. There is very strong evidence that Christianity arose here before the Romans came under Claudius's direction and the Welsh people were so devout as to sit down to meals in three so as to represent the Holy Trinity.

One other metal was also present in some measure in Wales, iron ore, which led around 700 BCE to the commencement of a new metallic age, the Iron Age. Iron would become the metal of warfare for then right up to the present day. With the arrival of this new age came a new people: the Celtic people, who now dominated most of the lands that bordered the Mediterranean Sea, now reached the British Isles; it is, of course, most likely that these events went hand in hand. Between 700 and 500 BCE the Celts advanced from their homeland in what is now Austria and controlled modern day Portugal, Spain, France and Eastern Europe from the Alps down into Greece and parts of Turkey. This was not an empire for there was no centralised point of control, no administration: these were tribal peoples who would fall out among themselves and only unite at times of great need. Eventually, the Celts would be beaten down by the slow, steady, but relentless spread of the Roman Empire until they were pushed into the margins of Western Europe, now Britain and Ireland, around 50 BCE. In the British

The upper Roman drift mine at Dolacouthi, now in the care of the National Trust.

Isles the Celts would have had comparative peace from the advancing Romans, who stalled at the prospect of venturing beyond the edge of the world. It took the Romans almost a century after conquering Gaul (France) and crossing the English Channel to successfully invade the British mainland, but there would not be peace among the Celtic nation; being a tribal people and perhaps ignited by the arrival of new tribes driven out of modern day Spain, Portugal and France, the Celtic tribes of Britain went to war with each other. Hand in hand with the new development of iron weapons and tools came advancements in agricultural techniques and farming which, when combined, meant that the people had the ability to produce more food and so sustain a greater population. In consequence their settlements became larger, and that in turn bought a need for more land in order to produce yet more food to sustain the growing population. These humble village-like and tribal-based settlements then took an enormous leap forward in social development: they chose to construct settlements that could be defended from attack. Small, successful centres of civilisation became targets of jealous neighbours or raiding tribes from further afield who took rather than nurtured what they needed to survive. They not only stole food, weapons, clothing and livestock, but also people to be slaves within their own settlements. The need to defend themselves with ever larger enclosures led the people of the Iron Age to construct hill-forts; these were the villages and then the towns of their day. They were always constructed on a high defensive position where the occupants would have excellent visibility. Their builders used the natural contours of the land and shaped the hilltops so that the fort was surrounded by a series of ditches and palisades, where guards patrolled day and night and where the populations inside could sleep safe knowing that their homes and the livestock they relied upon were safely inside their earth and wooden walls. Against one another, these hillforts were strong enough defences to prevent one Celtic tribe from overrunning another; against the might of the Roman war machine, the hillforts were entrapments within which the Celts would be trapped and beaten time and again, by the artillery arm of the Roman army.

Eventually the Celts were forced to submit and a period of calm descended upon Britain which would last for 300 years, until in the 360s the Picts and the Scotti begin a series of raids on northern and western Britain. Although these were repulsed, there were more raids in the decades that followed and the Saxons from mainland Europe began to raid the east and south coast of Britain. In 402 the Romans withdrew one of the remaining legions from Britain to assist in the defence of Rome and in 407 the final legion was withdrawn, leaving Britain defenceless. Word seems to have travelled fast and in 408 a series of raids by Picts, Saxons and Scotti left a trail of devastation across the land. By 410 Britain was independent of Rome and the time for defending herself was at hand. Over the next 170 years the Britons, who were now a race of Celtic-Romano-British people, would fight to stem the advancing tide of invaders. Picts and Scotti would invade from the west and north, while from the east a whole range of Germanic tribes, Saxons, Angles and Jutes, would strive to secure a foothold in eastern Britain. There were successes for both sides in the battles that followed, as we shall see, but at the battle of Dyrham in Gloucestershire in 577 the final British resistance was broken, allowing the Saxons to reach the Severn estuary and cut off the south-west of Britain (Somerset, Devon and Cornwall) from what is now Wales. Communication between these realms could now only be conducted, and at some risk given the amount of pirates, by sea. Now these areas were on their own, and this created a situation which would, given time, allow the country of Wales to be born as the people there became isolated from the rest of the Britons.

Trapped in their now independent kingdoms, the peoples of Wales, the South-West, Cumbria and the Strathclyde region developed their own identity; their language, their laws, their myths, their recipes and their dress slowly crystallised to form the peoples that were at the core of those respective lands for many centuries. In Wales the Britons became at one with their landscape, where they survived more than thrived, but they maximised the use of their natural resources of wool and meat from sheep, supplemented with fish from the sea so as to provide variety to their diet. Cereal foods were not easy to grow, except along the coastal fringes in the lowlands of the south, which was one of the only places in Wales where crops could be grown with any certainty of success. The high mountains provided a natural defensive barrier, making the steep river-cut valleys between them the only communication routes, and these were packed with dense deciduous oak forests, making the hinterland unsuitable for rapid communication.

Wales was a wild country both before and after the Roman occupation and some of the people returned to live in their Iron Age hillforts, where being situated atop the hills that intertwined with the mountains offered protection from any raiders or invaders. These hillforts once again provided the natives with a place of sanctuary for them to nurture their slowly redeveloping settlements. This harmony between man and his environment can be plainly seen in the way that the Welsh fought to deter would-be conquerors from invading their lands. Time and again the Welsh exploited those natural resources and used them against their enemies, meaning that they were very difficult to beat; when they discarded these assets and fought their invaders on their invader's terms, the results did not go in their favour. Throughout the period between the end of the Roman occupation and the arrival of the Normans in 1066, Wales was torn by a series of internal struggles as the princedoms fought for mastery, one over the other, while at the same time trying to fend off incursions from an array of raiding warbands. During this time of internal strife, the Welsh language developed, while at the same time bands of Welsh fighters fought as mercenaries alongside a variety of Saxon leaders who strove for their own mastery of England. As well as being raided, the Welsh also went on their own raids, penetrating deep into England to steal cattle and sheep before, in almost Wild West fashion, stampeding them back to Wales. This situation lasted for almost four centuries until by the late eighth century the King of Mercia, Offa, had completed the reconstruction and improvement of a former Roman earth wall, Offa's Dyke. This reconstruction was not so much a physical defensive barrier intended to keep out Welsh armies as a demarcation line, a barrier either side of which people knew whose law prevailed and woe betide anyone found on the wrong side without duly obtained permission. It is reported that a Welshman would lose his hands for theft on the Saxon side, while a Saxon caught in Wales was likely to be hanged. The dyke had the effect of reducing the number of raids that the Welsh made into England and it also set an official border; thus, in isolating the Welsh people from further interferences, it had the effect of sealing the Welsh with their own language, a point from which the various forms of the Welsh language have developed, down to the form in which we understand Welsh today. The great dyke allowed fast communication along its length and this allowed the Saxons of Mercia to prepare for any large-scale Welsh incursion before it arrived near their border.

It is fitting at this point when isolation occurred to look at where the name of Wales and the Welsh people comes from. Both words come from a Germanic, in this case Anglo-Saxon, root: the term *Wælisc*, which was used by the Saxons when referring to the Celtic Britons in persona, and *Wēalas* when referring to their land. The English words 'Wales' and 'Welsh' are really German words and were used by the Saxons to mean anything associated with the 'Britons', including the people of Cornwall and the isolated British settlements in northern England and southern Scotland. Interestingly, the Welsh name of Cymry, which they use to describe themselves, is also a word that was once used to mean their fellow Britons in the same areas of Cornwall, northern England and southern Scotland. The Welsh name for Wales is Cymru and both of these words are derivations from the Brythonic word *combrogi*, which meant simply 'fellow-countrymen', and which aptly sums up the connection of these small British kingdoms left isolated by the successful advance of the Saxons, who were their common enemy.

With the completion of Offa's Dyke, which was in 787 according to the Welsh Annals, the Welsh had (by making a nuisance of themselves) gained their independence, not by invasion or a long war, but by default. This freedom was further strengthened just a few years later by the first Viking invasions on the east coast of England. When these commenced at Lindisfarne in 793, they immediately drew away from Wales the eyes of any ambitious Saxons as they had to look to the east and their own defence. For the next three centuries the Saxon kingdoms

Offa's Dyke, east of Montgomery.

would be beset by an ever increasing threat from the east as the Vikings or Danes of Scandinavia and Denmark pushed for and finally gained land upon the east of England. The Viking threat also materialised on the west coast of Wales, where they allied with the Scotti as they sought to pick soft Welsh targets for plunder. The important thing for Wales was that she was now independent; the question was would the Cymry princes work together and forge a nation together?

Written Sources

The military campaigns in Wales cover over almost two millennia, and for the majority of those first thousand years there is a lack of first-hand accounts for most events that took place. There are some source documents that can be used, especially if one can cross-reference certain common pieces together. The issue is that some of the information is often contradictory; even the *Anglo-Saxon Chronicle*, which survives in several different versions, contradicts itself from one version to another in terms of dates, of place names and even of events, as mistakes or transposing of letters or lines during copying led to a lack of consistency. Many of these accounts were written down hundreds of years after the events had actually happened and at the will of a particular person, so the information may be biased or distorted. In the case of Gildas, much of his work is now questioned as fanciful. However, even an exaggerated or politically biased account of an event, even if recorded many years after it happened, is better than no account at all and at least provides a starting point for the researcher. Occasionally some contemporary chronicles were written, but the information that was recorded was at the whim of the scribe, so that only what they deemed important would be written down. As the majority of scribes and the learned men who could both read and write were associated with the Church, it is their ecclesiastical records and their view of the events that happened around them that have survived. The vital events that punctuate the history of a nation, the key battles that were fought, the births and deaths of kings, the arrival of a comet or the result of a terrible natural disaster, were sometimes captured onto parchment, but even then it might be in such scant detail as to confuse the reader as much as to aid him. Fortunately, events were captured in a second way, a more traditional way for the native inhabitants of Wales: the events that mattered to their people were archived as songs and tales in the oral tradition of the bards.

The battles and their history here have been pieced together using a huge variety of source materials both written and observatory and some of those written sources are open to interpretation as they were originally based on story-tellers' tales, the Welsh tradition of the Bard, which is still practiced today. However, oral history today is being given more credence than ever before, particularly when it can be supported by archaeological evidence, even if there are gaps in the chain of the evidence; if the facts can be established before and after that gap then the gap itself can be filled by logical interpretation and common sense. This reasoning is explained in the BBC *Timewatch* programme on 'Atlantis: The Evidence' first shown on television in June 2010. It was presented by Bethany Hughes and Irving Finkel (a curator in the Department of the Ancient Near East at the British Museum), who is a scholar able to read and translate the oldest writing in the world, the cuneiform inscriptions on the very small clay tablets from Mesopotamia. Irving Finkel made the point that the story of Atlantis, similar to the story of Gilgamesh, was kept alive by oral tradition until the time that it could be written down. The stories that were remembered were those that were 'too important to forget'. The destruction of Atlantis was so cataclysmic to the ancient world that it was still remembered in tales when Plato came to record it and so retell it 1,000 years later; he wanted to make both a philosophical point and an historical one so that people would remember the great civilisation that was wiped out in just four days. By the same reasoning, one can argue that it would not be surprising if Arthur was not remembered by the Saxons because he had repeatedly defeated them, so that when they came to record the history of their time in Britain some 300 years later in the *Anglo-Saxon Chronicle*, they would not want to bolster any resistance from the remaining Britons in Cornwall, south-eastern Scotland and Wales by praising one of their ancestral freedom fighters. In contrast, the surviving Britons would want to record the deeds of their great warlord to strengthen further resistance, even to the point of predicting his return when the needs of the Britons would be at their most perilous, the myth of Arthur being that of their 'once and future king'.

The planting of this simple expectation of rebirth raises the morale of those still fighting, giving the simple people of the time a belief, a will to carry on their struggle with some faith that they can be successful. This was a complicated time in which some people still believed in multiple gods and where almost every activity was seen as the result of a god's action or presence, whether you believed in one God or many. Christianity is not the only religion where the theme of resurrection runs deeps in the minds of the congregation that believe and follow faithfully. At the time of Arthur, the Britons were Christian and his legend mingled with what historical fact we do know, say that Arthur will come again to save the Britons when dire need is upon them. The same legend runs true for the disappearances of Edric the Wild and Hereward the Wake, both of which happened at the end of the Norman Conquest following their rebellions against William I. The disappearance of Owain Glyndŵr in the early fifteenth century also fuelled tales that he would one day return to free Wales from English tyranny. The John Frum cults, which have affected Tonga from the 1930s to the present day, show how people can easily be influenced by a belief that someone will return to bring them riches and freedom from their current plight.

For this reason, the Bardic tales recorded as poems, which were possibly used by Nennius in his attempt to produce an accurate history, are included where appropriate as their 'history' has been drawn upon along with other sources detailed below. Following the Norman Conquest, the documenting of Church activity and some of the political and natural events that occurred were further recorded in a whole series of chronicles, which was then carried on by medieval scholars until the amount of information increased year on year. By the time of the English Civil War we find pamphlets reporting the details of a battle, sometimes from both sides, within a few weeks of the battle having taken place. With such speed also comes propaganda, with exaggerations of the size of the enemy to explain a defeat or to bolster the impact of a victory. History is often written by the eventual victor of a war, and so when the Britons defeat the Saxons we find little information in the *Anglo-Saxon Chronicle*; Glyndŵr's successes against the English or the French successes against the English get scant coverage in the English medieval chronicles compared to English accounts of English success. In order to reduce the need for repetition, where reference is made to a particular point in a source such as an item in the *Anglo-Saxon Chronicle*, year 834, this has been included simply as (ASC), the year having already been detailed in the text.

The Anglo-Saxon Chronicle (ASC)

This is the most important single source for the history of England and Wales before the Norman Conquest. It is not a straightforward record; the years of the ASC run from 1 September, not January, so for some events if a month is not mentioned then it is not certain which of the two years that event may have occurred in. The chronicle itself is a collection of annals that are written in Old English and they record the history of the Anglo-Saxon people. The original manuscript was created late in the ninth century, most probably under the instructions of Alfred the Great, for whom the education of his people had become of paramount importance. From the original record, multiple copies were then made and distributed to certain monasteries across England so that they could all be independently updated and be a consistent record. Today, nine manuscripts still survive; some are whole, others only in part and sadly none of them are an original version; due to human error in the copying, some manuscripts do not quite match. The author's version is the revised translation by Dorothy Whitelock, published by Eyre & Spottiswode in 1961, which is the most complete modern version and which compares and cross references all of the major manuscripts that survive in one single folio.

Anglo-Saxon and Welsh poetry

There are two great Anglo-Saxon poems which have survived in writing from those dark days over a millennium go. The poem commonly known as *Beowulf* is known to many, if not from the original poem then from one of the film versions made for the cinema, which are now available in a DVD format. The poem is of epic dimensions, with well over 3,000 lines; it is thought to have been written between the eighth and the early eleventh century and because of its pagan themes Professor Tolkien believed it to be written close to the earlier date. This anonymous poem centres on Beowulf, who is a hero of the Geat people, one of the Scandinavian tribal peoples in the sixth century. In the first two parts Beowulf aids the King of the Danes, Hrothgar, and defeats the monster Grendel and then afterwards Grendel's mother in her own realm. There is then a third part, set some years later in his life when Beowulf is now a king and has to fight a dragon who comes looking for a stolen cup looted by one of Beowulf's slaves. The dragon is eventually defeated by Beowulf in its lair but the king is mortally wounded and is buried in an earth mound overlooking the sea. The story in verse gives great insight into the lives of the Viking people, how they lived, fought and also died, as four burials are detailed in the epic, parts of which have been shown to be consistent with the famous burial at Sutton Hoo. The third story formed the basis for parts of Professor Tolkien's *The Hobbit*, with parts of Bilbo's adventure with Smaug resembling Beowulf's experiences with the dragon.

The second poem is far less well known as it has not attracted the attention of the Hollywood producer, but it too is of unknown origin. It is entitled *The Battle of Maldon* after its subject matter and is thought to have been around 400 lines in total. The fact that Maldon was fought in 991 gives us an approximation of its creation, as the writer clearly had detailed knowledge of the events, and so the poem was originally transcribed sometime around the turn of the last millennium. Sadly, the beginning and the end are missing so that only 325 lines survive, but even so this gives us great insight into exactly how a Dark Age battle was fought, how men behaved on the day of the battle, and how the English (Saxons) arrived, formed up and fought against their Viking opponents. It also shows the shortcomings in the English strategy and how reliant the common man was on the leadership and strength of their local earl, in this case the hapless Byrhtnoth, and once the figurehead was gone it was very difficult for an army to remain steadfast.

The Welsh poetry comes from oral traditions, many of which were captured by the Welsh chroniclers and put into prose for their own 'historical works'. The best known collection in literary form is the *Black Book of Carmarthen*, which is a collection of early Welsh poems most likely to have been written out by a member of the Augustinian Priory of St John the Evangelist at Carmarthen. The collection appears to have been collated by a single scribe over a period of time as the poems are on separate parchments that have been bound together, but are written in a fairly consistent hand. This rare book contains poems on a variety of religious matters, as one would expect, but also poems that draw on traditions relating to Welsh heroes and also the legend of Arthur and Myrddin (more commonly known as Merlin). There is one poem, 'The Elegy of Gereint', which refers to the Battle of Llongborth; sadly, it is not known where this battle was fought, though it does mention Arthur's involvement in the battle, bringing some credibility to our knowledge of the name of Arthur as a warrior with Welsh connections. It is just possible that the Battle of Llongborth is the battle fought at Portsmouth that took place in 501 (ASC) and in which a Welsh noble was killed.

Archaeologia Cambrensis

This historical journal covers all aspects of the archaeology of Wales and the Welsh Marches from the earliest Prehistoric discoveries right the way through to the industrial and landscape history of the nineteenth and twentieth centuries. There is a wealth of archaeological information covering prehistoric monuments such cromlechs, chambered tombs and, for the historian, both hill-forts and castles. Battlefields are also covered, as well as Roman sites. There are also details on many religious sites and the architecture of churches and monasteries, and with over 170 years of articles it is an invaluable series of sources.

Asser – d. 908/909 (A)

Asser was a Welsh monk from St David's, Dyfed. Little is known of his early life, but in the mid-880s he was asked by King Alfred to leave St David's and join a group of educated men that Alfred was gathering to him at his court. In 893, Asser produced a biography of the *Life of King Alfred*. Later in the 890s Asser became the Bishop of Sherborne, in the heart of Wessex, so one must assume that Asser's work was approved of by the king. No original document survives, the last surviving copy having been destroyed by a fire in the Cotton Library in 1731. However, transcriptions had been made and as a result of the information that has been preserved in copy, we have a greater knowledge of King Alfred than any other Dark Age leader and given that Alfred's failures are recorded alongside his successes, it suggests that Asser gave his reader a balanced picture of his patron and the lives of the Saxons at this time.

Bede – c. 673 to 735 (B)

The Venerable Bede, as he is known, lived in the Saxon kingdom of Northumbria approximately fifty years before Nennius. He wrote a work in a series of five books which is titled *The Ecclesiastical History of the English People*, the *Historia Ecclesiastica Gentis Anglorum*. This work was completed in the early 730s, but much of it, as the title suggests, is a history of the Anglo-Saxon Church, commencing in 597 with St Augustine's mission to England. The opening book goes back to Roman times and includes some geographical detail on Britain at this time; there are also references to other early notable events in early English history. His apparent choice of only including information of which he was certain, or where he could make a moral point, has given Bede's work great credibility, portraying him as an early historian in the true sense. Sadly for the historian, Bede, by concentrating on the ecclesiastical side of life, has perhaps omitted details of some of the other aspects of Saxon society, so that we have gaps in our knowledge that he might have been able to fill if he had thought it relevant to do so.

Caradoc of Llancarfan – d. 1147? (CL)

Caradoc of Llancarfan is not to be confused with Caratacus and his wars with the Romans. Caradoc of Llancarfan was a Welsh cleric of the late eleventh and early twelfth century who is believed to be the author of the chronicle *Brut y Tywysogion*, 'The Chronicle of the Princes'. Although no medieval copy mentions him as the author, Caradoc was a contemporary of Geoffrey of Monmouth, the author of the *Historia Regum Britanniae*, the end of which refers to Caradoc as writing a continuation covering the period from 681 to Geoffrey's own time in the 1100s. Today, the details of the *Historia Regum Britanniae* are not seen as reliable source material and have not been further detailed here. Caradoc is also generally accepted to be the author of two other important biographical works, a *Life of Saint Cadog* and a *Life of Gildas*. The *Brut y Tywysogion* covers many aspects of life, wars and battles, great plagues of disease, the building of castles, raids of pagans, and the marriages and deaths of kings and princes, covering events not only from across the British Isles but also from parts of Europe.

Florence of Worcester – d. 1118 (FW)

As with so much that emanates from the Dark Ages, the details as to who Florence was and where he obtained his source material are open to speculation. Florence was a monk living in Worcester who was known as Florentius and he played some part, probably with another monk called John, in the creation and maintenance of a world chronicle that began with the creation of the world and continued until 1140. The names of the three key monks who are recorded in the list of monks in St Mary's chapter at Worcester when Samson was bishop there between 1096 and 1112 are Hemming, John and Florence. It may be that Florence was the researcher for the project and that John wrote up the information presented to him; this theory is supported as the hand of the scribe does not appear to change within the chronicle even after Florence's death is recorded therein in 1118.

Gerald of Wales (GW)

Born at Manorbier castle in 1146, Gerald of Wales would go on to become an important cleric and chronicler of his times, though his strong-willed nature would also bring him into conflict with both the monarchy and the senior clergy. Gerald was well connected to the powerful nobility of both Anglo-Norman England and Wales. He was the son of William FitzOdo de Barry (Barri) and so the common ancestor of the Barrys of Ireland; through his mother, Angharad, Gerald was related to Rhys ap Gruffydd, who was Angharad's first cousin. With such parentage, Gerald was clearly going to receive a strong education and his formative years were spent at the Benedictine house of Gloucester; this was followed by ten years of study in Paris from around 1165–74, where he studied the Trivium (grammar, logic and rhetoric), the medieval equivalent of the three 'Rs' (Reading, 'w'Riting and 'a'Rithmetic) from the English and Welsh pre-comprehensive education system. Gerald distinguished himself on an ecclesiastical mission to Wales and was rewarded with the title of Archdeacon of Brecon in 1174, which he held for two years. In 1176 Gerald was nominated as the Bishop of St David's by the chapter, who were seeking to break away from the control of Canterbury. Gerald's support for such a contrary move following on from Henry II's problems with Thomas Becket meant that his claim was not supported by Henry, who feared further Welsh uprisings if any more favour was shown to them. Instead, seeing a man who could be both potentially a useful talent and a threat, Henry II decided to keep Gerald close to him and his family.

St David's Cathedral, closely associated with Gerald of Wales.

The result was that in 1184 Gerald became a royal clerk and chaplain to King Henry II, his position of authority being reflected by the fact that he was given the responsibility of acting as the mediator between the crown and Prince Rhys Ap Gruffydd that year. Just a year later, Gerald was sent with Prince John on an expedition to Ireland, and this led directly to Gerald commencing a new career as an author. His first known work was the *Topographia Hibernica*, which was published in 1188, an account of the royal journey through Ireland with Prince John. Although entitled a topography, it is much more of a history and Gerald was to follow this account with his *Expugnatio Hibernica*, which is an account of Henry II's campaign and conquest of Ireland. Whether writing from his own experiences or from the position of seeking to justify the tyranny of his Norman family and masters, Gerald was extremely prejudiced against the Irish, whom he portrays as barbaric, incestuous savages. Whether this was Norman propaganda to justify their 'Christian' crusade against the native Irish people, or whether there were some elements of truth in his words is questionable. His abilities having been recognised while in Ireland, Gerald was then invited to accompany Baldwin of Forde, the Archbishop of Canterbury, on a tour of Wales in 1188, ostensibly to generate recruits to accompany Henry II on what would be the third crusade to the Holy Land. Henry was to die before the crusade embarked in 1189, leaving his son Richard I (later Richard the Lionheart) to lead the English contingent sailing for Jerusalem. The resultant works written by Gerald about his time in Wales are the *Itinerarium Cambriae*, published in 1191, and the *Descriptio Cambriae*, which followed in 1194. These two works on Wales are valuable historical insights into both Welsh and Anglo-Norman culture and contain references to the way that the Welsh lived and also fought, with detailed descriptions of weapons and their effects. Gerald would continue to write throughout his life and in his later years was again at odds with the monarchy, criticising them for the way they ran their country. For the fact that Gerald was prepared to write what he felt, even if it went against the grain and bought him into conflict with his betters, we must consider that there is a good deal of honesty within Gerald's writings even if some of it is biased at times.

Gildas – c. 500 to 570 (G)

The fall and conquest of Britain, the *De excidio et conquestu Brittanniae*, is a text in three parts written by Gildas in the mid-sixth century. Where he lived is open to debate, as some later Saxon sources say northern England and Ireland, and also connect him with having made a pilgrimage to Rome. Other, later, Norman sources state that he lived in the south-west of England and northern France, thereby having connections with Glastonbury, where he also mentions Guinevere which, like the finding of Arthur's tomb at Glastonbury just when the abbey was short of funds, is all a little bit too convenient. Gildas was a British cleric and he certainly lived after the first Germanic tribes, the Saxons,

Angles and Jutes, had arrived and settled in the east and south-east of England. The texts contain details of the Roman occupation and subsequent departure and the perilous state that the Britons found themselves in after that Roman exodus. In parts one and three of this work, he concentrates on the ecclesiastical aspect of British life and in particular he criticises the British clergy. Importantly for the military history of the times, he mentions with adoration Aurelius Ambrosius, who is described as leading the British resistance to the Saxons. The British victory at the Battle of Mons Badonicus (Mount Badon) is also mentioned and in some later texts the victory is attributed to Arthur.

Nennius – c. 796 – c. 860 (N)

This monk from Wales, who lived in the early ninth century, is believed to be the complier of the *Historia Brittonum*, a history of the Britons. He is thought to have lived in modern-day Powys, in an isolated mountain community where he lived in a Welsh princedom, and so outside the direct Anglo-Saxon way of life. It is likely that he used the earlier works of Gildas and other unknown sources to compile his work, and although some historians brand some of his work as invented, he should not be dismissed out of hand for several reasons. Primarily, it is believed he had access to sources going back to the fifth century that have now been long lost to us; these may have been written sources or, given his location and the tradition among the Welsh (née Britons) for recoding events orally, they may have been sources that were only presented to him in an oral fashion. In addition to these sources, Nennius himself is also the major source for the references to Arthur, and as we shall see below the Welsh connection and the story of Arthur are inseparably entwined. The *Historia Brittonum* is a puzzling series of texts which exists in different versions and it is unclear who really compiled them as some are attributed to Nennius and others to Gildas and the majority are not ascribed at all; for an historian interested in early Wales, they are an important source.

Tacitus 55/56 – 117? (T)

Publius (possibly Gaius) Cornelius Tacitus was born around 55 or 56 AD and lived for just over sixty years; the years of his birth and death are not known exactly. During his life he was a senator at the height of the Roman Empire and a prolific writer. He produced works on oratory as well as on the history of Germania and the emperors Tiberius, Claudius and Nero, but importantly for us he also wrote extensively on the Roman campaigns in Britain, including those concerning his father-in-law Agricola, one of the great Roman generals. In total, Tacitus wrote thirty books which have been divided by scholars into two groups, entitled the *Annals* and the *Histories*. Neither set of these books is complete as whole books are missing, but what has survived gives the reader information on a wide range of subject matter. As well as the military actions and campaigns, the complexities and brutality of normal Roman life are exposed as political ambition and the Roman attitude to the Christians and Jews is expounded. Tacitus is the main source for Caratacus and Boudicca.

The Weapons of War

Missile Weapons

Axe – Throwing (Francisca)

Information on the use of this weapon comes from two sixth-century chroniclers, Gregory of Tours and the Roman historian Procopius. Both sources state that the Franks, after whom this weapon was named, used a small throwing axe that had two very sharp sides on a heavy iron head. This axe would be thrown by the Franks as they closed on their enemy, hurling it at them just before impact. This tactic would have been used to achieve the same result as the skirmishers who hurled their javelins into a shieldwall, which was to weaken the shieldwall sufficiently for a frontal assault to stand a chance of breaking into the defensive formation. The axe was far more likely to cause serious injury to a defender or irreparable damage to his shield when compared with a javelin, which was more likely to cause injury to a man as the long, thin point flew into the heart of the shieldwall if it had succeeded in getting past the shields of the defenders. The effective range of such a weapon would be quite small, somewhere between ten and fifteen yards depending on the balance and design, and such was the skill of metal workers at this time that there can be no doubt that both would have been optimised to maximise the weapon's damage on impact with its intended target. How significant this weapon was is not clear, but it contributed to the success of the Franks, who eventually conquered most of former Roman Gaul, filling the vacuum there to create the country of France. There is some archaeological evidence from England that the Saxons also used this weapon, but whether they did so in anywhere near the same numbers as the Franks is as yet unproven. The Vikings certainly used a similar weapon, as the Sagas record, and perhaps the costs of its production in Britain or the minimal effect it had upon battles fought here made it uneconomic to produce and use such a weapon. A francisca would have weighed between two and four pounds and so was light enough to be carried through the belt, providing additional combat weapons should others get damaged. In addition, the lightness of the axe meant that it could be used in combat one-handed, while a shield could still be held in the other for protection.

Bow

By far the most well-known fighting force to come from Wales is the Welsh archer, synonymous with the longbow and the devastating effect it had on the French armies during the Hundred Years War at Crecy and Agincourt. However, the skill of the Welsh longbowman goes back long before the mighty yew bow was developed and although yew was used, is it not certain when it became recognised as the wood of choice. Gerald of Wales, writing in 1188, states that the Welsh bows were not made of 'horn, sapwood or yew, but of wychelm – not shaped or polished but rough-looking and unformed'; this might suggest that the Anglo-Norman English bows were perhaps made of yew as Gerald was surprised at how the Welsh bows were still made. There is no certainty as to when yew did become the wood of choice for longbows and whether the English adopted it from the Welsh or vice versa; certainly the bow was in use en masse by the southern Welsh for centuries before it was taken up by any other army, and with such experience would come refinement and improvement, so one would think that it would be the Welsh design that would be copied? Perhaps the term in general use for the great armies of the Hundred Years War should be the Welsh longbow and not the English longbow.

The earliest record of a casualty from a bow in battle is said to be that of Offrid, the son of Edwin, king of Northumbria, who was killed by an arrow shot from a Welsh bow during the Battle of Hatfield Chase in 633, when the Welsh and the Mercians clashed near Doncaster. Yet the majority of continental Dark Age bows were made of yew and were 6 feet or more in length, as archaeological finds in Nydam in Schleswig-Holsten (old Denmark) from the fourth to fifth century and Oberflatch in Germany from the seventh century testify. But bows were not made exclusively of yew there, as finds have also been made of fir and elm. The draw strengths of these finds have been estimated to be around 55 pounds, while a ninth or tenth-century bow found in Haithabu in Denmark is estimated to have an 80-pound draw. This appears to be evidence of improved technology as the bow was found to have a thick ovoid section at the centre, tapering from there to flared, flat ends, with an overall length of 6 feet 6 inches, showing that improvements had been made to give the bow more spring, making it more effective; at the same time as increasing the length, the weight was reduced by tapering the ends. There is much speculation over the numbers of bows used in battle in the Dark Ages. While many sources are rare, the Bayeux Tapestry has twenty-nine images of archers, suggesting that in the mid-eleventh century they made a significant contribution to an army. There is little or no evidence as to how far these basic bows could shoot; a longbow had an effective range of up to 250 yards, but that was at the end of the military evolution of the British design of this weapon, and so for this period the maximum effective range is unlikely to have exceeded 200 yards. Perhaps it was the cost of producing a bow that was prohibitive, but one would not think so given the cost of creating a shield or metal-edged weapon. The arrows that would have been shot would preferably have been made from ash, wood being traded to acquire ash if nothing suitable was available locally. It is possible that oak and other woods may have been used, and they would have all been up to 20 inches in length. The bowstring would be made from hemp or a similar fibrous material and would be protected by a natural glue or waterproofing agent such as lanolin, extracted from sheep wool, in order to protect the strings from absorbing moisture and prevent them softening, which would make the tension too weak to shoot with.

It is easy to see why the Welsh army consisted of bowmen and spearmen; with the resources of the natural forest all about them and sheep to provide lanolin to protect their weapons, they did not need to trade and look elsewhere for their arms. Perhaps this is why archers were only used in great numbers by the southern Welsh, the Scotti for example using none at all. There is some speculation as to whether the bows used by the Picts were composite ones, as evidence exists that such bows had been used in southern Scotland towards the end of the Roman occupation. Were these bows auxiliary weapons stolen from a Roman supply train or from an ambushed and defeated Roman unit in a successful Pictish raid, or is this further evidence that the ancestral Picts were the descendants of Scythians, for whom the composite bow would have been a familiar weapon? Although the bow that the Welsh used would only develop slowly into the lethal longbow later in the medieval period, the arrows themselves did develop. A metal bodkin arrowhead began to be produced; this had a small, thin, straight point, especially designed to penetrate the chainmail that so many of the upper class warriors wore from the ninth century onwards for their protection, and against which the older arrowheads were not so effective. In the medieval period, arrowheads were also refined further to allow them to do more damage to both armour and man when they hit home. Arrows were designed with a v-shaped point so as to hit and snap a chainmail link and still continue to penetrate into the body. Long, thin arrowheads could find the smallest chink in plate mail, and with so many thousands raining from the sky

Arrowheads and crossbow bolts from the author's collection.

some would slip through those gaps in the plate mail, be it the eye slit or an overlapping joint, and so incapacitate their victim.

Crossbow (Arbalest)

For four centuries at the start of the second millennium (c.1070 to 1470), this weapon would vie with the longbow to be mistress of the medieval battlefield; this is because although the longbow was easier to make, it was much harder to use and required the archer to practice daily to keep both the strength and the skill to make it an effective killing machine. In contrast, the crossbow was harder to construct, which made it much more expensive to manufacture and to replace if damaged, but it was a much easier weapon to use. The tension and strength to shoot a crossbow came from the winding mechanisms, not from the muscles of the user, and it was simpler to aim, for the wielder could just look down the sight. The crossbow bearer also required a minimal amount of training and so it could easily be used by new recruits, youths or even women or wounded men who were in a sheltered defensive settlement. In contrast, the longbow had to be individually tailored to the man shooting with it, the weight and size of the bow increasing in proportion to the strength and size of the bowman. There was, however, still one fundamental weakness to the crossbow in battle, a key factor that would be critical when the two weapons found themselves on opposing sides, and that is the speed at which the different weapons can be reloaded and shot. The crossbow, even in practised hands, could release just two quarrels per minute, whereas a similarly experienced archer could shoot as many as ten arrows in the same time. The other advantage the crossbow had, and which would become significant towards the end of the life of the longbow as a weapon of war, is that the crossbow could be made out of a number of woods, whereas yew was far and away the best timber for constructing longbows. By 1500 there was not a spare yew tree for sale in Britain or in Spain (as they had sold all the yew to England), and as for the rest of Europe, our enemies were not going to sell us their timber to equip the English army with.

The origin of the crossbow and how it came to be used solely by the Picts in northern Britain before the Normans widely adopted the weapon in the tenth century is a matter of conjecture. Certainly the ancient Chinese used the crossbow in large numbers and the only other ancient army to use it was that of the Macedonians, but their version was much larger, one that had to be set with an enormous windlass or winding key. It is possible that crossbows found their way to Britannia with Greeks who traded for copper and tin, or that it came from the Romans, but they themselves were late in adopting the crossbow as a missile weapon, and it was not until around 310 that trained units began to appear in the ranks of the auxiliaries. This was a period of great change for the Roman army, with the composition changing to include a greater variety of troops which, when combined, could cope with all the different styles of fighting that Rome's enemies used as they pushed and probed the frontiers of the Empire. The most likely source of crossbows would be from Pictish raids upon Roman defences or baggage trains that allowed them to steal examples and so learn of the weapon first-hand. The alternative again supports the possibility that the Picts brought the technology with them from Scythia, from where they would have had first-hand knowledge of the crossbow from their encounters on their eastern borders, where one of the Scythian tribes, the Hsiung Nu, fought against the Chinese armies of the Ch'in Dynasty. The strongest evidence for the use of the crossbow comes in the form of a crossbow nut made of bone and excavated at Bustan Crannog, Ayrshire, in 1880, but they are also shown pictorially on some Pictish standing stones.

The crossbow would be made from a variety of different woods, ash, hazel, yew and elm on occasion. It had a central stock (tiller) that had a groove for the missile quarrel (bolt) to sit in, with a trigger at the opposite end to the string attachment and with a winding device that the shooter wound to create tension in order to pull back the string, which would propel the missile forward when the trigger was released. Like all wooden objects, it would be treated with varnish to keep it waterproof and to save the wood from drying out and splitting, as linseed oil was used to preserve cricket bats before today's plastic coated varieties. The crossbow string would be made in exactly the same way as a bowstring and would be protected in a similar way against moisture. This illustrates how crucial weather could be in an era where weapons relied on the condition of natural materials; torrential rain would have made these stringed weapons next to useless.

The crossbow fired a quarrel, which was a projectile smaller than an arrow and a little larger than a medieval dart. This quarrel had a length of around 10 inches (25 cm) with a maximum range of over 300 yards, but again this range was at the end of its military evolution in the early Renaissance period and it is unlikely that, as good as the Picts were at both wood and metal work, their crossbows would have been as effective as the later European ones. For the medieval period, then, it would seem that the effective range would have been around 200 yards; it certainly seems to have come off second best when pitted against the longbow, where the rate of fire and longer range made the longbow mistress of the battlefield. Although most armies of this period were not heavily armoured, it was the penetrating power of the crossbow bolt that made it so effective in the later medieval period; we may never know whether the Picts' crossbows provided the tension to force home their bolts to the same degree. In the early to mid medieval period, only the Picts, and the Normans, used the crossbow at all and those troops made up just 10 per cent of their total force so this was not a weapon in widespread use, presumably because of the cost of construction when compared to its slow speed of fire. After the Norman Conquest, the crossbow was used more extensively by the Anglo-Norman armies until the 1180s. After that time it was the longbow which was preferred by the now 'English' army, while the crossbow would still be used in the hands of the many mercenaries, especially French, who were widely employed in the English armies.

Javelin

After throwing stones, the javelin, made from a piece of straight wood, is probably the oldest missile weapon on Earth. It was the first tailor-made projectile; to ancient man it was as significant as a jet rocket to a twentieth-century general, as the javelin allowed man to catch food that he could not get close enough to grasp with his bare hands. It is possible that the oldest javelin wound yet discovered is in the shoulder blade of a fossilised rhinoceros dated to between 300,000 and 500,000 years ago, unearthed in a gravel quarry near the village of Boxgrove, West Sussex, England. Seven archaeological finds of throwing spears located in a coal mine at Schöningen in Germany have been found to be spruce and date from 400,000 BCE. Given that humans created these projectiles early in their history, one can deduce that long before the Roman occupation of Britain, the manufacture of javelins for strength and flight must have been close to the optimum. The javelin was the ubiquitous weapon of the ancient world and continued in use right up into the Renaissance armies of Italy. Javelins were cheap to manufacture and were the common weapon for both infantry and cavalry; in some armies the whole force was equipped with them. The word javelin in English derives from the French word for spear, *javelot*, thus a *javeline* is a small spear. The word may be Celtic in origin and have come to the British Isles with those peoples as they migrated across Western Europe from their original home in Austria. A javelin or small spear was the universal weapon of this period; only a freeman was allowed to bear arms and the simplest was this light polearm, which could be used as either a throwing or close combat weapon. Javelins were designed for both throwing and for thrusting and so different styles will have been manufactured. A javelin was not as long or as thick as a spear, being only 5–7 feet (1.7–2.1 metres) in length, with the balance slightly heavier near the front to improve range and impact into the intended target; the wood used would generally have been ash or spruce. Over time, the humble javelin developed into a hand-held melee weapon as opposed to just a simple thrown missile weapon. It spawned a whole range of different weapons; some were simply longer versions of the wooden javelin, the spear and the pike for example. By increasing the length, more ranks of troops were able to hit their opponents' unit with their sharpened points at the same time. The other weapons that developed were 'pole-arms', which were short spears topped with a metal head, the shape of which changed to meet the developments in defensive armour; these different types of weapon will be examined in more detail below.

Musket – Matchlock

This gunpowder weapon appears towards the end of our chronology of Welsh battles and there were few encounters fought in Wales with this weapon. A musket fires a small lead ball by means of igniting a gunpowder charge secreted at the stock end of the weapon; at the bottom of the barrel, a small priming pan (with a neat sideways hole to the charge) allows raw powder to be poured into it ready for ignition. The musket's charge is ignited by simply placing a piece of smouldering match (match cord or thin rope made from hemp or flax) into the priming powder by means of a simple plunging trigger. As the reader can appreciate, these weapons were cumbersome to use and dangerous, with lighted match-cords and gunpowder always in close proximity to one another. These matchlock muskets had developed from the first real hand-held firearms, fifteenth-century 'handguns' which were literally small, cannon-like barrels mounted on wooden stocks. Gradually, these primitive weapons were refined into the arquebus, which was a shorter barrelled and shorter range firearm that found favour across Europe. The refinement of the arquebus into the matchlock musket led the latter to be taken up across the whole of the Continent. It was in this form that the musket would come to dominate the seventeenth century, gradually replacing the pike as the weapon to be used on the battlefield. Many people have questioned why the musket, which was so slow and unwieldy, replaced the bow as the weapon to deliver long-range volleys into the enemy. The answer is similar to that of the crossbow: the longbow took hours of training and then practice and a bow had to be tailored and continually upgraded in draw weight and size to suit the user. A crossbow or musket was a weapon where one size fitted all and so could be churned out from a factory where a simple production line allowed hundreds of weapons to be made in a short space of time. Although more difficult to master than a bow and arrow, once trained a musketeer could keep firing his musket as long as he had ammunition and powder and he would not tire as quickly as if he was loosing off his arrows. The matchlock musket dominated for almost 100 years, but was slowly replaced by the flintlock, which, when paired with its bayonet, became in trained hands the mistress of the battlefield.

Musket – Flintlock and bayonet

Around the end of the sixteenth century the flintlock, which was a much safer mechanism for igniting a firearm, was developed. Once the bearer had loaded a powder charge and a ball into the barrel, it was discharged not by a lighted match-chord but by a spark from a trigger in whose jaw was held a piece of flint. When the trigger was pulled, the flint snapped against a piece of steel and threw the spark straight into the priming powder. This was a far safer method of igniting the powder and saved the musketeer having to both carry and keep safe a length of lighted match-cord. Over the seventeenth century the flintlock slowly replaced the matchlock until, by the end of the century, the latter was obsolete. The musket was further enhanced by the invention of the bayonet around the 1650s, and although the early types of bayonet were of a plug variety that stopped the musket from being fired, as the flintlock developed so did the socket bayonet, which fitted over the muzzle. The bayonet led to the final demise of the pike, as the musketeer when shooting his musket could now defend himself with his extended musket and the spike of his steel bayonet. The socket bayonet and the flintlock became widespread throughout all the European armies by the start of the eighteenth century, when most western European countries became embroiled in the War of the Spanish Succession. These two weapons of war would become synonymous as the British army mastered them, allowing them to forge an empire on the battlefields of the world over the next 150 years. Born out of discipline and practice, the British 'thin red line' relied upon the infantry keeping up a standard rate of fire so as to keep the enemy at bay until they were sufficiently weakened that the British troops could charge them with their bayonets and complete the victory. It is fitting to remind ourselves at this point that the tenacity of the British army was forged from all the nations of the British Isles and that Scottish, Irish and Welsh men all played a significant part in the success of the British army.

Pilum

The Romans were unique among the ancient empires in developing the javelin into a weapon that would not only maim an opponent if he was hit but also render him defenceless if they missed the man but struck his shield. The pilum was the length of a conventional javelin, but the business end was not simply a sharpened wooden point or an inserted leaf shaped metal point but a long, thin rod of metal with a long, sharp metal point at the tip of the rod. After being thrown, if the missile hit the man then the metal rod was long and thin enough to penetrate deeply into the victim, either killing him or rendering him disabled, with the weight of the shaft pulling the stricken man down. If the pilum hit the shield, such was the weight of the shaft that the metal rod would bend as the weight of the shaft pulled down the shield, rendering the wielder of the shield defenceless. The other advantage of the pilum was that it could not be thrown back as the impact almost always caused the extended point to bend. The use of the pilum was limited to the legionnaires and the auxiliaries, while the skirmishers continued to use the light javelins, which gave them a slightly longer range but were not as effective against more heavily armoured troops.

Pistol

A foot soldier could not easily shoot a matchlock musket on foot with the time it took to load and shoot, so to give mounted men a chance to shoot at their enemy a more lightweight but robust weapon had to be developed and over the fifteenth and sixteenth century the pistol was born. It was in essence simply a smaller version of the musket, but because of the demand for an effective weapon to replace the crossbow, javelin and bow (which had been the traditional weapons of the horseman), an incredible array of different pistol designs were produced across the whole of Europe. The principle is the same as for the musket (a charge of powder and a small lead ball were loaded into a steel tube) but the variety came in the different methods of igniting the powder so as to cause the weapon to discharge safely while manoeuvring and fighting on horseback. The earliest pistols were created in Germany and Pistoia in Tuscany, Italy, in the 1540s. A wheel-lock mechanism was developed, possibly invented by Leonardo da Vinci, and of course Leonardo was born and lived in Tuscany and is renowned for his interest in military inventions. The wheel-lock is so called because it works by spinning a spring-loaded steel wheel against a piece of pyrite to generate sparks that ignite the gunpowder in a pan, which again travels through the small touchhole in the barrel to ignite the main charge of the firearm. Other mechanisms were invented, the snaplock in the 1540s and the snaphance in the 1560s, but the one that would revolutionise warfare was the flintlock, which was invented around 1600 as we saw above. The flintlock pistol became the mainstay of every cavalryman during the late Renaissance period and in consequence whole regiments of cavalry were formed that carried two pistols each, to allow them to ride up to infantry that did not have firearms and discharge both of their pistols at close range before retiring to the rear to reload. This system was known as caracoling, and allowed cavalry to shoot at blocks of pike and swordsmen uninterruptedly until driven off by foot troops armed with missiles or other, heavier cavalry.

Sling

This weapon was probably the second to be developed after the javelin as human hunter-gatherers would have used stone missiles to bring down birds and small mammals to eat, and it has been used in warfare for longer than any other weapon save for the hand-hurled stone. In the hands of a practiced exponent, the sling stone is a lethal weapon. The Bible tells us of David using a sling to bring down Goliath, and slings were used in the Spanish Civil War in 1936–9 and by the Finns against the Russians in the Second World War; it is still used by militants and protestors today, particularly in the Middle East. The Celtic armies that deployed in defensive formations before the Romans would have had as many as a quarter of their force armed with slings. Excavations at many hillforts have uncovered stone, lead and baked clay missiles, stacked ready to be used to repel attackers; Castell Henllys, an Iron Age promontory fort in South Wales, is a prime example. It appears, however, that the Dark Ages started to see the demise of the sling, as the bow steadily developed into the most effective long-range weapon, having the advantage over the sling that the arrow would penetrate armour and so do far more damage to the recipient than a bruise-inducing sling stone. The disadvantages of the bow, in that it was more expensive to produce and required specialised materials rather than just a piece of leather or twine and a convenient stone, do not seem to have stopped its advancement. It does appear that there is a slinger shown on the Bayeux Tapestry but the man is out hunting and not engaged in battle and therefore the sling may in fact be a lure to bring a tame bird of prey back to its master. The sling continued to be used in small numbers by the Anglo-Norman and English armies up until the end of the thirteenth century. The range of a sling made it an extremely useful weapon: in skilled hands it could out-distance any other missile weapon propelled by a man. In his account of the retreat of the 10,000, Xenophon stated that the retreating Greeks suffered severe casualties because their own arrows and javelins could not reach their Persian enemies, who used their slingers to outrange and bombard the Greeks from a safe distance. Interestingly, Xenophon later states that the Greeks formed a company of Rhodian slingers who, by using lead shot, were able to outdistance their Persian adversaries, who used larger but heavier natural stones. This suggests that at this time, 401 BCE, the effective range of a sling was greater than the bow. Although the sling gradually fell from favour in Britain, it continued to be used across Europe into the Renaissance period. The effective range of the sling is thought to be around 200 metres, though historians, including Chris Harrison, who has written extensively on early and medieval ranged weaponry, states that a skilled slinger, trained from youth, may have been able to achieve ranges in excess of 500 metres if the sling was matched by a quality cast-lead shot. The world record for the distance a slingshot stone can travel was set in 1981 by Larry Bray, at an incredible 437 metres. This information was taken from 'The Sling in Medieval Europe', in *The Bulletin of Primitive Technology* Vol. 31, Spring Edition, 2006.

Staffsling

The sling had a short revival under the Normans, who adopted a weapon that had originally been used in small numbers by the Macedonians in the fourth century BCE. The staffsling was simply a normal leather sling mounted on a short pole, some 3–6 feet (1–2 metres) in length; this allowed the shooter to achieve a higher trajectory and so a much greater distance than the traditional hand-powered sling. The extra power generated by the leverage and the whip in the stave also meant that a heavier shot could be propelled towards the enemy. The height and distance that could be achieved made these weapons popular for shooting incendiaries, both in sieges (to fire over the walls and into the defenders beyond) and, incredibly, in naval warfare, where a staffslinger could shoot an incendiary device from one ship to another. Staffslingers can also be used behind allied forces as the height of release would be around 10 feet

(3 metres) from the ground, allowing the missiles to pass over the heads of their own troops and into the enemy's ranks beyond, presuming that they had not yet come together in hand-to-hand combat. According to the Roman military writer Renatus, the effective range of both bows and staffslings was 600 feet (200 metres), with the benefit being that the staffsling's missile would be heavier and cause more injury when striking an opponent than those missiles shot from hand-hurled slings when reaching the same mark.

Hand-to-Hand Combat Weapons

Axe – Two-handed

The seamstresses who placed the cross-stitches into the Bayeux Tapestry have left us some fine examples of the design of the heavy two-handed axes which the later Anglo-Saxons used to defend England in 1066. We know the difficulty that William had in breaking through the Saxon shieldwall and how a combination of locked shields, a forest of spear points and axes whirling down onto the bodies and the horses of the Norman knights pinned against that shieldwall was a very effective defensive formation. The handle or shaft of the axe would have been between 3 feet and 4 feet in length and, like the medieval longbow, the weapon would be the length and weight to suit the wielder, as it was essential that he was comfortable with its weight to be able to swing it efficiently. The archaeological finds of axe heads show differing styles, thickness and size, indicating individual rather than consistent manufacture. The head of the axe would have been of a delta shape, the widest part being at the blade's edge, which could vary from 3 to 6 inches in the early centuries, gradually increasing in size to between 9 and 18 inches by the end of the first millennium. The narrowest part of the delta was where the axe head joined the shaft; this structure maximised the cutting ability in ratio to the overall weight of the weapon, thereby causing the maximum amount of injury for the minimum amount of effort. In some cases the edge of the blade has been fashioned from hardened steel that has been welded to the iron head, a most formidable weapon for battlefield execution. The 'crook'-like shape also allowed the axe to be used as a pulling weapon to wrest from a defender his own weapon or shield, to tip him off balance and render him prone to a spear thrust into an unprotected area of flesh exposed by his removal from his defensive posture. It also allowed a man on foot to hook onto and pull a rider off his horse, something the author has seen first-hand at a re-enactment at a living history weekend. The Viking sagas refer to the axe shaft being tightly bound in metal and leather and this would have served to provide the wielder with a better grip and also with protection, so that the weapon would be able to withstand the blows from his opponents should any fall upon the axe shaft. The Anglo-Norman armies continued to use this heavy infantry weapon up until the end of the twelfth century, after which it was replaced by the long spears and a steady increase in the variety of polearms, which were more versatile for both attack and defence than the offensive two-handed axe had been.

Lance

The lance makes an appearance in the eleventh century, when the Normans changed the traditional use of the javelin from a thrusting overarm or throwing weapon into a couched spear, tucked under the right arm of the knight and used to charge home and attack the enemy. The aim of the mounted heavy cavalry was not necessarily to wound with the weapon's point but to drive the recipient back from the shock of impact into the ranks behind, so as to allow the cavalry to break through the almost impenetrable shield wall and so turn and attack the weak rear of the enemy's line. The horseman was aided by a large kite-shaped or round shield which protected his left side as his horse bore down on the enemy; they were part of an integral team. From our knowledge, it appears that only the Roman-British cavalry at the start of the Dark Ages and the Normans at the very end of it were armies that used cavalry as a shock weapon. As the Anglo-Norman army developed, the knight continued to develop: armour improved in quality and the horses were bred and trained for war. This finally led to the development of the fully armoured knight, who would dominate medieval warfare until the end of the fifteenth century; the knight was master of the battlefield. However, first the longbow and then advances in gunpowder weapons would lead to the demise of the noble horseman on the battlefield as they were brought down by the volleys of arrows and then by the solid iron of cannonballs and the masses of musketballs. Some armies, notably the French, despite suffering horrendous losses in battle, continued to field large numbers of heavily armoured knights up until the early seventeenth century, when they finally abandoned their medieval style of fighting.

Pike/Long thrusting spear

These weapons are variants upon a theme, centred on a long wooden shaft that could be anything between 10 and 25 feet in length. A spear was normally up to 10 feet in length, a long thrusting spear up to 15 feet in length and a pike was most commonly between 15 and 18 feet long; all of these weapons were traditionally made from seasoned ash. These weapons were also used in the same manner, their wielders being grouped together in a formation where the unit was five or more ranks deep so that when used in conjunction with hundreds of others, a whole forest of sharp points could be brought into contact with an enemy unit at the same time. If the opponents of such a weapon have no long spears themselves then they are unable to reach their opponents and must either take casualties without inflicting any in return or retreat. The pike was first developed as an offensive weapon by the Macedonians under Philip II and then his son Alexander (who would earn the title of Great) as his well-balanced army, of which the pike phalanx was an integral part, would go on to conquer most of the known world in his lifetime. The wooden shaft had an iron or steel spearhead and that head was often reinforced with metal strips called 'cheeks' or langets, which ran down the head of the shaft and prevented the enemy from being able to chop off the point as it approached them. When the troops of opposing armies both carried similar weapons, the ensuing melee would be brutal as each side faced up and charged the other, the weapons of both sides reaching beyond each other's front ranks as they each pushed, trying to force their opponents to retreat. By the time of the Renaissance, the spears and the majority of polearms were replaced by the pike, which became present in almost all European armies and whose dense ranks were protected first by crossbowmen and then latterly by musketeers. However, as gunpowder technology improved, dense blocks of slow-moving infantry became easy targets on the battlefield for cannon to concentrate their fire upon. The effect of a solid 10 lb cannonball hitting a unit of pikemen ten ranks deep can be likened to a game of skittles as the iron balls carved great swathes through men, shattering anything they came into contact with as their violent passage crashed through the ranks and sometimes on into other regiments behind. The days of these long-shafted weapons were numbered and, instead of being a major weapon in their own right, they became an integral part of a foot regiment, where pikes and muskets worked together, the one protecting the other. However, even this role gradually became obsolete as the bayonet, when affixed to the musket, allowed the musketeer to become his own pikeman.

Polearms

As in all arms races, a new method of protection leads to the development of a new method of attack, which is exactly what happened with armour and polearms respectively. When chainmail was the principle protection, the spear, sword and axe were the offensive melee weapons and there was almost a balance where none of these weapons was mistress of the battlefield as the bow had not yet developed into the killing machine it would become. When plate mail began to appear, the traditional weapons did not have the same impact upon their opponent and these new knights began to rule the battlefield. The result was that a whole new set of weapons was developed to overcome this new defensive armour; some were designed for foot troops (the bill, glaive, halberd, poleaxe, guisarme and spetum), while others (the warhammer, the morning star, barbed mace and gordendags) were designed to be carried by a horseman. Taking the weapons that would be carried by the foot first, it is no coincidence that many of them have two different edges or weapons within the one design, and that many resemble some form of giant tin opener, which is exactly how they worked. Many had a hook-like feature with which they would try and pull their opponent over, and once down they would look for a weakness in the armour through which to insert the blade of the weapon so as to prise open the armour and allow a

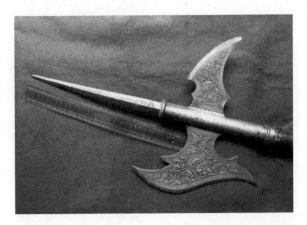

A halberd polearm head from
the author's collection.

telling thrust to be inserted through the space. English archers carried long, thin knives expressly for the purpose of being able to slide the blade in through the smallest of holes to dispatch their enemy. The mounted man's weapon had a shorter stock but the metal head was designed like a nutcracker to smash the helmet and the head inside with it, or to break open the armoured body of the target, either to break the joints which held the armour together or to unhorse the rider with the blow so that he could be dealt with by infantry moving up in support. Despite the power and destruction of the English arrow storm, the French knights and men at arms still rode into battle upon horseback while English nobility almost invariably dismounted to fight, preferring to be on their feet when the battle was joined. The ability of the English arrows to penetrate plate mail is plainly illustrated at Agincourt, when the cream of French chivalry was slaughtered in a single day by an outnumbered and for the most part lightly armed English force under Henry V, who used the wet conditions and the speed and agility of his bowmen to destroy the French army. Within a century both the longbow and plate armour would reach their zenith and then slowly decline, but one relic of this age survived into the Napoleonic era. The partisan was originally a form of short pike in the later medieval and Renaissance periods and it had a main bladed point and two side points at 90 degrees to the main point. Although it died out as a main weapon of war, it was still carried by all twenty sergeants within a British line infantry regiment; it served as a badge of rank but also as a tool for keeping the ranks in line and spaced properly, and in addition it was a stout defensive weapon which could be used when the regiment formed square to pull down enemy horsemen that attacked the squares.

Spear

This weapon was thicker and a little longer than the more common javelin and gradually replaced the lighter weapon before becoming the basis of the multi-headed polearm of the medieval and Renaissance periods. A spear could

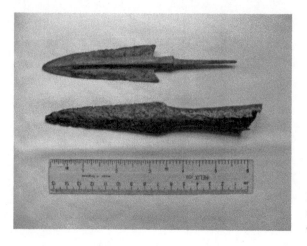

Bronze Age and medieval spearheads from the author's collection.

vary from as little as 6 feet to as much as 12 feet (2–4 metres) in length but most in this period would be between 6 and 9 feet in length (2–3 metres), with the metal tip ranging from 1 foot to 2 feet (30–60 cm) at the business end of the shaft. Generally the wood was ash and, being thicker and longer, the spear was heavier and more difficult to manoeuvre than the lighter javelin. The metal tip would be securely fixed to the wood and would have been effective as a slashing or cutting weapon as well as a thrusting point. The butt end of the shaft would probably have had an iron sheath to prevent it from getting damaged or splintering, especially as the wielder would at times grasp the rear and middle of the shaft in order to get great leverage when pushing at an opponent. The spear was ubiquitous because it had two great advantages over most other weapons of the time: it was far cheaper to produce than any other weapons and could be used with very little training, particularly important when massed blocks of spears and javelins were the mainstay of all armies at this time. The spear also had religious significance in some cultures, for it was the traditional weapon of the Saxon god Woden. The armies that tended to use the spear in this period were the Welsh, Picts, Scotti and finally the Normans, the latter developing its use as part of a co-ordinated and balanced army. The Welsh and Scottish armies went on to use the long spear with varying degrees of success right up to the end of the medieval period. As both these nations favoured the longer version of the spear, it may be why they were chosen as mercenaries to fight alongside other armies at this time, providing a sound, strong defensive unit. These spears must not be confused with the spears used by the ancient Macedonians and many armies in the Renaissance period who used pikes, which were up to 18 feet (6 metres) long.

Swords
The manufacture of a quality sword was a time-consuming process, requiring the gentle but strong hands of a proficient blacksmith. Purely from the time

taken to craft them, swords were very highly prized, so beloved by their wielders that they were often named by them, and lords would bequeath them as venerable gifts to their greatest followers, family or even to the Church. Prince Athelstan left to his brothers in his will some of his swords, one of which was his prized possession, a sword which some generations before belonged to the mighty Mercian King Offa. Swords are still mighty symbols of power; our own Queen Elizabeth today still uses a sword to dub someone as a knight. J. R. R. Tolkien, who was twice professor of Anglo-Saxon (Old English) at Oxford University, put much of his historical knowledge, gleaned from the Dark Age texts he translated, into making his world of Middle Earth far more plausible than many fantasy worlds that have tried to follow his complete example. Middle Earth's third age is a Dark Age setting and Tolkien's naming of all the important swords in his quadrology of books is a prime example of where fantasy is based upon historical fact and yet seems stranger than fiction. Archaeological finds have unearthed swords with personal names engraved upon them, names such as 'Leg biter' or 'Shield smasher'. The makers' names were also engraved onto the weapon, clearly an early form of marketing but one which has allowed historians to determine where swords were made and how they were distributed. The names of Ulfbehrt and Ingelrii appear in the ninth and tenth centuries, the former name quite frequently, including on a sword recovered from the River Thames. Early swords were, as has been demonstrated on the Channel Four television series *Time Team*, cast by the pouring of metal into a stone mould, after which it was filed and polished and the hilt crafted to produce a sharp-edged weapon comfortable for the wielder to hold. From such creations, it is possible to see a clue to the legend of the Sword in the Stone so closely linked to King Arthur. The Celts created their swords by twisting strips of metal together, heating them and hammering them into shape before adding another layer; the process was repeated with additional strips until there was sufficient metal – around 2 inches across and half an inch thick – to create an edge on each side; the metal would then be filed, sharpened and polished before a handle (pommel) was fixed to the tang sticking out from the top, still an important part of the whole weapon, making it far stronger. This pommel could also be fashioned into a weapon; fixed with a heavy knob of metal at the end, it both balanced the sword for use in combat and also gave the wielder a mace-like object with which to pummel an opponent and render him unconscious. To pummel does mean 'to beat upon the head' and the word clearly derives from this heavy pommel of a sword hilt.

Each nation had its own way of crafting weapons and swords were no exception. A Saxon sword was around 33 inches long, with a sharp edge on each side, and with a groove down the centre of each side of the blade to take away some of the weight without weakening the weapon. Viking swords were shorter, around 30 inches in length, and some were inlaid with other metals for design and elegance: tin, brass, copper, silver and gold have all been found inlaid within the hilt on excavated swords. As metallurgy skills advanced, swords moved from blades of iron to blades of steel, which were produced by continuingly heating, then cooling and then reheating the blade in a charcoal furnace. This allowed the smith to produce a much lighter but stronger sword. The Viking smiths of the tenth and eleventh centuries were, it seems, the most skilled in Europe in this whole Dark Age period, and significantly their swords had a much better balance, which meant that the blade could not only be used for slashing or cutting at an opponent but also for thrusting into an enemy without fear of the blade bending or snapping, something which could happen with a simple iron blade. It seems, however, that the Viking smiths did not invent these methods, but in fact honed their skills from their encounters in the Middle East. The Vikings traded through a network of rivers with the Byzantine Empire and recent tests carried out at the United Kingdom's National Physical Laboratory proved, by examining the metals of eleventh-century Viking swords under an electron microscope, that their steel originated from Herat, in what is now Afghanistan. By Norse law, all Vikings were required to carry swords and it is estimated that at this time a sword would cost the equivalent of ten or more fertile cows. Unlike a spear or javelins, which were cumbersome to carry, the sword could be worn on the person in a scabbard, which had its own straps to attach it to a leather belt that went either around the waist or over the shoulder as a baldric, and so the wearer was not encumbered by having to carry the weapon. The scabbard would be constructed of wood bound with leather and lined with fur or wool, which would be oiled to keep the blade clean and, very importantly, protected from any moisture, which would corrode and rust the blade. For the wealthy, the scabbard would be decorated as befitted the owner, with patterns or trappings to reflect their high status. Throughout the majority of this period the broadsword was the favoured blade, and it had been in use since around the sixth century; like all swords they varied in size, so the blade could be anything between 30 and 40 inches in length, some 2–3 inches wide and averaging around 4 pounds in weight.

In the medieval period the variety of swords increased as influences from the experiences of knights on crusade to the Holy Land were brought back to their own countries and the weapons they had seen were copied. The broadsword was now joined by two similar curved blades. The scimitar, which was long, but light for its size, was a curved blade, favoured by the Saracens, which tapered to a sharp point. There was also a heavier version, which may have been used by cavalry, which was the falchion; it too was curved like a scimitar but it was much heavier in weight and, with just one cutting edge as opposed to two, it would have favoured the downward chopping action of a mounted man. As the medieval period progressed, the size of swords grew; first the longsword or bastard sword, as it was sometimes known, which was between 40 and 50 inches in length, and then the enormous greatsword, which was between 50 and 72 inches in length with an additional handle length of around 20 inches. This enormous sword was a two-handed variety and would become the specialist weapon of German mercenary troops (Landsknechte) during the Renaissance period. It was so long that no shield could be carried, so the wielder was defenceless barring his skill in combat. At the battle of Norwich in 1549 the Earl of Warwick employed over 1,000 of these expert German swordsmen to deal with the Kett rebellion, where some 20,000 peasants had taken control of the city and the immediate countryside.

Armour

Leather was the simplest and lightest means of gaining some bodily protection and it could be made and shaped simply by soaking it in cold water and then keeping it damp until ready to be cut to shape, sewn as required and then gently dried to harden. Once set to shape and dry, it would be given a thorough waxing that would both protect and sheen the leather ready for sale or for wearing. This process could produce helmets, cuirasses (for the chest), leg greaves, saddles and even drinking vessels. Chainmail was expensive to manufacture, consisting of thousands of rings around two-fifths of an inch (1 cm) across, all of which had to be handmade and then linked individually through the next one. In the same way that a good blade could mean the difference between wounding and killing your opponent, a coat of expertly made chainmail could mean the difference between being bruised and being killed. A good suit of chainmail was a prized possession; it was the best protection a warrior could wear into battle for a thousand years but it was a heavy and cumbersome item to wear. Generally, there were two different types of chainmail worn in the Dark Ages, the byrnie and the hauberk. The byrnie was a mail coat which only came down as far as the waist or hips and weighed between 25 and 30 lb (10–12 kilogrammes). The hauberk was a full suit of chainmail, coming down to at least mid-thigh, sometimes to the knees and on occasion to just above the feet. Clearly the longer the suit, the more it weighs, so a full-body coat could weigh up to 60 pounds (27 kilogrammes) and was capable of taking a blow from an axe or a spear, especially if it was reinforced by a leather coat beneath it. Mail is thought to have originated from the Keltoi people (later the Celts of Western Europe) around 400 BCE and as it originated in Eastern Europe it is not surprising that it spread into those neighbouring kingdoms first. It was particularly favoured by the peoples whose armies were cavalry-based, Armenians and Parthians, people that dominated in the northern Middle East and western Asia at the extreme eastern end of the Roman Empire. Some units of the Roman army also used chainmail, so its use would have continued into the Dark Age period by both acquisition and emulation. There is speculation about just what proportion of an army would have worn chainmail but these coats were very durable and could be repaired by a skilled blacksmith. As many archaeological finds show, the Staffordshire Horde for example, these people were incredibly skilled and could work with many different metals, having the ability to create items both of outstanding beauty and brutal destruction. The final piece of chainmail to be considered is the coif; this was a chainmail helmet designed to fit over the head, rather like a balaclava helmet but with a long skirt that came down to protect the neck and head. This is likely to have had a padded cap to fit underneath the rings and so prevent chafing and help to cushion any blows that rained down upon the head of the person wearing it.

Tests by the Royal Armouries have shown that chainmail was very effective at dealing with the blows of medieval weapons, depending of course upon the quality of the manufacture. The problem with chainmail is its own weight, as a full hauberk worn with a coif could weigh up to 80 pounds (36 kilogrammes), with much of the strain bearing down on the shoulders. A strong leather belt around the waist would help to take some of the strain but even so the endurance of men wearing such protection to fight all day is a testament to their strength and stamina. Both English and Norman knights depicted on the Bayeux tapestry are shown wearing chainmail that comes down as low as the knees; as these are clearly hauberks and many are also shown with suits that fit over the head and neck, these warriors were wearing the best armour they could get, and it is clearly chainmail from the circular pattern portrayed in the cross-stitch. So to fight for 9 hours at Hastings while brandishing a weapon and supporting a shield to give further protection to the other half of the body means that their diet must have been good, their health must have been strong and their fitness must have been outstanding to be able to withstand such a drain on the body and still manage to fight. When the Saxons and Normans met at Hastings, those men were the cream of soldiery.

Chainmail was good at protecting the wearer from edged weapons, and only the finest of arrows could pierce the links to hit home on flesh. Maces and spears, certainly axes, could injure the wearer by breaking a bone beneath the area of impact, or by pushing the mail rings into the flesh to cause a wound and later infection. To combat this type of injury, a coat of thin leather armour or cotton cloth may have been worn underneath. Certainly the Scythians wore such an item, called a gambeson, as early as the fourth century BCE. The gambeson was formed by making two identical fabric shirts, which were then sewn together and filled with any absorbent material; ragged wool, linen and horsehair are all believed to have been used. As well as helping to absorb some of the impact, this clothing presumably absorbed any blood that might leak from a wound caused by a significant blow, reducing the discomfort of the injured man. Deer hide was worn by Vikings and is said to be quite as strong as chainmail when treated properly; when worn, this hide is much lighter than the metal and allows the wearer much greater flexibility and movement in the storm of battle. This quote from 'The Fight at Finnsburh', translated by Kevin Crossley-Holland, illustrates what damage armour could suffer in battle: 'Then Guthere withdrew, a wounded man; he said that his armour was almost useless, his corselet broken, his helmet burst open.' Some Roman units also wore scale or fish mail armour, named after the way the plates overlap each other like the scales of a fish. This armour had been around for centuries in various formats ever since the time of the Sea People's migrations and their wars with Ramses III in the fourth century BCE. It is easier and more economical armour to construct as it uses fewer materials and it is easier to replace as sections can be patched, with metal plates being re-sewn. It is also lighter than chainmail, with the plates being fixed to leather clothing rather than to each other. Despite being seen on mainland Europe, this armour does not seem to have been assimilated into the armies that fought for control of England, as not a single archaeological example has ever been found in Britain to support its use.

After the Norman Conquest chainmail continued to be used but it began to be supplemented with better helmets as advances in metalwork led to the production of small sheets of iron or steel which could be fashioned into helmets and so give greater protection to the wearer, sometimes at the cost of impaired vision. Much of this 'new' technology came back with the Crusaders from the Holy Land. Small sections of plate armour had been around for many centuries, again with the Greeks and Macedonians and then the Carthaginians and Romans making various types of armour from it, notably as metal cuirasses to protect the chest of the wearer; greaves were also fashioned from a single piece of metal. Plate armour was designed to be worn as a complete suit which interconnected and so protected the whole of the body. It also had the advantage of being around half the weight of a suit of chainmail, and as it was made to fit the build and shape of an individual it allowed a good fluidity of movement, vital when the wearer is going to fight in it. Sometime around 1300, the use of full plate armour by the aristocracy began to become more widespread; it was an expensive item to make and only the gentry could afford to commission such luxury but the new means of protecting the body found favour and the nobility of armies across Europe began to wear it. The interesting thing is that while the French continued to ride horses into battle while wearing their plate armour, the English knights would dismount and fight on foot alongside their bowmen. The increase in armour saw the development of new ways of getting through it, as discussed above in the section on polearms. In Europe plate armour would reach its peak in the late fifteenth and sixteenth centuries, but the arrival on the battlefield of cannon and muskets which could smash or penetrate the armour rendered it obsolete and yet another cycle of change in warfare began. Interestingly, plate armour reverted back to its former style and metal cuirasses were worn by the later Renaissance and seventeenth-century pikemen and cavalry. In this smaller form the protection lasted into the Napoleonic Wars, where it was worn by the elite cavalry regiments of many European nations, who were known by their armour, the aptly named 'cuirassiers'. It is interesting to note that chainmail endured for far longer than the plate mail that replaced it and, given its use for over 1,000 years, it must be considered the most successful body armour produced.

Helmets

The coif outlined above was not widespread and appeared only towards the end of the Dark Age period but spread rapidly after the Norman Conquest until full plate helmets arrived in the twelfth century. For the majority a simple leather cap was the best they could hope for. Those warriors of a higher status would seek better protection in the form of a metal helmet, though often with a leather cap underneath for both added protection and comfort, given the metal that encased their head. The title for this essential piece of protection comes from a Germanic word, *helm*, which means hidden, a reference to hiding the face of the enemy that you were about to encounter. At the start of the period, the late Roman helmet used by the forces leaving British shores was constructed of different sections of metal to protect the crown, nasal, neck and cheek areas of the head, the sections being riveted together. These helmets were known as Spangenhelms (a Germanic term simply meaning 'segmented helmet') and the design evolved into ever more elaborate variations, not quite as elaborate but not too dissimilar from the famous Sutton Hoo burial helmet unearthed in 1939. The seventh-century Benty Grange Helmet, discovered in Derbyshire in 1848 when an ancient tumulus was being excavated by Thomas Bateman, was the first Anglo-Saxon helmet to be unearthed in Britain. That helmet was constructed from iron struts, which met at the apex, where they were surmounted by a gilt bronze boar with garnets for eyes. The struts were once covered with horn pieces which were riveted together, the whole helmet covering a protective leather helm affording further protection. The boar would have been used to hold a plume of horsehair to finish off the helmet with a status decoration. In Norse mythology the boar was a symbol of Freya's role as the goddess of battle and such helmets with boar crests are described in the poem *Beowulf*. The Benty Grange helmet also has traces of silver from the rivets, and possibly from a simple cross that was fixed above the nose guard.

The cheapest and easiest helmets to make were leather ones made of *cuir bouilli*, though as outlined above, this shaped leather, in spite of its name, was not boiled but treated in cold water before being moulded to shape. Extra protection could be given by fixing metal strips to the leather to protect the vital parts of the nose and the top of the skull. Such light leather helmets would be the mainstay of the common soldier but they were often worn in battle as a first layer of protection by the wealthy, who would put a chainmail coif or a metal helmet over the top. The complex design and construction of the helmet seems to have declined towards the end of this period, with much simpler and more standard designs being seen among the majority of warriors. By the eleventh century a conical style of metal helmet was popular with the Danes and so the majority of Vikings, their Norman cousins and eventually the Anglo-Saxons would adopt this style of head protection or close variants upon it. This conical helmet was made from a single piece of metal which was strengthened at the front with a nasal guard to protect the face; this gave the wearer a fair amount of protection but also good visibility, essential in close combat, although with suits of chainmail and large shields it also meant that the exposed sides of the face were highly vulnerable spots on the body. As outlined above and as part of the advancement in the production of stronger and lighter armour, plate mail helmets began to appear in the late eleventh and early twelfth century before becoming an integral part of a complete plate mail suit of armour, though they were often worn over a chainmail coif to give double protection. The issue with a lot of plate mail helmets is the restricted vision that that added protection brings and the construction of long, thin, needle-like arrow heads was to allow for penetration into the narrow holes in the armour, the eye sockets being the most vulnerable part.

Shields

The shield was one piece of a warrior's equipment which did vary considerably from one army to another; the size, style and shape would all be different depending on the role that the warrior had in battle. The shield was used in warfare from the earliest known armies until it eventually died out in the eighteenth century. For some armies, the shields were similar; the Welsh, Saxon and early Viking shields all appear to have been round, with a central boss. In contrast, the Pictish shields were rectangular or square as well as sometimes round, though these round ones may have been captured ones. The Vikings who settled in Eastern Europe also developed rectangular shields. The shields of the spearmen were designed to protect their left flank while their right arm used the offensive weapon; the men in the line would link arms with the next man, presenting a solid wall of shields bristling with spear points, over which arrows would be shot and javelins hurled from the ranks behind. If missile-armed troops carried a shield then it was likely to be small and light so that they could use it to ward off any missiles that were shot at them, but were still able to move swiftly with it so as not to encumber them too much while they skirmished to get their own shots at the enemy. When the skirmishers themselves were shooting, they would drop the shield to the floor, ready to retrieve if they moved or were shot at again, while leaving themselves two hands free to shoot their weapons.

Traditionally, shields were made from lime wood but what archaeological evidence is available suggests that beech, larch, oak and pine were all used.

Because of the weight and being carried on one arm, the shield would be as thin as possible but protected with a leather hide cover and possibly a reinforcing metal rim, held in place with nails. The shields could vary in size between 2 feet (60 centimetres) and 4 feet (1.2 metres) and the majority would have a central metal boss that covered a void which was where the hand of the holder would grip the shield. The shield would often be braced with iron strips running across the planks of wood that would both hold the timbers together and protect the shield from direct blows; those covered in leather offered greater strength and protection. To the larger and heavier shields a long leather strap was attached, which went over the head and under one arm, and so allowed these heavier shields to be supported by the shoulder, which took some of the weight. The left hand of the warrior could hold the boss in the centre of the shield or use a leather strap attached to the far edge of the shield, in which case his elbow would fit into the space behind the boss in the very centre of the shield. It is not known if any shields were durable enough to last for the duration of a whole battle, where the shield would have been battered from the outset with an array of missiles and then impacted with axes and swords; an axe would surely have split many a wooden shield with the first blow. Some tests by re-enactors have shown that flat shields can split with the first blow of an axe despite having leather and metal reinforcements and that even a javelin strike can split the wood if it hits true. Flat shields have also been shown to be poor at deflecting missile weapons and sword blows. However, in contrast, a concave shield can be up to four times more effective at deflecting missile weapons. The shield was also an offensive weapon as well as a defensive screen, as the boss could be smashed into the face or body of the enemy to hopefully unbalance him and so allow a decisive strike to be made by a colleague supporting from behind.

Towards the end of the Dark Ages, a new kite-shaped shield was developed that would eventually have a slight curve to mirror the shape of the body, with the aim of protecting the whole of the left side of the user, legs as well as torso, and it would also protect the complete side of a man when on horseback. Was this development in response to more missile weapons being used in battle, which required a man to make more of his shield, or was it that the Normans were developing their cavalry into an attacking force that would become master of the battlefield? Certainly it was the Normans who most readily adopted this design and in the eleventh century the Saxons also adopted it, but this may well be due to the time that both Edward the Confessor and Harold Godwinson spent in Normandy. Throughout its length the Bayeux Tapestry shows all the combatants with kite-shaped shields, and the English defending themselves by altering the position of the shields to meet either missiles coming down upon them or men advancing towards them. What is not certain is whether this innovation applied to all Saxon infantry or just the select fyrd; it may well be that those of a lesser social standing in the ranks still used round shields. The Bayeux

Tapestry also shows a variety of shield patterns, animals, birds and patterned devices in different colours, a forerunner of the heraldry that would develop as the medieval world took over from that of the Dark Ages. It is possible that the Vikings and other tribes adopted colour-coded shields, perhaps either by ship or at the order of local jarls so as to allow ease of recognition and organisation when in battle or when returning to the ships for their voyage home.

The medieval shields changed to suit the amount of protection that the bearer had, so that as the quality of the armour and the helmet improved, so the shield got smaller but was still made of wood and leather. In the late twelfth century the shape of the shield changed to the iconic one we know today, the 'heart' shaped shield that has a flat top and two equally sized curved sides which meet at the perpendicular centre of the shield when drawn from the middle of the top flat surface. This shape of shield would dominate in England for the next two centuries until advances in armour and the size of weaponry made such shields impossible to carry for defence. These shields were also instrumental in displaying the accepted livery of a knight, which became vital when men were fully enclosed in armour and no facial features could be seen. The painting of a chosen livery which could then be handed down from father to son would

A buckler shield from the author's collection.

allow everyone to tell friend from foe as required. It is thought that this practice began in the early 1190s, during the Third Crusade, when men began to paint motifs upon their shields while advancing on Jerusalem, and as there were rival factions and disputes it seems that some rules were agreed among the nobility from each country and the system of heraldry was born. The incredible thing is that the whole process seems to have taken place almost overnight; one day there was no system for heraldry at all, then a short time later, with no apparent declaration, there is in place the language, the approved colour scheme, the ways of identifying sons and all of the rules required to control a fully hereditary procedure and they are all in place as if it had been there forever; it is one of the great mysteries of history. These heart shields would continue in use in France and Britain but in other parts of Europe troops used a whole variety of shield shapes; hearts, ovals, diamonds and triangular shields were all tried at some time. The traditional round shield designs were also still used, as well as a small half-curved one which was used by some light cavalry. Towards the end of the medieval period some footsoldiers began to use a small round shield, almost like the Scottish targe, except that this new shield was made of metal instead of the usual wood, but was light enough because it was only around 15 inches across. This shield was called a buckler and was designed to be used by swordsmen. The buckler could either fit upon the left arm by means of a strap or be held in the hand by means of a grip; the idea was that it could be used to deflect aside an approaching weapon, allowing the bearer to counter-thrust with his own sword.

CHAPTER 3

Warfare in Wales

Having looked at the variety of weapons that the different armies used for war, let us now turn our attention to the people that used those weapons, the different races that fought in these battles that will follow, and the structure of the armies that they constructed to try and conquer the land of Wales. Almost every nation that ruled England would at some point try to conquer Wales; some would succeed and others would not. The whole history of Wales is, as we shall see, a series of attempted invasions which were punctuated by periods without intervention from outside, some of those periods lasting hundreds of years. We begin by looking at the Welsh armies themselves and how they responded to invasions from both land and sea.

Celtic Armies 55 BC–AD 75

The first recognisable 'Welsh' armies were formed by the ancient Celts, who governed their own tribal communities across Britain and who we know lived in considerable numbers in what is now Wales. As we saw in the previous chapter, the Celts arrived in Britain in a series of migrations from southern and central Europe, settling here in tribal communities centred on hillforts which had proved to be solid defensive structures for the Celts for centuries. It was not until the first-century BCE Roman army arrived, with its artillery for bombarding the forts from below and its testudo formation for approaching and breaking into palisaded defences, that these former strongholds proved indefensible, causing them to be abandoned on mainland Europe. To get some idea of the importance of these defensive settlements to the Celts in Wales, one only has to look at the numbers recorded; in total there are over 3,000 hillforts in Britain and almost 600 of those are in Wales, so 20 per cent of the hillforts were built on only 9 per cent of the land mass, showing how densely populated Wales was compared to the rest of the country. Many of these hillforts were located in so strong a position that they were re-occupied after the Romans had departed when strong defences were once more required against the advancing Germanic tribes. The Celts were a warrior nation; they thrived on conflict and saw individual acts of bravery in battle as the way to obtain glory and so advance within the tribe. They almost all fought with a javelin, carrying a shield for protection. This desire to fight as individuals was fine when taking on other tribes with similar values; when such warriors come up against a disciplined Roman army that works together as a killing machine, the ill-disciplined army cannot compete – a pitched battle would almost certainly result in a Roman victory. However, when the Celts ambushed or isolated small Roman units then the outcome was less predictable, as the Romans could not bring their coordinated, tried and tested tactics into action. A Celtic army was made up of four distinct types of warrior, among whom the elite were the two-horse charioteers, who made up around 10 per cent of the army. These light, fast and highly manoeuvrable machines were used to approach and harry the enemy formations as the single crewman hurled a succession of javelins from close range into the enemy ranks to try and encourage them to make a rapid charge and break up their solid formation. The driver of the chariot would bring the vehicle round time and again to allow all of the javelins to be thrown before retiring to their own lines to restock their chariot with more javelins so that the attack could be repeated. These chariots were not designed for charging into the enemy; they were built for speed in both attack and retreat. Another 10 per cent of the army was made up of light cavalry; these mounted men were also armed with javelins and a shield and fought in open order designed to skirmish with and harry the enemy, picking off stragglers and avoiding contact with more heavily armoured men that would defeat them if they clashed. The third element were the missile troops; around 20 per cent of the army would be slingers, whose role was to wear down the enemy with wave after wave of stones so that they would be weakened by the time the main element of the army charged home. The remaining 60 per cent of the army were tribal warbands, groups of men in large numbers who were all effectively from the same clan and who fought as group. Some of them would have been fanatics who fought naked to show that they were not afraid of dying in battle and who have demanded to be at the front of the charge. These great hordes would wait until they deemed the enemy had been galled by the other three elements of the army, then the whole force would charge en masse into the enemy ranks, hurling their javelins as they ran and drawing their long swords to follow up on impact with the enemy line.

Roman Army 55 BC–AD 410

The Roman Empire was founded upon the steadfastness of the army, which was structured into legions, each of which would contain about 6,000 men when at full strength. The legion worked as a complete unit (almost like a modern limited company) where everyone knew their part and was made to feel a part of the whole. The legion had a hard-core of heavily armoured fighting men (its legionnaires) with auxiliary units, who were the scouts and the light troops, to protect their flanks. The legion also contained non-combatants, medical personnel and a variety of administrators who took care of all the logistics, food, pay and the matters of supply. There were farriers to look after the horses and a structure of command in which everyone knew their place and the men respected and honoured the legion they were a part of. The Roman army was a paid army, it was trained and its men had good accommodation that consisted of tents when they were on campaign and barracks when on garrison duty. Above all, it was a professional army that was well organised and disciplined, where her generals were able to learn from their mistakes in battle and make sure that they were not repeated. It is this professionalism that sets aside the Roman army from all of the other armies that it encountered; in its organisation, the Roman army was almost as structured and controlled as the modern armies of the world today. Coupling that strength of structure with the ability to remain flexible in their approach to warfare gave the Romans a huge advantage over the untrained nomadic peoples and tribal hordes that prowled around their borders. Great versatility was shown by the commanders in the field, who were able to react and bring in new ideas in order to counteract any changes in the tactics of their enemies which were causing the Romans a problem. For example, when the Romans invaded Dacia they found themselves receiving horrendous injuries at the hands of the Dacians' falx (a scythe-like chopping polearm weapon), so they strengthened their helmets and altered their body armour to deflect the blows and so limit the impact of the Dacians' hitherto master weapon. And if they could not alter their armour, then the Romans could amend their tactics, as the following example shows. When encountering fully armoured men on fully armoured horses (cataphracts) in the deserts of Persia, the Romans struggled to cope with the shock of impact that these extremely heavy cavalry caused as they smashed through the Roman lines, the Roman arrows and pilums failing to stop the cavalry charge. Having suffered in several encounters, the Romans were ready when they next faced the seemingly indestructible horsemen. In preparation, the Romans dug shallow pits in the sand, screened by some of their light troops so that the enemy could not see what the Romans were doing while deploying. These pits were then covered and camouflaged so that the Roman hidden inside could not be seen. When the advancing horsemen rode over the pitted ground, the Romans were able to thrust their blades up into the unprotected part of the horse, thereby bringing them both down with one blow. In terms of composition, the main strength of the Roman army was the legionnaire, and many people will have an image in their mind's eye of the archetypal Roman soldier with the large rectangular shield (curved in order for it to fit around the body) with a red front, seen in such films as *Ben Hur* with Charlton Heston and *Gladiator* with Russell Crowe. These legionaries were indeed the stolid, strong, highly disciplined heavy infantry found at the core of every Roman army, armed with the pilum and trained to work as a team: advance; throw the pilum; advance; thrust the shield into the enemy and stab with the sword; advance; thrust the shield into the enemy and stab with the sword; advance – and so it went on, the mechanical, methodical killing machine driving all before it. Although the legionaries made up between 50 and 80 per cent of a Roman army depending on the campaign and the enemies they were facing, they could not win battles on their own and the rest of the army was made up of troops to support the legionnaires. There would be heavy cavalry, ready to charge home and exploit any enemy weakness, and light cavalry whose role was to skirmish and drive away other skirmishing units working for the enemy. There would be units of archers, slingers and light javelinmen who, like all missile troops, would be tasked with depleting the enemy's ranks by shooting or throwing into the densest part of the enemy ranks to weaken them before the legionnaires attacked. The Romans even had light artillery that moved with the army when on campaign. These were ballistas, giant crossbows, which could accurately shoot large bolts for hundreds of yards and strike enemy units that could not even see what was shooting at them.

Many times the Romans encountered both localised field defences and fully enclosed ramparts surrounding a hillfort, the latter seemingly impregnable. The Romans developed a formation called a 'testudo' (tortoise) which, as the name suggests, involved the legionaries holding their shields above them to ward off any missile attacks, while the legionaries at the front, protected by their colleagues behind, were able to either chop at and pull down any defences with their hatchets or fight off defenders protecting the defences. This formation was practiced in training so that on the field of battle it could be quickly formed,

Old Oswestry Hillfort, showing the size of the ramparts.

ready for an assault. Tacitus states that this method of assault was used against the Celts in Wales under Scapula as he tried to quell the Celtic revolts. The key to the Romans' success was the fact that they had a balanced army that worked together as a cohesive force and could cope with almost any type of enemy attack thrown at it.

British Army 410–475

The first true British army was only in existence for a very short period of time, when the people of Britain were alone, abandoned by the withdrawal of the Romans, and had to fend for themselves. This army lasted from 410 until 475 and was composed of militia forces that were still heavily influenced by the late Roman model. The militia provided units of heavy and light infantry and heavy and light cavalry, all of whom would have been armed with javelins and shields. This core of trained troops was supported by additional units of light cavalry and light missiles troops armed with bows and slings. One can appreciate that following a Roman model the army was well-balanced and although not as heavily armoured and as well-equipped as their former masters, the British if well led were able to give a good account of themselves.

For some time the regional centres and their financial activities proceeded as they had under the Romans and this produced some revenue through taxation which provided sufficient monies to fund the militia. It was when these financial systems broke down towards the middle of the fifth century that there were insufficient troops to defend the country against the frequent sea-borne raids made by the Scotti (Irish) and the Saxons in addition to the overland Pictish expeditions which came from the north. It was these incessant attacks that forced the British leader Vortigern to take drastic action and invite some of the very people that were invading, the Saxons, to act as co-defenders of the realm.

British Army 476–580

The second type of British army emerged in direct response to the growing Saxon threat. The Germanic tribes, having been invited to fight by Vortigern in 449 as mercenaries to help stem the tide of Pict and Scotti raids on British settlements, quickly turned on their new employers, having realised from their early exchanges how weak and vulnerable the Britons were. The Saxons now invited more and more of their Germanic families and friends to join them in Britain, an action that led to a major change in the whole history of Britain. The Saxons soon got a foothold in the east of Britain and continually looked to expand their territory. The British were forced to abandon the majority of their eastern cities and return once more to their hillforts, the settlements that their ancestors had taken refuge in at the time of the first Roman invasions. These hilltops were now refortified, the stockades rebuilt and the gateways strengthened. In some places walls or ramparts were erected inside older fortifications to reduce the overall area that had to be defended, which illustrates that the number of people involved and needing protection was less than in the first century (400 years earlier), when the same forts were last occupied, suggesting that a decrease in population had occurred towards the end of this period. From the remnants of these western migrations, an army developed that was fighting for survival with its back firmly against the western shores. This army was the one that Arthur would have commanded and in composition it was very similar to the previous army, save that the militia had gone and that the troops supplied were the loyal forces of minor kingdoms ruled by princes and warlords. This patchwork of small territories was led by warriors, men who could hold together the social structure, albeit on a local level, as Britain's footing shifted from a controlled, commercial trading nation to a series of princedoms on a simple war setting.

There were three key elements to this army which brought it a string of successes over the Saxons, who at this time still relied solely on a mass of javelin armed infantry. Firstly, the armies in the west began to use a spear rather than a javelin, giving them more solidity and a longer reach in melee, something that continued with the Western British and Welsh armies. Secondly, there was still a strong cavalry force, presumably using every piece of available equipment that remained after the final break down of the post Roman administration. Finally, the army still had a core of missile troops, mostly bowmen but supported by some slingers, who would have been able to inflict casualties on the Saxons without a great risk to themselves as the Saxons had very few, if any, long-range missile troops of their own. These three things combined to make this British army a very strong one and, being so well balanced, it could undertake in battle either an offensive or a defensive strategy. Sadly, following a series of catastrophes in the sixth century,

Late Roman or British cavalry in a reenactment at Wroxeter.

which we will look at in chapter five, 'The Britons 430–577', the British fell out among each other, after which there was a steady decline in the unity of the British defence as the country further fragmented. When the Saxons advanced with renewed vigour in the 570s, the remaining British forces could no longer match them in battle, though this may have been due to being vastly outnumbered. At Dyrham in 577, the British were heavily defeated and their remaining realm split into fragments on the Western extremities of the British Isles.

Welsh Army 580–1420

The Welsh were mostly unsuccessful in battle when fighting on their terms, as they did not evolve or change to meet new technological challenges and advances in warfare. The simple fact is that it hardly changed at all; the basic composition of the army that fought against the Saxons in the 570s and the Vikings in 800s was almost identical to that which rose behind Owain Glyndŵr in 1400 in the last great rebellion for Welsh independence. The Britons were now trapped in isolated pockets in Brittany, Devon and Cornwall, Wales, Strathclyde (covering Cumbria and south-west Scotland) and Dal Riata (sometimes spelt Dalraida), which covered the northern tip of Ireland, the rest of western Scotland and some of the western Scottish isles. These peoples would eventually evolve into the Bretons, Cornish and Welsh and all have survived to this day, the others eventually becoming absorbed into the English and the Scottish peoples. Their problem after being isolated was one that none of them could overcome: no single state was strong enough to be able to force a corridor through to another kindred realm and so lead an assault to reunite the territories that had been lost. Today, the people descended from these kingdoms are known as 'Celtic' people. However, that term for these peoples was not coined until 1707, when Edward Lhuyd used it to describe the derivation of the Indo-European language that had evolved into the three separate stems, Gaelic, Cornish and Welsh, which were being spoken at that time, and which are still spoken today.

The structure of the army which the now-isolated Britons in Wales forged deviated at some point so that those Britons in North Wales formulated armies that were almost opposite to their kin in the south. The two separate armies are quite distinct: the southern Welsh army consisted almost entirely of infantry bowmen, while the northern Welsh army consisted almost entirely of infantry spearmen. Both armies had a small contingent of light javelinmen that would act as skirmishers in support of their more numerous comrades. Similarly, both armies were always short of cavalry, so that in an army of say 1,000 men, probably no more than between 50 and 100 would be mounted and very few would have protective armour. The luxury of good quality weapons, shield and armour came from trophies taken from opponents as victory in battle always provided fresh horses and much needed metal weapons and varying amounts and quality of armour. This was a time when nothing was wasted, so as well as food, money and weaponry, the bodies of the defeated men would be stripped of every useful item of clothing, if not to be worn then to be traded or sold later. The differences between the compositions of these two armies meant that when combined in a united cause, as under Owain Glyndŵr, they were formidable and a match for any opponents, as we shall see in due course. Sadly for the Welsh as a nation, the princes tended to squabble among themselves, and rather than looking to ally with each other to see off invaders, they would often ally with raiders, such as the Vikings, in order to challenge Welsh prince rivals. One device that the Welsh used to great advantage to move men and supplies very swiftly, was water. Small boats, which could carry about four men, and coracles, which normally carried just one man and his weapons, were used. The light, shallow-drafted craft could be paddled on almost any of the Welsh rivers, and their use allowed men to be able to travel silently to arrive below the walls of castles or underneath bridges ready for an assault or an ambush.

Welsh Clothing and Uniforms

For the vast majority of this period, there is very little evidence for any styles of clothing worn by the Welsh during the Dark Ages and into the medieval

Small Welsh skin-covered boat used for river transport, built like a coracle.

period. Gerald of Wales states that the Welsh people were for the most part very poor, having very basic homes with just thin rushes on the floor and insufficient coverings for a bed. Sleeping together and with a fire constantly burning was the only way that they could keep warm. These were days long before any kind of uniforms; the vast majority of the Welsh, whether they fought or not, would have been dressed in their simple day-to-day peasant clothing, which was a shirt and a long piece of woollen plaid akin to the clothing worn by their distant cousins, the Highlanders who followed the Stuart cause as Jacobites between 1689 and 1746. It is not insignificant that these two 'Celtic' peoples had dressed the same for many centuries. Few had shoes or boots and many fought and marched barefoot and even bare legged. In the later medieval times, the Welsh were still as poorly dressed, though lords like Owain Glyndŵr and other Welsh princes and gentry who had experienced life in England would have had their own livery and some, but by no means all, would been able to equip their entourage and perhaps men of their wider household in a livery or colours that reflected their coat of arms.

Scotti 200–846

The Latin word for the peoples that inhabited modern-day Eire (Ireland) when the Romans ruled Britannia was *Scotti,* and from this source come our modern words of Scotland and Scottish. Some of the Scotti left their homeland at the time of the Roman occupation of Britain to raid the west coast of Wales and the north-east and south-west coasts of England in search of plunder. Sometimes they would fight against the local population and sometimes they would fight alongside them as mercenaries. Eventually they formed their own Kingdom of Dal Riata, which would grow to include the modern-day area of Antrim in Northern Ireland, most of the Hebrides and the western mainland of the Highlands of Scotland. This brought the Scotti into conflict with the peoples they had apparently initially sent to settle in Scotland, the Picts. Eventually the Scotti would grind down and overthrow the now indigenous Picts, combining with them after decades of war to form the mainstay of the ancestors of today's Scottish people. The Picts, as we shall see below, were strong for around 600 years, but eventually lost out to the more organised and expanding Scotti until these two races were united in 846 under Kenneth MacAlpin and a new, united 'Scottish' army was born. The Scotti were one of the two armies of the Dark Age period that still used chariots, a light two-horse vehicle similar to those of the Picts. Julius Caesar was surprised when he saw the Celts were still using chariots in 55 BCE as they were a weapon that had disappeared from land warfare in the Mediterranean centuries before. No doubt, any armies encountering the Scotti or the Picts would have been similarly amazed at seeing such an unusual method of fighting. The military activity of the Scotti was initially raids against western Britain, but from their kingdom of Dal Riata there was almost incessant war against the Picts, which only ended when the Picts were heavily defeated by the Vikings in the early 800s, allowing the Scotti to finally defeat their neighbours. Over the next 200 years a mixture of Scotti, Picts and Viking settlers would forge the kingdom of Alba, which we know today as Scotland. A Scotti army did not have much flexibility, because its only horsemen were light chariots and its shock troops were only a small bodyguard of hostage kings' sons – brought to make sure that people left at home toed the line. There were two large infantry contingents, one of noble warriors and one of lower class warriors, all of whom were armed the same, with javelins and shields, but little or no armour to protect them. The only skirmishers they had were some light javelinmen and a few slingers.

Norse-Irish 846–1300

The Vikings raided the Irish mainland with the same frequency that they did everywhere else in Europe and for a hundred years the native Irish had a torrid time as they lived in fear of ever more violent raids. Eventually, as with elsewhere, the Vikings settled down in their own villages to become craftsmen, traders and farmers, and by 950 they had established colonies on waterways at Dublin, Wexford, Waterford, Limerick and Cork, the major cities of the island. The Vikings never fully colonized Ireland, reflecting again the pattern elsewhere, seeming to be content to settle on coastal lands reminiscent, perhaps, of those lands that they had left behind. These Vikings gradually became integrated into the local population, even fighting in the internal wars between the different realms of Ireland. This gave rise to a new combined army which would last for 450 years, well beyond the Dark Ages, and one that would fight to defend Ireland against the Normans, who looked to be the first nation to take complete control of the Emerald Isle. The native Irish were by this time better armed than before, having added two-handed axes to accompany their javelins, but they still had very little, if any, armour. The vast majority of troops were still armed with javelins, but the nobility and some of the Bonnachts (troops maintained by the nobility, effectively mercenaries) would have had the two-handed axe as well as javelins. Reinforcing the army would be units of Vikings from the mainland or from outlying islands so that huscarls, bondi (small landholding farmers serving their lord) and some archers brought more flexibility to the overall force. This army would remain unchanged until around 1300, when cavalry began to make an appearance, altering the structure of the force. This army was made up from a combination of troops, with the Irish and Viking settlements working together, and does not appear to have used many other nationalities as mercenary troops save for the two predominant types of Welsh infantry, archers and spearmen, two types of troops lacking in the Norse-Irish ranks – Wales was their closest source of available mercenaries, though at times the Norse-Irish aided Welsh princes.

Norman 888–1072

To the modern mind, an army of Normans conjures up William the Conqueror and the Battle of Hastings, but these warrior lords of northern France had been a growing power since the late ninth century. Their name and the region of northern France they came from are synonymous with one another as they both come from the Latin *Nortmanni*, which means simply 'Northmen'; the Normans were simply descendants of Vikings that had landed, pillaged and then settled in the northern coastal regions of France in the early eighth century. These Normans were no different to the Vikings that had settled and increased the power of the Scotti until the amalgamated Irish-Viking invasion force was destroyed at Brunanburh on the Wirral in 937. A similar derivation is to be found with Russia, for the name given to the Northmen that settled there was *Rus*. The Normans used the same ships as their ancestors, swift, shallow of draft and easy to manoeuvre, the perfect tool for expanding your frontiers by sea and by 1154 they controlled most of southern Italy, parts of North Africa and Malta. Unlike their ancestors, the Normans abandoned the axe at just the same time that it was being adopted by the Anglo-Saxons for their most important troops, the huscarls, who were a lord or king's most loyal band of fighters. Although the Normans ditched the axe, it was for a positive reason: they replaced it with two innovations that they brought to the late first millennium battlefield. The first was to make the horse the dominant force of an army. Now ridden by armoured men with large shields, the horses were trained to charge into and break through an opposing force's defensive line. The ubiquitous javelin, which every army carried, was replaced by a heavier spear that became the lance when used on horseback. The Normans developed their tactics so that they charged home with the lance couched under the right arm and their shield protecting the whole of their left side, making their charge all the more devastating when it hit home. The second innovation was the organisation they brought to their tactics on the battlefield. The Normans went back to the days of the Romans and the early British and fused together a combination of differently armed light missile troops and heavily armed shock troops so that they had the means to deal with any type of enemy. These well-balanced Norman armies consisted of mounted knights, heavily armed javelinmen and missile troops who were variously armed with crossbows, bows and staff slings.

The final innovation that the Normans brought to warfare was the wooden motte and bailey fort, the forerunner of the medieval stone castle. Already in widespread use in Normandy, William I dispensed patronage after his successful invasion to the lords who had been loyal to him and they began their lordship with the construction of numerous motte and baileys. These Normans were determined to stamp their new authority upon the land and there were hundreds built; many of their remains are still visible today, particularly along the Welsh borders. Some remains are just the mound – or motte – a conically shaped hill with a flat top where the wooden, later stone, square tower – the bailey – would have sat; others are complete, such as at Clun in Shropshire. The first of the great stone castles, the Tower of London, still stands today. However, 1066 was not the first time that the Normans and Saxons came to blows in England. When Edward the Confessor returned to England in 1041, following his exile in Normandy, he brought with him a Norman-educated mind and also many Norman counsellors, including a small number of knights, some of whom established a small 'English' cavalry force. Some of the Normans were even given lands, most famously Ralph, who was established as Earl of Hereford by Edward and charged with the task of defending the Welsh Marches and making war upon the Welsh, who were still at this time raiding Mercian lands. It is interesting to note that in these early exchanges the Normans failed to make any headway against the Welsh, suffering defeat and embarrassment at the hands of the Welsh spearmen and bowmen, a lesson Harold Godwinson would have done well to note, but sadly for Saxon England he did not, a lesson the Normans would be taught again when they invaded Wales, having conquered England.

Picts 250–846

The emergence of the Picts as a nation is still fairly mysterious. They are first recorded in two panegyrics in the early fourth century; the latter, addressed to Constantine by an unknown author, mentions the Caledones and 'other' Picts, indicating that they were branches of the same people. According to Bede, the Picts arrived from Scythia in a just few small vessels, arriving first in modern-day Northern Ireland, where they sought refuge having missed their intended destination of southern Britain. The Picts were instantly turned away by the Scotti, who suggested that they should travel north-east to a land where they would find room to settle, adding that they would come to their aid if they encountered trouble. We have already seen above, when we examined the weaponry of this period and mentioned the stelae evidence of the Pictish stones, that there is some evidence that the Scythian theory does hold up. In addition, we must consider three more facts. Firstly, the Picts were known as the painted people, as they painted their bodies with tattoos, as did the Celts before them, and they would also fight naked to let the spirits of their drawings protect them in battle. By pure chance, Scythian tomb excavations in Pazyryk, in the Altai Mountains in Siberia, have revealed painted bodies complete with tattoos. These bodies were frozen incredibly quickly after burial by the penetration of running ice water into their graves which then refroze, preserving the skin and its tattoos. The Scythians were painted people who we now know spread far from their Steppe homelands and travelled as far as the north German plain, as well as east into China and north into modern day Russia and the Ukraine; it was little hardship to move a similar distance west. Many of the eastern symbols are of animals and horses and are comparable to those found in Scotland, where Pictish symbols are often influenced by horses and human-horse pictorials – most fitting for a race whose ancestors lived in the saddle on the steppes of Asia. Secondly, the Picts were the only race in Britain where the women were expected to fight alongside their men, just as the Scythians are reputed to have done. The final piece of evidence comes from a written document signed by the Scottish aristocracy and Church hierarchy in their declaration to the Pope, penned at Arbroath in 1320. In this declaration they urged the Pope to see Scotland as an independent country, separate to the English peoples to the south, because, so the declaration claimed in the second paragraph, 'Scythia was their former homeland,' proving that they were a different people to the Anglo-Saxons. So were these people from the steppes of near Asia? One day we may know for certain.

From a military perspective, the Picts are the most varied and colourful army of the Dark Age period and have left their mark on the Scottish landscape because so many of their standing stones have survived, showing in pictograms events from their history. The carvings show three different types of horsemen, chariots and both light and heavy cavalry, and also crossbows – they were the only Dark Age army to use such a weapon. These detailed carvings are some of the few testaments that we have to their very existence. The most notable is the Sueno stone near Forres, which is probably a cenotaph. In terms of their success upon the battlefield, the Picts raided deep into England from the third century onwards and joined in raids on Wales and the Welsh coast. On their home soil they fought with success against the Scotti and the Saxons from Northumbria, as well as against the Vikings. The Picts are one of the few nations in the Dark Ages to have a balanced army, their mobility provided by units of light chariots and light cavalry, their strength in steady infantry armed with spears and javelins supported by light units with missiles fired from crossbows and bows; when the battle was at a crucial point, the Picts had a reserve of heavy cavalry to deliver the hammer blow at a weak point in the enemy ranks or to reinforce any apparent weakness in their own line.

The land of the Picts stretched from the River Forth north to the Western Isles, across to Orkney and Shetland and across the whole of north-east Scotland, where their strongest realm, Fortriu, lay. They were accomplished seamen and there exists on just one stone, the St Orland's Stone in Angus, a carving of an oared longboat, but the fact that a third of their realm was made up of islands must mean that they had some reliable ships in order to administer it successfully for so long. As with other areas of Britain, the Pictish people, living in such unsettled times, looked to use naturally defensive positions such as steep hilltops or narrow coastal promontories as bases for their homes and their court. These would have been improved by adding enclosing ditches, palisades and ramparts. The outcrop fort at Dundurn has three such phases of fortification, all built between 500 and 800. There are also several examples of Picts reoccupying earlier Iron Age forts, for example the vitrified fort at Craig Phadrig, so called because at some point in its destruction the fort was set alight creating such heat that as the palisades burned, they melted the local stone, coating the remaining rampart in a glass-like glaze. The Picts both allied with and fought against the Scotti and they also used Saxons and Vikings as allies, particularly in their wars with the Scotti. Ironically, the Picts would be defeated by a major Viking raid in 839 that destroyed their aristocracy and weakened them to such an extent that the Scotti were able to defeat them once and for all and so unite Scotland. The battle is recorded in the Annals of Ulster for the year 839, listing the deaths of the Pictish King Eoganan and many more of his household. The site of this battle is unknown, but given that so many of the Pictish nobility were wiped out in one battle, it is likely that the battle had to be fought near a major stronghold of their realm. Such a place lies near St Fillans, in the very centre of Scotland, where the major Pictish stronghold of Dundurn Hill stands, which remained the place of Pictish kings up to the death of King Giric in 889. For the Welsh, the destruction of the Picts removed the threat of their raids, as the new kingdom of Scotland looked to raid by land south towards the Saxons and not further afield by sea.

Saxons 447–1066

The term 'Saxons' is a generic name for a whole group of Germanic tribes from the Rhine basin, the plain of northern Germany and the Danish peninsula, who migrated west in the late fourth and early fifth century. Due to the demands on the land of an increasing population, a need to grow more food meant that there was a need to find fresh places to settle and the situation became critical. Indeed, Bede stated that these migrations emptied that whole region of people, such was the migration west, only for it to be filled by Scandinavian peoples who were moving south. The reference to Angles, Jutes, Frisians and upper and lower Saxons under the broad name of 'Saxons' led the people on the fringes of Britain to call them Sassenachs, a term still used in colloquial Scottish today for the English people, and we will also use the broad term of 'Saxon' throughout the book to refer to all of these Germanic settlers. A Saxon army consisted of just two main types of troops, both of whom were infantry. There would be noble javelinmen, who were well armoured and carried a stout round shield, and for every one of those there would be three or more low-class javelinmen, unarmoured, save for perhaps some form of leather waistcoat, and carrying a shield for protection. There were little or no cavalry in the Saxon armies and just a few missile men to skirmish in support of the shieldwall, which was the only offensive weapon such an infantry-dominated army could generate. However, the Northumbrians were known to use horses and whether this was to allow the army to move quicker or whether they actually fought as cavalry is open to much speculation. This army reflects the Saxon states that gradually settled into their distinct areas before waging civil war with each other as each tried to become overall ruler of England. The only change to these armies came around 640, when some Welsh spearmen and a small number of Welsh bowmen were used as allies by the armies of Mercia or Wessex when fighting other Saxon and Viking enemies. The Northumbrian Saxons sometimes allied with the Picts, but only when they were not fighting their conspicuously painted enemies to the north. Following the uniting of the Saxons under the reforms of Alfred of Wessex, and later of Ethelred the Unready, England was able to count upon a standing army that could be called out at need without disturbing the essential food production that manual agriculture in these times demanded. As well as creating the huscarls, who were the king or commander's personal retinue and administrators for a given area, there would be a strong, select fyrd of armoured infantry made up from the thegns, as well as the general fyrd, which were the lower class of troops. These troops were all used to being mustered for campaigning and would have had rudimentary training and weapons drill to make them an effective fighting force. The ability of the fyrd at Hastings to withstand almost 9 hours of Norman assaults and missile bombardments shows the great discipline that had to have been instilled in them at some point, so some training clearly existed. The importance of the army to the Saxon monarchy is illustrated in the laws of the day, where a Saxon thegn (equivalent to the level of a village squire) was required to fulfil a *heriot* (death duty) on his land in the form of a gift to the monarch. This consisted of four horses, two saddles, four shields, four spears, a helmet and a coat of mail. Effectively, the death of the thegn meant his small retinue went to the king to allocate to fresh troops at need. There is much discussion as to exactly how well armoured the greater number of troops were in these massed infantry ranks and the assumption is that the well armoured and better trained troops took the front and second line of the shieldwall, and that the less well armoured general fyrd took the rear ranks, supporting their comrades in front with strength and muscle when the crunch of impact came. The missile troops were still few in number compared to the massed infantry that formed the shieldwall, but archers and slingers would skirmish, shooting in support of the shieldwall, either from the flanks or, if the height of the ground allowed, shooting over the top of the dense infantry lines.

Vikings – Danish and Scandinavian 790–1100

The development of the longboat was to bring to Dark Age conflict what the helicopter would bring to modern warfare. Looking to arrive with the dawn or the tide, or preferably both, the Vikings would creep quietly inland, floating up river estuaries ready to pounce on a fresh target, some unsuspecting and previously ignored settlement ripe for the plucking. An examination of the Vikings' progress shows that the vast majority of their attacks, and their then settlements, were alongside waterways. The Vikings' advancements in ship-building gave them the ability to launch these lightning fast raids against targets located many hundreds of miles from their homelands. Many times these tactics prevailed and they were able to wreak havoc on their surprised and defenceless victims, but on occasion, as we shall see at Buttington in 893, penetrating unsupported so far inland could go disastrously wrong. Initially their attacks were simply raids, where they looted villages and churches, picking off any soft targets for material gain and often carrying off prisoners to become slaves, which were a valuable source of income. Later, they made more organised invasions to establish and settle in small communities along the coasts of France, Ireland and England. Eventually, great armies came in hundreds of ships, making wholesale invasions with which they would eventually conquer and control their own lands in England, Ireland and France. In 1880 the Gokstad ship was excavated in Norway, giving a valuable insight not only into the detailed construction of these exceptionally crafted oak ships but also into some of the organisational elements of this Dark Age military transport. The ship carried sixty-four shields, thirty-two on each side, giving a combative force of at least sixty-four men, and there would have been officers and possibly crew inside as well, so perhaps eighty men in total. From the perspective of recreating a Viking army of this period, the archaeologists were able to determine that the shields were alternately painted yellow and black, giving an indication that both a ship's and a crew's shields may have been colour coded to allow ease of recognition, particularly important for a large force such as Harald Hardrada's, which invaded York in 1066, when many hundreds of ships were involved. The shields of King Olaf, who was a Christian Viking, were painted white, upon which crosses in a variety of colours were painted. The Vikings won a great number of their battles, especially when given time to form up, such as at Maldon (991) and Fulford Gate (1066); it was when they were caught off guard and unable to form properly, such as at Stamford

Bridge in 1066, that they were soundly beaten. The reason the Vikings may have been so successful in battle against other shieldwalls is that they adopted a formation similar to the testudo used to such great effect by the Romans, notably in Britain against Caratacus at his last stand in 51. The boarsnout (*svinfylka* or *Svinfylking*) would have required considerable practice and men of great strength and bravery, as they would lead the attack, so it is most likely that it was conducted by the huscarls. These men were chosen and trusted bodyguards and as such they would have had more opportunity to practise this manoeuvre. The formation was formed by the men locking their shields together, with the outer men protected by the inner with shields held up to stop missiles raining down upon them. To the front would be the greatest warriors, who would smash into the enemy's shieldwall looking to punch a hole through it, allowing the lighter armed troops following behind to exploit the gap and so get behind the enemy's shieldwall, rendering it useless. In the Viking way of life, it was expected that every able-bodied man should have their own weapons, each according to his status. The Vikings' army consisted of no cavalry, though horses were stolen in raids and used to cross country between settlements and their ships. The mainstay of the army was armed men with two-handed axes, supported by lower class warriors with javelins; they also used a small number of bow, sling and javelin skirmishers to support their shieldwall. The Vikings fought all across Europe and their allies reflect their penetration into other civilisations, for example Welsh, Scotti, Picts and Franks. In spite of their defeat at Stamford Bridge, the Vikings remained a threat throughout the remainder of the eleventh century and were involved in the Battle of Priestholm in 1098 when, rarely, a three-way battle occurred.

Anglo-Norman 1072–1181

Following the completion of the Norman Conquest, during which William I had been forced to crush the Saxon rebellions in Shropshire, East Anglia and the north of England with savage brutality, the new English king amalgamated the two armies. The foreign mercenaries that had aided William in his conquest were now gone, and so those contingents of troops were replaced by the remnants of the fyrd, and this gave the already strong Norman-style army an even greater solidity. The majority of the troops still wore little armour; only the select fyrd, the knights and some of the mercenaries could be classed as heavy infantry. Many of the armoured knights that made up the cavalry were those French and Breton mercenaries who had fought in the invasion and who had been given both titles and land for the aid in the expedition. Their descendants would continue to fight as knights in the royal cause, forming much of the aristocracy that would in time become part of the established nobility of

The shieldwall was used by most Dark Age armies; this one is performed by Cestrefeld.

England. This duality of William and the close connections between France and England would both unite and cause conflict between the two nations until end of the fifteenth century. The Welsh repeatedly fought as mercenaries throughout this period, sometimes on opposite sides. The issue for all of these first Norman kings was that they had no standing army, so that if there was a rebellion or the threat of invasion the king had to pay men to fight for him which often meant acquiring mercenaries from abroad, often from modern-day Belgium, whose men were renowned spearmen and known then as Flemings.

English 1181–1455

Eventually, Henry II realised that this constant drain on the exchequer could not be maintained. In 1181 he issued a proclamation, the Assize of Arms. Under this law there was an obligation for all freemen of England to both possess and bear arms in the service of both king and country. All were obliged to swear allegiance to the king, and if anyone failed then vengeance could be brought upon them, from the confiscation of land or possessions to the 'severing of limbs'. This assize was merely the reintroduction of the old Anglo-Saxon fyrd duty, which allowed a king to call out his men at time of need. With the advances in armour and weaponry and the stipulation in the assize as to exactly what military equipment each man had to supply, according to his rank and wealth, the king would have an accurate idea of the size of the force that he could muster and what its potential strength and composition would be. With a stipulation as to the arms now to be provided and improvements in both metal armour and weapons, the English army began to increase the amount of armour it wore and the number of archers it fielded. The armoured knights were now

Units of polearmed men forming for battle.

fully armoured and the fyrd were replaced by militia and companies of archers supplied by counties such as Cheshire and Shropshire. The Welsh, Flemings and Norse-Irish continued to provide mercenary spear and javelinmen, so the assize did not supply all of the troops that the monarch required. After 1310 the chainmail began to be replaced by the plate mail discussed in chapter two and the composition of the armies changed again. By the 1350s all of the knights were now wearing plate mail and riding armoured horses bred and trained for battle. The lighter javelinmen and spearmen were now gone, as were the majority of the long, thrusting spears; in their place the infantry of an army was now made of one third polearms and two thirds archers. The army was almost entirely English though it was still supported by small numbers of mercenaries, Welsh spearmen, Welsh archers, German pikemen, and French crossbowmen, but these were now a small percentage of the overall numbers involved and were hired for their specialist skills, not to make up for shortfalls in the rest of the army. Throughout the period the armour continued to get heavier and the variety of polearms to deal with the armour became ever more varied. In most battles the English knights chose to fight on foot rather than on horseback and everywhere the English and Welsh longbowmen and their storm of arrows wreaked death and havoc among their enemies; unfortunately, sometimes they would also wreak havoc and destruction upon themselves.

Warfare in Wales

One can see from the armies and enemies of the Welsh peoples that there was in some cases a sharp contrast between the two different forces. When examining the battles involving armies in Wales, one has to allow for these differences and understand how their choice of ground differed, one to the other. The invaders would be seeking to catch the Welsh unprepared in their unprotected homesteads or on flat, rolling terrain that suited the well organised and disciplined troops of the Roman and Norman armies. On the other hand, the Welsh troops would be looking to draw their enemy onto poor terrain, a marshy valley floor with steep-sided hills to restrict their deployment and allow the Welsh to ambush or surround them. Certainly, the Welsh army was one that was constructed for defence and it was never more dangerous than when upon its own soil. The dense blocks of spearmen supported by cavalry and missile troops made it a formidable force in the rugged terrain of Wales, where the steep mountains with narrow valleys in between (often with wide marshes and fast flowing rivers within them) meant that there could be no fast movement for an invading army. Routes of march were therefore restricted to known valleys, which could be staked out by the local Welsh troops, who then, almost unseen, stalked and harassed the enemy from the mountain slopes above. Where necessary, the narrow valleys could be defended with blocks of spearmen while missile troops shot arrows into the enemy's flanks from the hills above with the cavalry poised, ready to be unleashed should the enemy line begin to falter so that the horsemen could deliver the final blow. One reason that the Welsh army did not change over a 900-year period was because it did not need to change; the ambush tactics it used and the missile and melee weapons it used were perfectly suited to that type of engagement. When the northern spearmen were combined with the southern bowmen, they were a very effective defensive army.

For the greater part of this period, from 44 until 1200 (when the first organised lines of longbowmen started to deliver their telling volleys of missiles into the massed ranks of their opponents to cause death and injury), the majority of battlefield casualties were caused by people fighting at very close quarters. Groups of men in lines several ranks deeps, or in some cases individuals, would come together at the end of either a controlled or a fanatical charge, bent on wearing down their opponents through the strength of their combined numbers and the volume of destructive blows they could bring to bear upon their opponents. If it was a set battle, where both sides could see each other, once the initial volley of arrows, slingstones and javelins had been exchanged, the two sides would charge home, each expecting the crunch as they came together.

If it was an ambush, which as we shall see many of the Welsh battles were, the first that the ambushed force would know of the presence of an enemy

Steep-sided, wooded valleys aided the Welsh ambush tactics, as here in the Glyn Ceiriog Valley.

was when they were hit either by an avalanche of javelins, arrows and stones from people that they could not see, or when they were hit as a hidden enemy emerged from the undergrowth around them to smash violently into their flanks and rear. In these wars, this was the time when the majority of casualties were caused, as people hit and thrust at each other, standing right in each other's faces. Each combatant would see the whites of their opponent's eyes gleaming from the dark recesses of a helmet or metal head-guard if they were lucky enough to have one. The men would smell each other's breath and see the sweat, blood and dirt on their faces, faces that wore an expression of grim determination which stated in simple terms, kill or be killed. All of this would be taken in by the warriors in fractions of a second as their weapons, shields and even their bodies crashed together time and time again. Only when the Dark Age and early medieval wars had ended did battles involve longer periods of missile exchanges as first the bowmen and then the cumbersome musketeers shot from both armies at one another, but even then a point would come in the battle when the two sides would bear down upon the other, resulting once more in massive melees as each side tried to wear down their opponent and so drive them from the field.

CHAPTER 4

The Celts and
the Roman Tide

Background

When Julius Caesar led the first Roman expeditions to Britain in 55 and 54 BC, he landed each time just north of Dover, somewhere close to Deal or Walmer. Britain was seen as the edge of the known world and although several voyages of discovery had been made there in the previous 400 years and reports had been made of the island and its rich metals, few of these reports were accepted as the truth. Although trade in tin and copper had existed for around 1,000 years, much mystery still surrounded the island and its inhabitants. Caesar knew that at least some of the tribes in Britain were Celts, as some of them had assisted the Gauls (the Celtic people of France) in their war against him. Caesar had only just conquered Gaul and such was the speed of that victory that he was wary of pushing further north for yet more conquest in case there was a rebellion behind him by those tribes that had only recently submitted to Rome. In fact, when Caesar tried to find out from merchants and sea captains something about Britain, those he questioned were reticent about divulging any details of the landing places or the minerals to be found there, presumably because the traders feared the loss of their livelihood if the Romans took control of the country. Despite a series of setbacks, Caesar eventually succeeded in making two successful landings in consecutive years and on both occasions, after establishing a bridgehead, fought a series of battles at which the Romans drove off the Celts but did not defeat them. The appearance of an elephant with a howdah atop and men shooting arrows from it caused panic among the Celtic horses, causing the Celts to retreat. The Celts, seeing that in a pitched battle the Romans were all but invincible, resorted to guerrilla tactics, harrying the Roman foraging parties and using their fast chariots to cause casualties and then flee. Caesar was amazed to find that the Celts still fought with chariots and wrote about them at length in his reports of the campaigns. Caesar also discovered that there was much inter-tribal warfare and played one tribe off against another as he sought tribute and allegiance from the more powerful tribes. In September 54 BC, and with the threat of winter on them and having already suffered casualties crossing the Channel due to the ferocity of the wind and tides, Caesar was anxious not to stay longer than necessary and so he called time on his second expedition and all of the Romans left and returned to Gaul, where the seeds of rebellion in Caesar's absence were already geminating. Tribes that paid homage to Caesar in his presence now sent reinforcements to their 'cousins' in Gaul to aid that rebellion. To the Senate in Rome, succeeding in getting to Britain at all carried such kudos that a *supplicatio* or special thanksgiving of twenty days was awarded to celebrate the successful report received from Caesar.

This surely suggests that the Romans must have known of the mineral wealth of Britain to attach so much importance to Caesar's news. Having received Caesar's report and having seen the reaction to it, one might have expected that the island of Britain would be invaded for a third time within the near future; no doubt the tribal leaders of the Celts also expected the return of the Romans after two expeditions in two years, but the anticipated invasion never came. The series of brutal civil wars that occurred either side of the assassination of Julius Caesar commanded the attention of all the senior politicians in the Senate. When the second triumvirate of Octavian (Augustus), Marcus Aemilius Lepidus and Mark Antony subsequently triumphed over Cassius Longinus and Marcus Junius Brutus, the key conspirators against Julius Caesar, the collapse of the Republic and the foundation of the Augustan dynasty followed. These events combined to put Britain extremely low on the list of priorities for the newly crowned emperors and as a result the Celtic lands were free from military interference for almost 100 years. Trade links, however, had been established and these flourished in the intervening years, during which the Romans sought to maintain a watchful eye without interfering in internal Celtic politics so long as their trade continued and peace was maintained.

The death of Cunobelinus (the Cymbeline of Shakespeare's play of the same name) brought to prominence his two sons, Togidumnus and his more famous brother Caradoc (Caradog or Caratacus). When tensions rose among the Celtic tribes, those who had shown favour to Rome with tribute now expected some protection, while Caratacus and Togidumnus demanded they leave the country. Against all expectation, the emperor in Rome was now Claudius, who came to power after the assassination of his mentally unstable nephew, Caligula. Claudius was proclaimed emperor in 41 by the Praetorian Guard, the personal bodyguard of the emperors. Like all emperors, Claudius would have wanted to make his mark and the pleas from the pro-Roman tribes, including the Atrebates, may have been the catalyst he needed to divert attention away from Rome and the recent assassination. Britain was a territory on the border of the empire to which an expedition could be mounted with some certainty of success. The Rhine frontier was established and secure and further expansion to the east was impossible at present and would require an enormous investment in both time and men and would be far too expansive; but troops could be taken from the Rhine to invade Britain. The Roman army had gone through a series of improvements since Caesar's day; a strengthened helmet and segmented armour had improved the personal protection of each soldier. The army was now at the height of its power and efficiency and Claudius issued a directive that Britain should now be conquered.

Celtic tribes of Britain before the Roman conquest

When the Romans looked at Britain in 43, the island had changed little since Caesar's visit; the land was still divided unequally into irregularly shaped geographical areas, each of which was dominated by a particular tribe and ruled by the tribal chieftains. Although divided into small areas, the country as a whole was prosperous in terms of trade, especially the fertile lowlands in the south, growing grain that was always essential to feed the populace of Rome. To the north of an imaginary line across Britain, which roughly corresponds to the orientation of the Cotswold Hills, abundant cattle and sheep were farmed and there were dense tracts of woodland in which wolves, bears and wild boar still roamed. Aulus Plautius was appointed to lead Claudius's invasion force; he was a man of considerable experience, a very organised general who knew how to lead and get the best from his men. This was no preliminary sortie but a full-scale invasion with an army of four legions, around 24,000 legionaries, which was supported by a similar number of auxiliary troops, the lighter cavalry and skirmishers. To carry so many men and the stores that would be required as well as horses for the cavalry, the fleet would have been enormous, probably 1,000 vessels at least, and it sailed in three separate convoys. The first convoy's aim was to secure the safety of the landing site for those men that would follow and these first ships landed at Richborough in Kent, within a few miles of Caesar's original landing site. They quickly secured the area, building ditches and dykes as the bridgehead behind which the other two convoys could land. The second convoy to land then expanded the initial bridgehead with more defences further inland, and this allowed the final convoy of stores and equipment to land in total safety. The whole operation had gone smoothly and was the Roman equivalent of the Allied D-Day landings in Normandy in 1944.

With his army safely landed, Plautius swiftly expanded his localised area of control and sent out extensive scouting parties to ensure that there was no major threat in the vicinity. Satisfied that it was safe to advance, Plautius advanced and soon encountered the main Celtic resistance force, which was drawn up on the banks of the River Medway, blocking the Romans' crossing and their advance westwards. The Romans would not have committed all of their troops to this advance, and one can assume that a legion and the equivalent number of auxiliaries would have been left to guard the shore-fort that would have been constructed before any troops departed into the interior. As explained, the Roman army was a professional one and nothing was left to chance. Roman military policy dictated that an army was to construct a defensive outpost every evening to secure their quarters against attack. The shore fort at Richborough would have been vast given the number of men and the amount of supplies stored to equip and support them. The Romans would not have wanted to risk leaving valuable supplies aboard ship, in case a storm should wreck them. The Roman force would have therefore been around 30,000 men. With an estimated British population of 1.5 million, there were roughly 150,000 men able to fight.

There is a suggestion that the Celts put 100,000 men into the field, but that is extremely unlikely as the 150,000 men able to fight were spread across Britain, not just in the area of south-eastern England needed to challenge the initial Roman advance, and some tribes were not hostile to the Romans. However, it is unlikely that the Celts would have risked battle without a sizeable force of their own, so given the size of the Roman army it is not unreasonable to suppose that there were at least a similar number, say 30,000, of Celts also present. Caratacus and Togidumnus led the Celtic army that watched the Romans approach. These generals were familiar with their own Celtic warfare and would no doubt have reinforced the river bank with sharp wooden stakes at all the known crossing points, and by standing on the opposite bank of the river they would undoubtedly have felt that they controlled a secure defensive position. They had no recent experience of the professionalism of the Roman forces that faced them and what now ensued was one of the most important battles in British history. Having assessed the Celtic positions and reconnoitred the river both north and south of his current position, Plautius split his force into different detachments. He sent his Batavians north and they crossed the river at a deeper place which was well out of sight of the Celts' left flank, while Plautius' main force diverted the Celts' attention by making as if to cross the river in front of them, which separated the armies. The Batavians crossed the River Medway where the depth of the river was such that the Celts would not have imagined anyone could cross in safety. Having managed to cross in spite of the depth, the Batavians successfully outflanked the Celtic line which, according to the Roman Dio Cassius, they attacked at once. The Batavians targeted the Celtic horses to prevent the Celts from using their chariots and cavalry to either counter attack the Romans or to escape swiftly from the action.

Hearing that the Batavians had succeeded, Plautius now launched his main attack – possibly aided by lightweight boats or tents filled with straw for buoyancy – directly into the waiting Celtic hordes, where they would have been met with a hail of javelins as they crossed. The young Vespasian (later emperor himself) took part in this assault as Plautius sent two legions across the river. The fighting lasted for what remained of the daylight hours but the resistance of the Celts was not broken. Given the superiority of the Roman soldier man for man when measured against the Celtic tribesman, Caratacus's and Togidumnus's force must have been the 30,000 men suggested above, if not more; the Celts had seen the mighty obstacle of the river crossed, they had been outflanked, lost a lot of their horses and were fighting the best army in the world and they had not crumpled in a whole day's fighting. When night came both sides must have regrouped and Plautius took that opportunity to send in the third legion, which he had been holding in reserve, across the river to reinforce Vespasian's bridgehead on the west, Celtic, side of the river. When the battle resumed the next morning, the resistance of the Celts was finally broken and the whole army fled north-west to cross by known paths across the Thames marshes and so escape the pursuing Romans. Casualty levels are unknown but they must have been significant on both sides; two large armies fighting hand to hand for around 12 or more hours must have inflicted heavy losses on each other. The decision to flee on the next morning may also have been to do with the Celts falling back on their knowledge of their own territories before their losses became critical. The Batavians had crossed the River Medway the previous morning, which perhaps indicates that time of day was the lowest tide point. For the lightly armed Celts, who would know the tide times of their local rivers, it may be that they had to flee at a certain time to a prearranged signal in order for them to cross the Thames marshes before the Romans could pursue. For whatever reason, the withdrawal of the Celts surrendered the field to Plautius and he was able to secure his Medway crossing, leaving him free to push on westwards. With the main force of the Celts fled, Plautius sent word to Rome for Claudius to come and claim his triumph at Camulodunum (Colchester), the capital of the Trinovantes tribe who inhabited the area of modern Essex. The emperor duly obliged, arriving on an elephant to impress those that knelt before him. The Imperial visit lasted sixteen days, during which there was no conflict reported and Claudius was honoured by the surrender to himself of eleven of the British kings, though these kings were tribal rulers and not a British monarchy. Not all of the kings paid homage, however; Caratacus had escaped and he fled west out of reach of the spreading Roman tide and all the time he tried to rally support to stand against the Romans, first with the Dubonni and then with the Silures. It is not certain whether Togidumnus was killed at the Battle of Medway or whether he chose to become an ally of the Romans as his name crops up again as the loyal ruler of the client kingdoms of the Regini, the Atrebates, the Belgae and the Dobunni once the initial invasion of Britain had been consolidated.

The defence of the River Medway highlights the difference in the approach to warfare of the respective commanders. The Celts would have examined all of the terrain between the Thames crossing just east of modern day Tilbury (a vital bridging point for those wishing to head north) and the shore fort established by the Romans as their supply base at Richborough. With secure defences and ships armed with ballistae which could cause casualties from a long distance, the Celts knew that there was nothing to be gained by attacking the Romans in their new encampment. They also knew that the Romans would not risk marching south and then west along the coast, which might overstretch their supply lines. Therefore, the logical route that the Romans would take was a march due west leading them to the River Medway, which was the most suitable terrain for holding back their advance. Importantly for the Celts, such a position also allowed them an escape route north-west across the Thames marshes should they be defeated. Now, as we know, this is exactly what happened and the Celts were forced to use their escape route; the Celts had not expected the Roman army to be able to cross the defended river, particularly as they had received casualties in crossing. The Celts, despite using all of the right deductions in making their plans, had failed to take into account that they were not fighting another Celtic army but the fully equipped and versatile army that had by then conquered all of the Mediterranean world. The other Celtic tribes of southern Britain, who resisted the Roman hand of kinship by tribute, would make the same mistake. Seemingly unaware of how Julius Caesar had effectively dealt with Celtic hillforts in Gaul, the Dubonni, Belgae and Durotriges tribes rechecked and refortified their own hillforts as Plautius steadily but relentlessly advanced across the country toward them. Each of these tribes surrendered in turn as each fort fell to the bolts of the Roman ballistae and, where necessary, the Roman testudo. In some archaeological excavations, namely at Maiden Castle and Hod Hill, both in Dorset, ballista bolt heads have been found concentrated in the area of the largest and therefore the chieftain's hut; at Maiden Castle one skeleton was found with the bolt head still embedded in its spine and this can be seen in the Dorchester Museum. This shows that Roman intelligence was sufficiently comprehensive to allow their artillery to be located to target the hierarchy of the defence of the settlement, introducing psychological warfare into the campaign. Naturally, it was in their favour if the Romans could encourage a hillfort to surrender without a frontal assault, saving them from the inevitable casualties that such an attack on so strong a fortified settlement would bring.

Plautius had masterminded a brilliant campaign and by 47, just three years after landing, the whole of southern Britain from the Severn estuary to the Humber was under Roman control. Effectively all of the land south and east of a line that matches the great Roman road, the Fosse Way, which ran from Exeter to Lincoln, was now producing goods for the empire and the Romanisation of Britain had begun. Plautius had quite rightly earned a holiday and returned in triumph to Rome, where his achievements were acknowledged. However, his successor Publius Ostorius Scapula was not made of the same metal and upon his arrival in late 47 he was greeted with news of rebellions from both east and west of Plautius's new border. In 47 the Iceni in East Anglia were unhappy at being made to surrender their weapons as a client kingdom of Rome and there was a small revolt which was quickly quelled, but it led to the installation of Prasutagus as king; his wife was Boudicca, and this political manoeuvre would have a significant effect on the short-term future of Roman Britain.

The capture of the hillforts and the displacement of tribal populations as the Romans took political control of the areas they conquered naturally drove some men of fighting age to seek refuge in a suitable area from which they could continue their struggle – that place was Wales. The upland terrain and the dense vegetation in many of the river valleys meant that the Romans had not yet risked a large-scale invasion of the country; after all, in three years they had achieved a great deal and with no natural boundary to their new-won kingdom, any further expansion could only be undertaken once the appropriate forts and the supply lines to those forts were established and secure. Caratacus, like many other exasperated warriors, eventually reached south-east Wales, coming to a large tract of land under the control of the Silures. The Silures were determined not to submit to Roman rule and instead of waiting for the inevitable Roman advance, they decided to take the fight to the Romans; for the first time the people of Wales were going to become militarily active.

Despite Caratacus having been the king of the Catuvellauni in eastern Britain, on reaching the Silures he seems to have become their king for two years until he moved further north. References are made in several sources to the fact that Britain had 'High Kings' since its foundation under Brutus, references that historians have considered fanciful and connected with a 'foundation' myth similar to that of Romulus and Remus for Rome. It is possible, given that Caratacus took over every tribe he joined, that there was among the Celtic tribes a hierarchy that came into play, giving him the right to lead them. Although tradition does not directly connect him with any of the High Kings of Britain, maybe Caratacus was one of these High Kings. If not, then perhaps Caratacus had family connections. There would have surely been inter-tribal marriages between these tribes, so it is possible that Caratacus was somehow related to the Silures through marriage. Maybe it is far simpler than that; according to Tacitus, Caratacus was a proven fighter who had won 'many an indecisive and many a successful battle' and this would have appealed to the Celts' warrior culture. One thing is certain: Caratacus, having retreated before the Romans for four years, brought with him up-to-date knowledge of how the Romans fought and how they were organised, the way that they foraged and the size of the forces involved – these very facts may have elevated Caratacus among his peers. For the next two years, from 47 to 49, the Silures took the fight to the Romans by waging a guerrilla war, picking off small units, ambushing supply trains and causing as much inconvenience as possible while minimising the risk to themselves. In 48 Scapula invaded North Wales and in a short but successful campaign succeeded in subduing the Deceangli tribe. However, before Scapula could reach Ynys Môn (Anglesey) and take on the Druids who held sway over the mystical beliefs of the Celts with their religious practices, he was forced to withdraw along the north coast of Wales. A revolt broke out among the Brigantes, who were the largest tribe in Britain, a tribe whose land covered a vast swathe of the modern-day north Midlands, Lancashire, Yorkshire and Cumbria. The Brigantes had always been loyal to the Roman overlords and a rebellion in so large a tribe brought Scapula back to quell the unrest before it could spread beyond his northern border; he needed peace to be maintained there or the whole province could be lost, given the recent risings elsewhere.

One of the problems for the Romans in Britain was the lack of natural boundaries such as the Rhine, which served as their eastern European boundary, and so order in Britain had to be maintained through the two things that Scapula could control: manpower in the form of strong patrols, and the construction of solid, defendable towns or forts. To counter the growing inconvenience of the Silurian raids, the Romans established a legionary fortress at Gloucester, on the edge of the Silures' territory, in 49 with the aim of using it to both deter any eastern incursion by the Silures and then as the base for their own campaigns into South Wales. Sensing that the balance of power was changing, Caratacus once more fled north, this time into the territory of the Ordovices, where he continued to recruit willing warriors to his cause. By waging a guerrilla war, Caratacus was able to inflict minor losses on the Romans, but he could not score the major victory that he knew would be required to throw the Romans out of Britain. Although the Silures and Ordovices were still actively engaged in fighting the Romans, as more and more tribes succumbed to become a Roman client kingdom, it seriously weakened the Celts' chances of ever seizing control of Britain back for themselves. With the Deceangli, the neigbours of the Ordovices, being the latest tribe to submit, it surely brought home to Caratacus that the Celts that remained free had to act before they were surrounded on all sides. Having made up his mind to fight, the question was where? Where could Caratacus entice the Romans to fight with a major army, rather than a single legion, and yet give his army the chance of success?

51 Cefn Carnedd/Llandinam – Caratacus's Last Stand

We know about this battle because of the detailed account of Tacitus; the key sections translated from the Latin follow:

> The army then marched against the Silures, a naturally fierce people and now full of confidence in the might of Caractacus, who by many an indecisive and many a successful battle had raised himself far above all the other generals of the Britons. Inferior in military strength, but deriving an advantage from the deceptiveness of the country, he at once shifted the war by a stratagem into the territory of the Ordovices, where, joined by all who dreaded peace with us, he resolved on a final struggle. He selected a position for the engagement in which advance and retreat alike would be difficult for our men and comparatively easy for his own, and then on some lofty hills, wherever their sides could be approached by a gentle slope, he piled up stones to serve as a rampart. A river too of varying depth was in his front, and his armed bands were drawn up before his defences. Then too the chieftains of the several tribes went from rank to rank, encouraging and confirming the spirit of their men by making light of their fears, kindling their

hopes, and by every other warlike incitement. As for Caractacus, he flew hither and thither, protesting that that day and that battle would be the beginning of the recovery of their freedom, or of everlasting bondage. He appealed, by name, to their forefathers who had driven back the dictator Caesar, by whose valour they were free from the Roman axe and tribute, and still preserved inviolate the persons of their wives and of their children. While he was thus speaking, the host shouted applause; every warrior bound himself by his national oath not to shrink from weapons or wounds. Such enthusiasm confounded the Roman general. The river too in his face, the rampart they had added to it, the frowning hilltops, the stern resistance and masses of fighting men everywhere apparent, daunted him. But his soldiers insisted on battle, exclaiming that valour could overcome all things; and the prefects and tribunes, with similar language, stimulated the ardour of the troops. Ostorius having ascertained by a survey the inaccessible and the assailable points of the position, led on his furious men, and crossed the river without difficulty. When he reached the barrier, as long as it was a fight with missiles, the wounds and the slaughter fell chiefly on our soldiers; but when he had formed the military testudo, and the rude, ill-compacted fence of stones was torn down, and it was an equal hand-to-hand engagement, the barbarians retired to the heights. Yet even there, both light and heavy-armed soldiers rushed to the attack; the first harassed the foe with missiles, while the latter closed with them, and the opposing ranks of the Britons were broken, destitute as they were of the defence of breast-plates or helmets. When they faced the auxiliaries, they were felled by the swords and javelins of our legionaries; if they wheeled round, they were again met by the sabres and spears of the auxiliaries. It was a glorious victory; the wife and daughter of Caractacus were captured, and his brothers too were admitted to surrender.

For a battle fought 2,000 years ago, this is a lot of evidence, and as the author emphasises, it is where the armies ended up that is the key thing. From that information we can work backwards and arrive at a logical starting point for where the fighting began and conclude the most likely places for the initial deployment of the troops and the site where they came together. Let us break down the evidence: we know that the Romans ended up on top of the hills that the Celts were initially deployed upon and that some of those Celts escaped, Caratacus included, even though he was with his men close to the river. The escape of some of the Celts is a vital clue to the actual site as many of the alternative sites to the one that the author proposes here, the Breidden Hills for example, are isolated and do not allow an easy and versatile escape route to allow the Celts to swiftly flee the battle should they be defeated. On the hilltops above Llandinam there is a small upland plateau which covers around 30 square miles; it is punctuated by a series of rolling hills, many rising to around 1,700 feet, with a series of passes and small valleys in between.

The majority of a Celtic army, with chariots and horses ready for them at the top of the hills, could have slipped away without any danger of pursuit; the heavy Roman infantry may have been able to ascend the hills but cavalry would have had to have been led; they certainly could not have been ridden up the hills and they would have not been sent forward to climb the hills until the battle was clearly won – there was no place for an assault by any horse in this battle.

We also know (and this is very significant for the location of the battle) that the hills varied in their slope and shape so that some parts could be scaled (this is where the makeshift walls were built) while others would not have been attempted, but those heights would have been safe places for the Celts to rain missiles down upon any Romans below. The hills around Llandinam do have several small stream-cut valleys where the land is less steep and it is easier to climb and ascend the heights than elsewhere. The Romans, we know, were able to push the Celts back up the slopes of the hills once they had used testudo formations to enable their troops to reach and smash the makeshift defences. These makeshift walls were therefore the first time the Romans and Celts came into hand-to-hand combat; before that it would have been slingstones, arrows and javelins that would have greeted the Romans once they had crossed the river. Stepping back further, we know that the Romans forded a defended river of uncertain depth but actually crossed it without issue. Therefore, wherever the Romans marched from was the opposite side of the river to the battle. We now have to take a big step

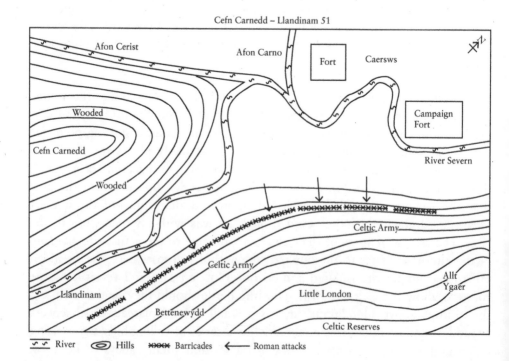

Cefn Carnedd – Llandinam 51

back and consider: would the Romans have attacked such a steep and precarious position unless there was something they wanted? Tacitus wrote that the position 'daunted' General Scapula, such was the defensive strength of the Celtic lines and it was the men who wanted to fight and were sure of carrying the day. Why? Let us go back to our earlier question: where could Caratacus fight the Romans and stand a chance of winning? The battle in 51 was not an accidental battle that happened as a result of two armies meeting on campaign; this was a pre-planned battle and Caratacus had to get it right because he knew he would only get one chance. Sitting opposite the author's chosen site is a small, low hillfort, Cefn Carnedd; the author believes this was the bait for the trap. The hillfort, although strong enough for Celtic warfare, was not strong enough to withstand a Roman assault, being a fraction of the size of forts like Maiden Castle that had fallen with comparative ease. However, the issue for the Romans was that it was a long way into Wales, 45 miles from Wroxeter along the Severn Valley, and having to pass many hills topped with hillforts all the way: a march right into the heart of Ordovices territory. It would seem likely that Caratacus, who was the wanted man of Celtic resistance as far as the Romans were concerned, would have deliberately drawn the Romans further and further up the Severn valley; feints and small raids would have goaded the Romans and confirmed to them that this is where all the rebellious activities were coming from.

The Romans knew that the tribes in the Welsh mountains were the only thing stopping them from completing their conquest of Britain below what is now Scotland; armed with the knowledge of the area in which they needed to operate, an expedition would have been planned. Such a campaign would not have been undertaken lightly and one can understand why it was two years after Caratacus had joined the Ordovices that the Romans finally marched west to deal with those who opposed Roman peace. Scapula would have sent

The larger than normal Roman campaign fort at Caersws.

The smaller Roman fort still within Caersws today.

sizeable auxiliary cavalry patrols along the Severn Valley long before any full-blown expedition would have begun, allowing them to reconnoitre the route and to gauge the numbers of Celts to be dealt with. One can imagine Caratacus resisting the desire to attack these vulnerable Roman patrols and instead drawing these scouts ever further into Wales, always along the valley, until he lured them to his lair, which would have been Cefn Carnedd. The hillfort, being isolated with valleys on either side, would have been a death-trap for himself and his army if Caratacus had tried to use it to take on the Romans, but as a temporary base, with smoke rising from the huts on top, it would have certainly been enough to convince the Roman patrols that they found Caratacus's base. Once the patrols had been led several times to the same place by slightly different routes, no doubt Scapula, on reading the reports, would have taken the bait and laid his plans accordingly.

Caratacus's own scouts would have waited for news of a major Roman army heading west, and when that news came, Caratacus would have called in the thousands of men who wanted to fight for their freedom, including the Silures, who came into Ordovices territory as Tacitus explains. Below Cefn Carnedd the River Carno joins the River Severn and the flow below the confluence is naturally deeper and faster; above the confluence, the rivers are both fordable in places, dependant of course on rainfall and flooding. Importantly, the area around the River Severn at this point displays a stony bottom not an alluvial one; even today, many flat stones can be clearly seen along the sides of the river when walking the valley floor. As Tacitus tells us, the Celts had piled up stones close to the river to serve as temporary ramparts; they would not have had either the time or the necessary wagons to bring in the stones from elsewhere, so any materials they used had to be present already; this again testifies to Caratacus's thorough preparation in picking everything to suit his army and nothing to suit the Roman one.

The village of Caersws sits at this confluence and in Claudius' reign a larger than normal Roman campaign fort was built just outside the modern village at Llwyn-y-Brain. This was later followed by a much larger fort which remained occupied for over 300 years. The campaign fort built around the time of the battle was below the hillfort of Cefn Carnedd, situated on a small hill east of the current town and protected on two sides by the River Severn. The Romans, in true fashion, would have built their fort at Caersws to act as their base so that they were ready for every eventuality: a rallying point if they were defeated and their home if they were victorious. Caratacus would have abandoned Cefn Carnedd shortly before the Roman army appeared, but would have most likely kept there a few of his strongest men, perhaps some of his fanatical warriors, in order to keep the pretence going that Cefn Carnedd was his base. With men appearing on the palisades and keeping the smoke rising from the hut fires, the hill would to all intents and purposes look occupied. In the period between the scouts disappearing and the main Roman army appearing, Caratacus would have organised his men to prepare the temporary stone defences at the bottom of the small valleys that allowed access up the steep hills to the south; he may have had them there for some time, screened by some form of foliage. His men would have lined the slopes immediately above the river, the higher slopes and the very tops of the hills above and either side of the modern-day village of Llandinam, on the opposite side of the River Severn to the Romans. Caratacus had by now done all that he had undoubtedly promised to his men; the only question now would be whether the Romans would still be prepared to attack when they saw that Cefn Carnedd had simply been a ruse and that Caratacus did not have merely a handful or raiding rebels, he had an complete army. Tacitus tells us that it was the ordinary men that wanted to attack, to

The Roman view of Caratacus's position above Llandinam.

The steep hills at Llandinam, where the Celts would have baited the Romans and where the battle was fought.

see through the campaign that they had trained for, and one can understand the ordinary Roman soldier in the ranks. Trained for fighting they would have been just itching to get at this enemy; for years these Celtic rebels had been killing their comrades in ambushes silently annihilating small scouting units and picking on isolated farmsteads developing near the Roman border; doing anything they could to rob the Romans of a feeling of comfort and security.

Compiling all of the evidence outlined above together (the larger than normal Roman campaign fort; the isolated and extremely vulnerable Cefn Carnedd hillfort; the size and placement of the river; the stony bottom of the River Severn to allow the temporary stone ramparts to be constructed; the irregular but steep and high hills and finally the fact that a fair number of the Celts escaped), there is only one out of all the favoured sites that meets these conditions, and that is the hills of Yr Allt Gethin above and behind Llandinam. Interestingly, there are cairns scattered around this plateau, so it is possible that mass burials may have taken place sometime after the battle, when the Romans had left the site. Although the hills are steep, there are access valleys which would have allowed an easier march to the summit; these are known today as Cobblers Gate and Little London. What we don't know is how many men fought in this battle. It is believed that Scapula had two legions and equally as many auxiliary troops, so between 20,000 and 24,000 men. Given previous battles and skirmishes in the eight years since the Romans had landed, a general would not have risked advancing so far into enemy territory without a sizeable force and Scapula had half of the Romans in Britain with him, just what Caratacus would have wanted. Some historians see the lack of Celtic casualties as an indication that the army was smaller than the Roman force; the author believes that Caratacus's force was in fact larger and that the lack of casualties was due to their ability to escape after retreating back up the hill rather than being caught by the pursuing Romans, which is when most casualties in battle occur as the beaten enemy retreats without putting up any resistance; a rout does not seem to have occurred in this battle. Caratacus would have wanted a large army so as to be able to exploit any weakness that might occur in the Roman attack; if the battle was going his way then Caratacus could send in every man he had to finish off the Roman army; if the battle was going against him then his men could retreat up the hill. As the ground was too steep for horses, all of the steeds could be kept at the top of the escarpment ready for an evacuation of the army before the bulk of the Romans could reach the top.

Putting all the above into a chronological flow, the Battle of Llandinam (rather than Cefn Carnedd) would have unfolded something like this. The Romans, upon the completion of their camp, would have slept at least one night there (maybe many more), with their allotted guards keeping a constant watch each night – they would never risk being taken by surprise. Each day, having completed an early morning scout and getting the all clear from his mounted auxiliaries, Scapula would discuss his plans and, having decided to attack, would have prepared his legionaries for the assault on the hillfort of Cefn Carnedd immediately ahead of them. Caratacus, his long-term strategy now coming to its conclusion, would see the Romans planning to advance from the fort and signal for his men remaining in Cefn Carnedd to abandon their posts and join the rest of the army on the other side of the river. Meanwhile, at the same time the main force of Celts start to descend the hills behind the river, taking up a defensive position, while even more warriors appear on the hilltops above. For the first time the full extent of the situation dawns on Scapula; he is many miles into enemy territory, he has a fort, but if he retreats there he will be isolated and there are perhaps many more Celts to come. As he has no means of assistance in the short term, he could be totally cut off and defeated before any other Roman patrol arrives. If he tries a fighting retreat then he does not have the comfort of a fort and the volume of supplies stored there and the enemy would have the advantage of the high ground from which to assault him

Caratacus's view from Little London, looking down onto the Severn Valley.

The rolling uplands of Yr Allt Gethin, across which the Celts could escape.

most of the way back to safe Roman territory. Scapula's men, who have been under pressure for years from the near-constant, probing Celtic attacks that were designed to wear them down, were clearly keen to get on with the battle; they were not daunted by the sight of so many of the enemy as they knew that their training as a coherent fighting force could beat this army of brave but incohesive individuals. His mind made up by the strength of his men, Scapula decides to attack.

The Romans' infantry advance was likely to have been in three columns; two would have been delegated to assault the hills where they were less steep, but this was also where the stone ramparts had been assembled to slow down their advance, shown on the map. The third column would have been a reserve drawn up in a dense line. On either flank, light cavalry would have been posted to ensure that the columns could not be outflanked. Ahead of all these heavy troops would be units of skirmishers that had crossed the river first and shielded the rest of the army while it crossed the River Severn behind them. As soon as the Romans were in range, the Celts would have let fly with thousands of slingstones and javelins; raining down from the heights above, the slingstones would have been particularly effective, doing significant damage to any unprotected flesh they hit. The Romans, having forded the river into the teeth of this storm, would have then formed testudo and marched relentlessly forward to the stone ramparts before eventually breaking through them and carrying on up the gradually steepening slope of the hill. We have no idea how long this struggle lasted; with almost a mile to cover of steadily rising ground and fighting every step of the way, it must have taken the Romans several hours to get out onto the hills above. There they would have been met by fresh Celtic warriors, perhaps the greenest or the youngest of the warriors; eager for their first taste of battle, freshness and agility would be their only assets against the experienced Roman legionaries, tired though they no doubt were after a fighting climb to the crest of the hills. As more and more Romans reached the plateau and fewer and fewer Celts were reappearing, Caratacus would have given the order for everyone to retreat and while those clear of the Roman soldiers would have fled, pockets of Celtic fanatics, brightly painted in their blue woad, would have fought to the death, taking Roman soldiers with them, aiding their comrades to escape. This final conflict matches with Tacitus's description of events and fit the circumstances that followed as a good number of warriors escaped to return to the Silures in order to fight again in the future; the battle may have been lost but at a price to the Romans. Not all of the Celts escaped; Caratacus's wife and family were taken and he must have found that a hard thing to accept, but he had proved again to the Romans that he could not be taken lightly: he could plan a campaign as efficiently as any Roman general and if the conditions were right then they could give the Romans a bloody nose and get away with it and there were not many generals that could make that boast.

Before we examine what happened next, let us consider the other locations that are considered potential sites for this battle and the reasons why they fall short. The key mistake that many historians seem to make is assuming that the battle was fought with Caratacus defending a hillfort, when in fact he was not. He had seen and learnt that every hillfort fell to the Romans almost as if they had a key to the door. Had the last stand of Caratacus been a hillfort then everyone would have been killed or captured and we can say with total accuracy that that did not happen, otherwise Caratacus would not have escaped and the rebellion would not have continued afterwards as the fighting men alongside him would have been permanently removed from further action, either being killed or sold as slaves.

The Breidden hills: the River Severn here is not fordable, though the hills are approachable without the need to cross the river. There is no Roman fort of the right age close to the site and the soil is alluvium so no stones are at hand to construct temporary walls alongside the river. The hill is isolated and Caratacus would not have chosen a position from which the fleeing Celts would be unable to escape.

Clun or Purslow near Clun: This site was favoured by the much-respected battlefield historian A. H. Burne, but the site suffers from three fundamental issues. Firstly, the River Clun is too shallow and narrow to be a significant river, even after torrential rain; it is hardly to be considered an obstacle, even allowing for modern drainage improvements. The river bed is again of alluvium, as is the valley floor; again, no natural exposed stone is available for constructing defences. Finally, there are no natural escape routes for a large army fleeing in haste; many of the hills descend quickly into valleys into which fresh Roman auxiliary cavalry would have ridden and caught any fleeing Celts with ease.

Coxall Knoll: This site suffers more than the others because the hill is again isolated and can be totally surrounded, so Caratacus would not have risked being caught here. The River Teme is shallow enough here to walk through in sandals but it does have a few stone outcrops; if the other factors had fitted then it might have been feasible. But such is the local terrain that a Roman army would not have even been required to cross the river before assaulting the hill. Finally, the knoll itself is very small in area; unlike the Breiddens, which are several miles long and could accommodate an army of at least 20,000 Celtic warriors, the fort atop Coxall Knoll is so small that such an army would have had difficulty in finding room to even stand inside it.

The village of Caersws still has a square grid system of roads and the two forts are visible, one on the very edge of the settlement, the other in the fields to the east. Both are accessible by both vehicle and on foot. The hills behind Llandinam are less accessible; as the battle was fought along a frontage of some distance, it is not possible to say exactly where a visit should be focussed. The roads that lead up on to the hills behind can be climbed on foot or in a vehicle and the views from the top are stunning; one can imagine the Celtic warriors fleeing across the upland range and disappearing before the Romans could catch them all.

Caratacus fled south-east, west and then north, succeeding in reaching the Brigantes tribe, who had recently revolted against Rome, and presumably, with news of their fight with the Romans, he hoped to stir the great northern tribe to spread the rebellion and give the Romans a war on two fronts. Sadly for Caratacus, Queen Cartimandua placed the British leader in chains and, showing her loyalty to Rome, handed him over to the Romans. Once in Rome and reunited with his family, Caratacus pleaded his case that he should be allowed to live and not executed like so many other captured slaves. His plea was listened to and recognised and while Caratacus lived a comfortable exile in Rome, Scapula was once more beset by revolt; under constant pressure, he died in 52, worn out by trying to maintain Rome's dominance (according to Tacitus). Worse was to follow for the Romans as the Silures, hearing of Scapula's death, now increased their attacks on Roman positions, no doubt using the knowledge they had gained from the action above Cefn Carnedd. Before the new governor could arrive, the Silures repeatedly attacked Roman troops who encroached into their territory; two auxiliary cohorts (with around 500 men in each) were wiped out and the XX Valeria Legion under Manlius Valens was attacked in open warfare. They even attacked and inflicted a number of casualties on a Roman force attempting to construct a new fort in Silures territory, possibly at Clyro, Powys, near Hay-on-Wye. To stop these attacks, Didius Gallus had been duly appointed governor and between his arrival in 52 and his departure in 57, he not only managed to restore order and keep the Silures in check but also succeeded in supporting the Roman ally Queen Cartimandua, who was now at war against her husband Venutius over the fact that she had divorced him in order to be with his armour bearer; the incensed Venutius waged war for the next seventeen years, eventually triumphing over his former wife when her call in 69 for aid from the Romans was only partially met. Tacitus states that Venutius was another sound tactician, like Caratacus, and he now became the leader of British resistance.

60 and 78 Menai Straits – Gwynedd

Following Gallus's sound consolidation of the Roman position, Suetonius Paulinus was appointed governor in 58, and he continued to build upon the foundations laid by his predecessor. Information gathered from over the decade would have pointed many times to the island of Ynys Môn as the place where rebellions were nurtured. Ynys Môn (or Mona or Anglesey as it is also known) was the traditional home of the Druids and the place to which many of the remaining Celtic warriors may have fled as it was the furthest point from the Roman-controlled parts of England and Wales. For the Romans it had long been a target, earlier expeditions having failed to reach it. Now, with Venutius in rebellion against his wife, it was also too close to the Brigantes' territory to be ignored. The Romans probably feared some great revolt against them if Venutius and the remaining Celts on the island became united. In 60 Paulinus led a large expedition, presumably through Deceangli territory, to the heights opposite Ynys Môn where, after their long march, they would have prepared their camps before resting and planning the attack. The only route was a direct one and meant crossing the Menai straights and assaulting the gently sloping hills opposite where the Celtic army would be waiting for them. Tacitus once more provides the details for what happened next.

> By subduing the mutinous spirit of the Britons he hoped to equal the brilliant success of Corbulo in Armenia. With this view, he resolved to subdue the isle of Mona; a place inhabited by a warlike people, and a common refuge for all the discontented Britons. In order to facilitate his approach to a difficult and deceitful shore, he ordered a number of flat-bottomed boats to be constructed. In these he wafted over the infantry, while the cavalry, partly by fording over the shallows, and partly by swimming their horses, advanced to gain a footing on the island. On the opposite shore stood the Britons, close embodied, and prepared for action. Women were seen running through the ranks in wild disorder; their apparel funeral; their hair loose to the wind, in their hands flaming torches, and their whole appearance resembling the frantic rage of the Furies. The Druids were ranged in order, with hands uplifted, invoking the gods, and pouring forth horrible imprecations. The novelty of the fight struck the Romans with awe and terror. They stood in stupid amazement, as if their limbs were benumbed, riveted to one spot, a mark for the enemy. The exhortations of the general diffused new vigour through the ranks, and the men, by mutual reproaches, inflamed each other to deeds of valour. They felt the disgrace of yielding to a troop of women, and a band of fanatic priests; they advanced their standards, and rushed on to the attack with impetuous fury. The Britons perished in the flames, which they themselves had kindled. The island fell, and a garrison was established to retain it in subjection. The religious groves, dedicated to superstition and barbarous rites, were levelled to the ground. In those

recesses, the natives [stained] their altars with the blood of their prisoners, and in the entrails of men explored the will of the gods. While Suetonius was employed in making his arrangements to secure the island, he received intelligence that Britain had revolted, and that the whole province was up in arms.

Paulinus's first view of Anglesey and the screaming Druid defenders.

The Celtic view of the Roman positions before the Romans crossed the Menai Straits. The bridge was built by Telford in 1826.

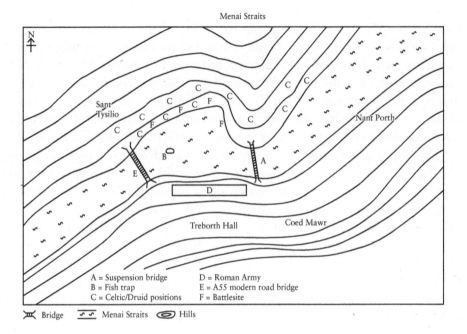

The details for this battle could not be clearer or simpler; at one point the straits between the island of Ynys Môn and the mainland are quite narrow, and with study the tides can be understood to make a crossing easier. The Romans had prepared for the crossing well, with boats to transport themselves across while the horses were able to swim or wade. The Celts seem to have favoured their gods rather than their javelins and slingstones, and at first the shrieking and wailing of the Druids does seem to have had an effect upon the morale of the Romans. Once galvanised into action, however, the battle quickly turned into a massacre and after the initial onslaught of javelins and other missiles there does not seem to have been any kind of resistance from the Celts and the Romans were able to commence the systematic destruction of many of the Druids' sacred sites. There being no doubt about the battlesite and the action that followed, there are questions regarding the numbers involved. References on the subject suggest the Roman force was quite small, with 10,000 to 12,000 quoted. Yet the easy way in which the Celts were defeated and the fact that whole areas of the island could be laid waste suggest a much larger force than that. Given the distance from the safe Roman territory and the potential size of the enemy they were looking to encounter, and the subsequent ease of victory, the size of the expedition is unlikely to have been less than 20,000 fighting men. Ynys Môn covers an area of 276 square miles and would require a sizable force to chop down and desecrate every Druidic temple. While busy in the execution of his victory, Paulinus received word that a major rebellion had broken out in the east of Britain; for the moment Wales had been reprieved. What happened next is also open to question.

Tacitus states that a garrison was placed on Ynys Môn to keep control of the island and stop any further Celtic rebellions, but two things challenge this fact. Firstly and most immediately, Paulinus needed every man he could muster to head back south-east in order to quell the rebellion, which would have grown larger (and rightly so) with every report that reached him. Secondly, and perhaps more telling of the true situation that Paulinus left behind him on Ynys Môn, a further expedition had to be undertaken in 78 to secure the island once and for all.

The rebellion among the Iceni began after the death of their king, Prasutagus, who had in his will left his territory jointly to both the Roman Emperor and his two daughters. The Roman authorities annexed the territory, demanded their taxes and seized property; Boudicca, the queen, backed up her people and objected. What happened next is well known; Boudicca was flogged and her two daughters raped. Insult and injury combined was the spark needed to ignite an already angry tribe into full-scale rebellion. The Iceni were joined by the Trinovantes, and in a wave of fire and the sword the Roman towns of Camulodunum (Colchester), Londinium (London) and Verulamium (St Albans) were razed to the ground; everything Roman was burned and what could not be burned was smashed. Many thousands were killed and the army under this apparently feisty queen grew to an enormous column, full not only of combatants but also their wives and children, among which trailed a convoy of carts filled with the treasures they had stolen. It is very difficult to estimate the size of this force, but it would have been in the tens of thousands and not an easy sight to miss with the noise, smell and dust that such a force would have generated as it marched. While Roman Britain burned, Paulinus raced south with every cavalryman he could collect on route from Ynys Môn, but he arrived

The sloping hill to the shore where the Celtic army waited and the Druid women cursed the Romans, but to no avail.

too late to save London and so he turned to head back north along Watling Street (which, when completed, would run all the way from Richborough to Ynys Môn) in order to meet the legions marching south who had instructions to rendezvous with him. Boudicca had an enormous army and would have been making for another soft target, but we do not know which one and it is clear that she was not marching along Watling Street or Paulinus would have encountered her twice, and this throws into question the commonly held belief that the encounter between the two armies took place there. Why would Boudicca march along a Roman road towards a fully equipped enemy when her success (and with it the need to feed her now enormous host) had been found in attacking weak, poorly garrisoned towns? That debate is not one which space allows here, as a whole chapter (if not a book in its own right) could be devoted to such a debate. Suffice to say as regards this book on Welsh battlefields that in the author's opinion the host was making for Wales to link up with known tribes that had in the recent past resisted Roman rule, namely the Silures and the Ordovices, the Welsh Celts having maintained the banner of freedom for the longest time. This may well explain the next Roman move as Paulinus now requested help from Exeter (where the II Augusta legion was based) so that they could march north and join up with the Romans in pursuit of Boudicca's force.

However, at Exeter the acting garrison commander refused to march as the city itself was besieged by the Dumnonii, who were in revolt, and he could not risk leaving the city undefended. Eventually, at an unknown location somewhere within the modern-day Midlands, the Romans managed to catch Boudicca's Celtic host and the Romans chose a narrow-fronted battlesite where Tacitus's description of a defile with a wood behind and an open plain in front leaves little for the historian to go on! The question of the size of the force again raises its head; Tacitus speaks of 10,000 armed men, but he also speaks of large cavalry units on the flanks and there were auxiliaries too; maybe by armed men he meant the legionaries, the true heavy infantry, while all the lighter auxiliaries and horsemen would maybe have been equally as many. Given that the infantry of the army was marching from Ynys Môn and Paulinus had gathered cavalry from every source en route then surely his force was larger than 10,000 men? It may have been as many as 20,000 – after all this was a battle that Paulinus could not afford to lose; if he lost, then Britain was lost. And what of the Celts? After the battle, Tacitus claims that some reports listed 80,000 dead; if every woman and child accompanying the army was slain then such a number is not unreasonable, but as regards combatants then perhaps there must have been at least 20,000, but probably more, with 30,000 not out of the question. Paulinus was certainly outnumbered but had chosen his ground well; with a narrow frontage and a curving wood and hill behind him, he knew his men could not be outflanked in battle and the overwhelming numbers of the Celts would not give them an advantage on a narrow frontage.

The arrogance of the Celts, and of Queen Boudicca herself, was to think that a straightforward frontal assault by poorly armed tribesmen would be able to smash the best fighting troops in the world when they were formed up and ready for the attack. The result was never in doubt from the first charge; the Romans advanced and killed, advanced and killed, and the Celts panicked and turned and then became trapped among their own seething numbers. Pushed back against the ring of carts from which their own families watched the battle like spectators at the Coliseum, the Celtic rebellion was extinguished before them. The Romans were not without their own losses; some 400 Romans were dead and around 800 were wounded; and away from the battlesite, three cities had been annihilated and goodness knows how many villas and farms had been ransacked. It was time for the Romans to take stock; after almost twenty years of Roman occupation Britain had taken an enormous step backwards and Wales was still untamed. For Celtic Britain, the chance to destroy the Romans fell with this last great rebellion; it is doubtful whether Caratacus or Venutius would had fought the Romans on a field of their choosing – they would have used the army that Boudicca had gathered to far greater effect by drawing the Romans into a situation where they would have had to fight the Celts on their terms and then they might have triumphed.

The destruction of Boudicca's revolt and the effect it had upon the Romans in Britain was so traumatic that for ten years the Romans undertook a massive programme of rebuilding and consolidation. When the dust had settled and the armies were replenished, it fell to Emperor Vespasian (who had been involved at the start of the very first campaign in 43) to resume and complete the planned conquest of Britain. In 71 Petillius Cerialis was appointed governor, followed by Julius Frontinus in 74. Frontinus established a fortress at Isca that is still visible today as Caerleon in South Wales. Here, the II Augusta, who had failed to march in aid of Paulinus, was stationed and under Frontinus they subdued the mighty Silures in the face of the enemy's bravery and the hostile terrain (according to Tacitus). Building upon his success, Frontinus began the construction of another fortress at modern-day Chester (Deva). The mighty city of Deva, where the plain of modern Cheshire and the mountains and hills of North Wales meet, only split by the River Dee, provided the Romans with the base from which to complete their conquest of Wales. In 78 Julius Agricola, who had been appointed governor to succeed Frontinus the year before, assembled an army to march on Wales. He first advanced into Mid Wales and subdued the Ordovices before turning north to Ynys Môn. The Celts on the island do not appear to have been aware of his approach and, unlike 60, there were no hordes of screaming women to try and deter the Romans from crossing. Agricola ordered his auxiliaries to swim across, probably by a low dawn tide, and launched a surprise attack on the inhabitants. This time there would be no mistake; the island surrendered to Roman rule and after over thirty years Wales was subdued and the conquest of Britain complete.

Conclusions

As with all rebellions, there have to be two things for it to stand a chance of succeeding. Firstly, there must be unity among the populace so that they all rise together; secondly, the rising has to coincide with weakness or uncertainty among those in power against whom the people are intending to revolt. In 51 the time was right because Scapula was nervous of the rebellions that were breaking out and his health was not good, as we know he died shortly afterwards. In 60, when Boudicca led her Iceni in revolt, Nero was so frustrated by the news coming out of Britain and the expense at maintaining the province that he was seriously considering abandoning the province altogether. On each of these occasions, if just a few of the smaller tribes or two of the larger ones such as the Brigantes and the Iceni had risen alongside the Silures then the history of Britain, and indeed the world, would have been completely different.

The Menai Straits at their narrowest point between the Island of Anglesey and the mainland of Wales are spanned by Telford's famous suspension bridge, and fortunately for the visitor there are observation areas where the visitor can park their vehicle and absorb what it meant to the superstitious Romans to cross the waters and invade the sacred isle of Ynys Môn. At times the water surges through the gap with frightening speed and a Roman fish trap that was built to corner fish as they changed their course to move with the changes of the tide is still visible today. To the Romans, who crossed to Sicily and built bridges across the Rhine, the Menai Straits must have seemed narrow, but they were also aware that Britain was an island of greatly fluctuating tides and of sudden mists and violent storms, and crossing this narrow race of waters would have been a victory in itself for the generals that masterminded it. The whole island of Anglesey is steeped in rich history, with sites that pre-date the Romans, and it is worth further research before visiting.

The hills where Caratacus chose to entice the Romans into an uphill assault and the place at which Boudicca's rebellion was crushed by Suetonius Paulinus are two battlefield locations that have remained lost to the military historian for many centuries; who knows what new technologies in archaeological research might bring to the debate in the future to qualify one site over another. These were two of the largest battles ever fought in Britain and certainly, in the case of Cefn Carnedd, perhaps the biggest battle ever fought in Wales. The author believes that the site around and above Llandinam is to date the most likely site for Caratacus's last stand and he would welcome knowledge on any artefacts found within that area or if there are any plans to do a battlefields survey of the area.

Following the Romanisation of Wales along with the rest of Britain, there followed a period of calm and stability across the land, which was not broken until the 'barbarian' raids began in the fourth century. However, one mighty rebellion took place across some areas of Britain and certainly across most of Wales during the time of the occupation. Around the year 190, and believed to have been started and spread by Lucius, who was a king of the Silures in South Wales, Christianity took hold and spread through Wales quite quickly. This was around 200 years before Constantine made Christianity the official religion of the empire.

It is very rare that a battle is fought at exactly the same place and even rarer when the two battles are from the same time period; there are a few sites in England where this happened but just the one in Wales. The two Roman crossings of the Menai Straits make a visit worthwhile, not least for the beautiful scenery, which can be seen from both modern bridges that span the famous channel which helped protect the island. The Roman stone fish trap in the middle of the straits stands out as a marker. For the record, in England, St Albans in 1455 and 1461 (Wars of the Roses) and Newbury in Berkshire in 1643 and 1644 (English Civil War) are the two places in England where two battles were fought. In Scotland, Falkirk does have two battle memorials but they are to the rising under William Wallace in 1298 and the Jacobite defeat of the Government troops in 1746.

429 Alleluia Victory – Dee Valley near Llangollen

Before we conclude the chapter on Roman battlesites in Wales, there is one more battle for us to consider that was heavily influenced by Rome, but which occurred twenty years after the Roman legions had abandoned Britain and it was clear that they were not returning. The victory, as the name of the battle suggests, was a victory for faith rather than arms and like Cefn Carnedd its location has never been certain, but unlike Cefn Carnedd, which only has one really strong candidate, the Alleluia battlesite has four, though only three are strong enough candidates and they all have valid but different reasons why they might be the site.

The actual facts about the battle are quite simple. Before the withdrawal of the Romans, Britain had long been a Christian country and Constantine's affirmation of the religion merely strengthened the belief. The theology of the Church was based upon the concept of original sin within man and that therefore a child had to be baptised into the family of God, and on the belief that it was impossible to have a sinless life without committing to Christ. In Britain, however, a monk named Pelagius had a much more modern view of theology, in which he basically preached that man was to all intents and purposes 'good' and therefore had a freedom of choice as to whether he committed a sin or not. This liberal belief was of course far too much for the Roman Church; in a world where deities, demi-gods and heroes had all been commonplace for thousands of years, there was now one God, whose influence had to be seen in all things, therefore it was man who was sinful and God who had the power to save and protect man. However, Pelagius's doctrines proved popular and there was such consternation in Rome that St Germanus, a former Roman army officer, was sent to Britain with other bishops to suppress the Pelagian heresy before it could spread further; the thought of giving people freedom of choice was a step too far for the fifth century, but it shows that throughout history there have been remarkably far-sighted individuals, many of whom, including Pelagius, have been victimised for their beliefs. St Germanus would have toured Britain, spreading the Roman faith, and he must have been somewhere in North Wales, not far from the River Dee, where he was baptising people in a makeshift church and pool using wattles. During this ceremony news came of a 'barbarian' raid; presumably it was the Scotti, the Picts or the Saxons, though it may even have been a combined raiding party of all of these. Whatever its origin, the raid would most likely have come from the sea. Raiding pirates would row up river estuaries, knowing that at some point they would come to a settlement, whether that was by leaving their ships and walking or being able to row all of the way.

Any of these settlements were now easy pickings; with the Roman army gone, there was only some local militia to defend the population and the idea of hiring Saxons to defend them had not yet entered into British thinking. On hearing the news, and no doubt seeing the fear in the eyes of his flock, St Germanus volunteered to organise the defence; the people would not have been without weapons but these would probably have been basic farm tools rather than swords and javelins. With his military background, St Germanus took the people out of their settlement and led them up unto the surrounding hills, well above the river below. Like many river valleys in Wales at this time, the valley would have been thick with vegetation, especially at a lower level, much of it deciduous oak forest. On the slopes, hidden from view, the Britons waited for the raiders to appear. The Britons were presumably down-river of their settlement, because otherwise their homes could have been pillaged without them being able to prevent it. In silence they waited for the raiders to arrive and the signal from St Germanus to rise. Eventually, through the trees below, the raiders could be seen leaving the water's edge and starting to fan out along the slope below them. On receiving St Germanus's signal, the whole host rose as one and cried out, 'Alleluia, Alleluia, Alleluia!' The event is recorded in the *Life of St Germanus*, a text by Constantius: '... and the great cry rebounded, shut in by the surrounding hills. The enemy column was terrified; the very frame of heaven and the rocks around seemed to threaten them ... they fled in all directions.' In panic, the terrified heathens ran back towards the river, many drowning in their haste to escape; the sources, including Bede, state that it was the Christian faith that caused the raiders to flee, and no doubt the echoes from the surrounding hills convinced the raiders that they were greatly outnumbered. But one cannot imagine that these tough sea-faring raiders would have simply thrown themselves into the river and drowned. One must assume that an experienced officer like St Germanus would have encouraged the people to harry the raiders as they fled, no doubt hurling rocks and stones at them if not directly chasing them with their improvised weapons to complete the rout.

Tradition has always linked the battle with two towns. The first is St Albans, north-west of London, where St Germanus was known to preach, but a raid on a strong Roman walled town that was so far from the coast was most unlikely. This coupled with the fact that there are no high hills with steep river valleys

The author at the monument to Maes Garmon near Mold where there are neither steep hills nor a deep river valley.

The low hills of Maes Garmon at Mold would hold no terror for a raiding army.

Dee Valley Alleulia Victory

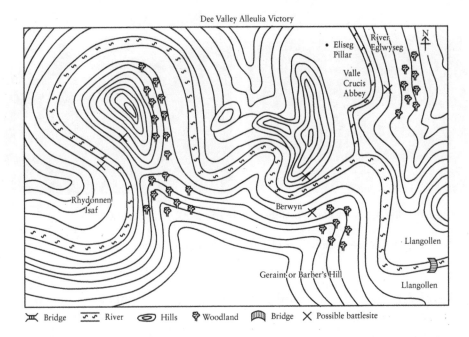

Bridge   River   Hills   Woodland   Bridge   ✕ Possible battlesite

running through from which to frighten off an impending attack, makes this city extremely unlikely. The other settlement is Mold in North Wales, where the low hill and field of Maes Garmon lie just a mile west of the town, complete with a small monument to the victory. Although there is a sizeable river close to the site, there are only low hills on all sides and the valley is not enclosed enough for any echoes, as the author can testify. The terrain is suitable for a battle from any age, being a mixture of rolling pasture with low ridges running at angles across it, but none of these ridges can claim to be surrounding hills and there are no rocks or echoes to startle even the rabbits that grazed in the fields. There are, however, two much stronger candidates. The third claimant of the four is one of the spurs along the Ceiriog Valley, which is a river-cut valley that runs broadly west to east from its head near Llanarmon Dyffryn Ceiriog to Chirk, near where the River Ceiriog joins the River Dee. Llanarmon has a close connection with St Germanus, as the village church is dedicated to St Garmon; there has been a church on the site since the fifth century, the first one reputedly being built to commemorate the battle. In places the sides of the valley are steep and the hills are high enough to qualify; the echoes also work well. There are two main issues, however, with the site; the valley goes nowhere, and with the river so small it is difficult to see why a raiding party would leave the major river, the Dee, and follow a tributary. This brings us to the second issue; the river is not deep and even in flood it is easily fordable for the best part of its short length, and so narrow is the valley and its catchment area that modern agricultural drainage would not have made a significant change to the river at all.

Above left: Glyn Ceriog valley, possibly the site of the Alleluia Victory.

Above right: St Garmon's church at Llanarmon DC in the Ceiriog Valley.

This leaves us with our fourth, final and strongest claimant to the site, the Dee valley around Llangollen, but the question as ever is: just where did this cacophony of noise take place? Fortunately, not all the valley is suitable, but it is a long valley, and there are several places where this harmonised attack could have taken place and where all the relevant factors clearly come into play: the deep river, the steep-sided valleys for the echoes to work, and places where at the time sheltered settlements would have been. Even the towering hills of rock (which Constantius mentions) are all present. The most likely places are at Berwyn, a mile north-west of Llangollen; at Rhwel, 2½ miles north-west of Llangollen; and at Carrog, which is 4 miles further upriver than Rhwel. All of these sites have hills and echoes can be achieved at them. One other possible site exists between Berwyn and Llangollen, where the north–south valley of the River Eglwyseg joins the Dee. Within this narrow valley sit two important recognised historical sites: the first is the Valle Crucis Abbey, which gets its name from the second site, the Pillar of Eliseg, which sits just north of the abbey itself. The Cistercian abbey was begun in 1201 and survived until the Dissolution of the Monasteries under Henry VIII in 1537; the magnificent ruins are well worth a visit and one can imagine the delight of living in such a beautiful and serene location, surrounded by beautiful mountains. The Pillar was once a magnificent stone cross before it was defaced by Parliamentarian soldiers during the English Civil War; there are sufficient legends about the Pillar of Eliseg for a book to be compiled upon them.

One legend has it that St Germanus blessed Vortigern during his time in Britain and the cross was erected to commemorate both the event and the great victory over the heathens. Perhaps it was as the story says; Vortigern needed all the help he could get at the time as the country was suffering from more and more heathen raids. Such a monument to such a victory would have raised morale

Looking towards Carrog, one possible site of the Alleluia Victory in the Dee Valley.

The steep-sided and wooded Dee Valley near Berwyn.

The ruins of Valle Crucis Abbey with the steep valley hills behind.

The Pillar of Eliseg in the Valle
Crucis Valley, just north of
Llangollen.

when the people were feeling particularly vulnerable, particularly as the Church could emphasise the role that Christianity played in the victory; this would reflect against both the heathen invader and the Pelagian Heresy. Traditions and fables, while not hard evidence, should not be dismissed completely out of hand; grains of truth lie in many tales that have been handed down through word of mouth, especially when such few written records were kept. Valle Crucis has as good a claim to the site as any of the others in the Dee Valley around Llangollen. This battle would therefore almost certainly have been fought in the immediate vicinity of the modern town of Llangollen, and perhaps the site of the cross has as good a claim as any to be the correct place. Maybe the cross was erected to commemorate the place where the barbarians were sent reeling simply by the power of Christ and the faith of his followers, and then over time the legends of other heroes were intermingled with St Germanus.

All three main sites can be visited by road and there are appropriate places to park a vehicle and observe the steepness of the cliffs and the narrowness of the valley. The reader will quickly observe why some locations do not carry a sufficient threat to terrify a marauding warband, while in others one can positively think, 'The battle could have happened here.' Maes Garmon at Mold and the Glyn Ceiriog Valley are agricultural areas with rolling fields and woodlands, whereas the Dee Valley, although mostly rural, has the important town of Llangollen at its centre. The town is a popular tourist attraction, with a world-renowned international Eisteddfod and a host of industrial, religious and cultural attractions to keep the visitor amused in addition to musing over where the battle may have taken place.

CHAPTER 5

The Britons 430–577

Background

In the earlier chapter on the history of Britain, we mentioned how Britain declined after the Romans left and the strong central administration began to break down as the country disintegrated into a series of small kingdoms, which in turn started to vie with one another for control of Britain. Those principalities, realising their own vulnerability, then began to ally with, or to use mercenaries from, these invading tribes to protect their own interests.

The turning point came in 428 when Vortigern made the same mistake that the Romans had earlier made with the Goths: in order to bolster their own beleaguered forces, Vortigern invited a number of Saxon mercenaries to support him – perhaps he had met such men on ships that came to trade and seen their fighting potential, or perhaps he had invited them via a merchant who was trading between the two countries. Either way, the Saxon mercenaries answered Vortigern's call, and Gildas states that the first to come were 'three cyulis of Saxons', a *cyulis* being a keel or warship, so perhaps as few as 120 or as many as 240 men arrived, sailing up the Thames to London. Vortigern seems to have overlooked the fact that it was the Saxons who had been raiding the eastern mainland of Britain for so long that the Romans had been forced to build the Saxon Shore Forts to protect the eastern seaboard and the precious supplies of grain and metal ores stored there before they were shipped off to the Empire. However, the deed was done and the door had been opened wide, allowing the Saxons into Britain. One is given an insight here into the size of the armies involved in military campaigns after the Romans had left. Gone are the days of Caratacus and Suetonius, with armies 20,000 strong; at the time of Vortigern, clearly, if three ships of Saxons, at most 240 men, could make a significant difference to a campaign, the armies involved in Britain had to be small, perhaps no more than 1,000 men a side.

By using mercenaries, it is most likely that Vortigern was attempting to continue the Roman policy of making an army from another nation into a *foederatus* or federate state. The principle was that in return for assisting the Britons, the Saxons would be given a small area of land in which to settle, thus providing a buffer zone between the Britons and the raiders or pirates. It was the use of Goths as *foederati* in Romania that ultimately led to the Goths rebelling, and their rebellion became the first in a series of catastrophes that dominoed through the Roman provinces and led to the final collapse of the Western Roman Empire. Following the introduction of Saxons into Kent in 428, the situation deteriorated further and the Romano-British fled west and the remote lands of Cornwall (Dumnonia), Cumbria and Wales became the bastions of Britain, where Christianity was their religion. In the face of everything they knew and held dear now crumbling around them, the people clung to the one constant in their life: their faith, a faith that would be particularly strong in Wales.

Over the next few years the civil war intensified across Britain, bringing hardship to the common people, with both war and famine spreading from the east. Many people abandoned the former Roman towns and headed west to join the British communities in the more remote parts of Britain, as far as they could get from the eastern shoreline. This migration centred on any places where the people felt safe and, as we touched on earlier, the re-occupation of some of the Iron Age hillforts began in earnest. Archaeological evidence has shown that during this period almost seventy Iron Age hillforts were reoccupied, 85 per cent of them in the west of Britain. As in all times of strife among petty kingdoms, alliances were made both through marriage and by military oath. Some kingdoms rose from their Celtic tribal routes, such as Dumnonia, which covered the south west peninsula of England between 425 and 450 under the stewardship of King Conomor. Such was the remoteness of Dumnonia that it would remain a bastion of the Britons for most of the Dark Age period, able to preserve its own language, Cornish. Wales, too, was able to

The Breidden Hillfort, reoccupied after the Romans left, dominates the Severn Valley 1,000 feet below it.

defend itself. Such was the pressure from the Saxons that the Britons did not need any further incursions, but between 440 to 450 there were an increasing number of Pict raids, the loss of the Roman garrisons in the north of England allowing the Painted Men from north of Hadrian's Wall to penetrate further south than ever before. Their raids were followed by yet more famine, which in turn led to more infighting among the Britons.

In desperation, in 446, the Britons sent word to Rome and begged for aid against the Picts, who were now their main threat, but they received no help. Rome itself was now embroiled in a war against Attila and his hordes of Hun horsemen. In desperation, Vortigern now begged both the Angles and the Saxons (ASC says 'the English') to come and help Britain. In 449 the first Germanic tribes came; three ships of Saxons under Hengest and Horsa landed at Ebbsfleet and defeated the Picts wherever they encountered them. However, the Saxons sent word home of the cowardice of the Britons and the excellence of the land and then the floodgates were opened. The war against the Britons had begun. The Angles came from Friesland and the Schleswig area of Germany. The Jutes came from Jutland and the other Germanic tribes of the Lower, Anhalt and Westphalian Saxons joined them; there was a mass migration into Britain. In 455, the Saxon brothers who were supposed allies of Vortigern fought against him at Aegelesthrep, but Horsa was killed and with no clear winner of the battle being mentioned in the ASC, it may have been a British victory – but the ASC does say that Hengest's son Aesc joined him. A year later, at an unknown location, Creacanford, somewhere between Kent and London, the British were trounced, apparently losing 4,000 men in the battle – a very great number of casualties for a battle in Britain at any time during the Dark Age period. The battle-weary Britons retreated into London with what men remained from their army. As repeatedly happens throughout this period, there then came a lull in the fighting. It seems that time and again the armies of both sides fought themselves to a standstill and had to rest to regroup. The Britons would use the time to reinforce the lands that they still held, while the Saxons began establishing settlements on the ground that they had captured. The Saxons would use these settlements as bases in which to recruit, train and equip their tribal army. These new recruits would be their own up-and-coming sons from tribes already established in England, or fresh migrants would have been invited to come and join them from their former homelands. As soon as one side was ready with sufficient forces for another campaign, hostilities would begin again, with the Saxons looking to push the boundary of their territories ever further to the west as they sought more land for their allies back in what is Germany today.

After nine years of void in the ASC, the record goes on to tell of decades of defeats for the Britons, beginning in 465 when Hengest and Aesc defeat a British army at Wippedesfleot, slaying no less than twelve chiefs of the Britons for the loss of just one thegn, who is named as Wipped. Presumably the place they fought was named after the Saxon as a mark of respect for a highly regarded servant. It is another eight years before the next victory, in 473, but neither the location nor any details are recorded, simply that the Britons fled from the Saxons as if from fire. The fragility of the British defences is clearly shown by an event in 477 when Aelle attacked the south coast near Pevensey with just three ships, each commanded by one of his sons, Cymen, Wlencing and Cissa, and these few warriors took the area without any marked resistance. The ASC was a record of the times according to the Saxon view of the world, and like all history written by the victors, there may be some exaggeration or some bias in the reporting, as is shown by naming the one Saxon thegn who was slain at Wippedesfleot but none of the twelve British kings who died. The years with no record may hide Saxon setbacks, and certainly the picture becomes more confused when the Saxons in 491 took Pevensey. In theory, it had already been taken fourteen years earlier, but the ASC clearly states that Aelle and Cissa besieged it, took it and killed every single Briton within. This perfectly illustrates just how confusing this period is, even when you have written evidence. This confusion is heightened by what happened next, for at this time of despair a saviour came to the aid of the Britons, a man known today as Arthur. The question is what comes next? Is it British mythology or British history? Clearly, the two are entwined so that one is not sure how much is truth and how much is fiction. One thing is certain, though: someone, at least for a time, was able to stem the advance of the Saxon hordes and unite the people in a common cause.

Arthur

There is insufficient space within this book to cover in depth all of the possibilities, theories and beliefs which the name of 'Arthur' conjures up for examination. It is unlikely whether anyone in the history of Western Europe has generated so much speculation and so many volumes of written works to support one theory or another as to his existence, his deeds and his legacy. What written references we do have are very short and must be tempered by the age in which they were written and what the needs of the writer were at that time. The more complete references to him are interwoven within the Welsh bardic tales, those compilations of Welsh history and folklore which have been told, and retold, handed down from master to pupil down the centuries. It is from these oral Welsh histories that were eventually written down that we know anything of Arthur at all. We do not know who Arthur was: a warrior or a king? We do not know where he lived or how long he may have lived for. There are scores of books on this subject, some of which are detailed in the appendices as I have referred to them for this work; the theories they contain range from

Arthur being everything from a warlord to a king, originating from Scotland, Wales, Cumbria, Shropshire, Cornwall or Sarmatia, whose campaigns were fought in Scotland, Cornwall, Wales, the Midlands, Kent and East Anglia and possibly even in France. What we do know of Britain around 100 years after the Romans retreated is that someone who was clearly a Briton and who had a secure base within Britain was giving the Saxons a very hard time in battle, so much so that the Saxons were eventually halted and it would be several generations before they were strong enough to again consider expanding their western frontier.

The name of Arthur fits the persona of this unknown person well, and for the lack of any alternative we shall use the name Arthur to represent this clearly charismatic man who single-handedly galvanised resistance to stem the advance of the Saxons. Indeed, there may have been more than one man, perhaps a succession from father to son with just the name being retained. From all the available evidence and theories put forward by a host of authors, it is this author's opinion that Arthur's territory was most likely to be found in South Wales, one of the safer British kingdoms, as it had been for the Silures so many centuries before. Protected by the nature of the terrain and the massive Severn estuary to the east, and with a south and west facing sea, it was as far away as possible from the Saxon strongholds in the east. Arthur was clearly able to bring together the normally divisive British kings, uniting them against their common foe, the advancing Saxons, because he is described as having been 'chosen' to lead them. He was therefore a natural leader, clearly respected, and most likely he was appointed as the main warlord (*dux bellorum*) of the remaining British kingdoms. He must have been a skilful tactician, able to inflict crushing defeats on the advancing Saxon enemy, for according to Nennius there were twelve battles listed as victories in which Arthur led the Britons.

If all the battles listed below are correctly attributed to Arthur, then he was capable of fighting long campaigns the length and breadth of western Britain and the location of South Wales as a base becomes even more significant. Most importantly, Arthur is not only portrayed as the saviour of the Britons but also as defending the Christian faith against the advancing pagan Germanic peoples. Nennius states that the twelve battles Arthur fought were as follows:

Then it was, that the magnanimous Arthur, with all the kings and military force of Britain, fought against the Saxons. And though there were many more noble than himself, yet he was twelve times chosen their commander, and was as often conqueror. The first battle was in the mouth of the river which is called Glein. The second and third and fourth and fifth on another river which is called Dubglas and is in the region Linnuis. The sixth battle on the river which is called Bassas. The seventh battle was in the forest of Celidon, that is Cat Coit Celidon. The eighth battle was near the fort Guinnion, where Arthur bore the image of the Holy

Virgin, mother of God, upon his shoulders, and through the power of our Lord Jesus Christ, and the holy Mary, put the Saxons to flight, and pursued them whole day with great slaughter. The ninth battle was fought in the city of the Legion. He fought the tenth battle on the shore of the river called Tribruit. The eleventh battle was fought on the hill called Agned. The twelfth was a most severe contest, when Arthur penetrated to the hill of Badon. In this engagement, nine hundred and forty fell by his hand alone, no one but the Lord affording him assistance. In all these engagements the Britons were successful.

As with all things Arthurian, there is an on-going debate as to where these twelve battles might have been fought. While there are clearly rival claimants for all these battles, there are some which can clearly be linked to places in western Britain, where the British kingdoms were fighting to defend both themselves and their religion. The sixth battle, Bassas, can be linked with Baschurch in Shropshire, a watery site with meres and pools not far from the river Severn and the city of Wroxeter, just outside modern-day Shrewsbury. Importantly, Wroxeter was an enormous site covering 200 acres and was a major Roman stronghold and it was also occupied long after the Romans left, including rebuilding work; Wroxeter marks a central position for armies wishing to move into either mid or north Wales or also into Cheshire. The seventh battle, at the forest of Celidon, that is Cat Coit Celidon, has been identified with the Caledonian forest, which at one time stretched across most of western Scotland. The Welsh tradition puts the battle close to the Scottish border and a convenient landing place for ships, so the battle could have been fought in the Penrith to Lockerbie area, just north of the Solway Firth. The eighth battle, fought near the Fort Guinnion, gives rise to a host of possible locations but the most likely western one is outside of the walled town of Venta, which would be the modern Caerwent in Gwent, South Wales. The ninth battle appears to

The imposing Roman remains at Wroxeter today, which were still inhabited after the Romans had left.

have been a siege as it was in the city of the legion. There are two Roman towns known by that name, Chester on the North Welsh/English border and Caerleon upon Usk in South Wales. As Mount Badon, the last and greatest of Arthur's victories, was fought in South Wales, the author believes that this City of the Legion battle was fought in the ruins of the old Roman settlement of Caerleon as the Saxons attempted to attack Arthur deep in his own heartland. Yet once again he managed to thwart their attack by keeping them penned in close to the sea, from where the Saxons had most likely come.

For the Saxons to attempt a seaborne attack at this stage of the campaigns would seem reasonable, as their recent attempts by land had all clearly failed. The tenth battle suffers not only from a lack of location but also from the fact that it can have many different meanings in translation, from being a riverbank to a sea shore. The battle is mentioned in the Black Book of Carmarthen, in the *Pa Gur*, a Welsh poem from the eleventh century, which states the battle may have been fought by the legendary foster brother of Arthur, whose name was Cai Hir, the tall. The battle is also associated with the Severn at Gloucester and the Eden at Carlisle, again all locations close enough to the sea to have been reached by ships. The eleventh battle, Agned, has, in a tenth-century version of Nennius, the alternative name of Breguoin, which may well be the Roman town of Leintwardine in Herefordshire, which is astride the main Roman road that runs from Caerleon to Chester via both Leintwardine and Wroxeter and as such was Arthur's main route from north to south along what has always been border country. This also strengthens the earlier claim for there having been a battle at Baschurch. Even some historians who favour Arthur fighting in eastern England have to conclude that the eleventh battle was most likely fought close to Leintwardine, as it was another former Roman settlement and once more close to the Welsh border; the battles keep linking Arthur with either places that can be reached by Roman roads or by sea.

The tidal River Usk at Caerleon, possibly one of Arthur's battlesites and likely to have been one of his ports.

We also have to ask ourselves, what is the significance of the reference to Arthur carrying the banner of Christ upon his shoulder? It is possible that shoulder may be an incorrect translation and instead it should read his shield, or perhaps the shield protected his left arm and therefore his left shoulder? Alternatively, it could mean that Arthur wore a cloak which had a Christian symbol upon it, presumably a form of cross. To understand this Christian message, it is important to go back in time and understand that Britain, during the 400-year Roman occupation, had well established pockets of Christian following among its peoples. In the reign of Henry VII, historian Polydore Vergil, and after him Cardinal Pole, both staunch Catholics, affirmed in Parliament that Britain was the first of all countries to receive the Christian faith and maintain it against the Romans, who were initially pagan in belief, worshipping many gods, and the persecutors of Christians. Bede mentions Lucius, who was the client king of the Silures, one of the many such kings who were tolerated throughout the Roman Empire where the Romans believed it was better to have a local tribal king on their side to perform the often difficult diplomacy that was required in local affairs, rather than using their own men from far across the Empire. They had perhaps learned from previous impositions, remembering what had happened when they had tried to impose their own rule on the Iceni tribe when they did not want Boudicca to become head of that Celtic tribe. On record, we know that Lucius wrote to Pope Eleutherius (174–89) asking for permission to become a Christian who lived in Britain and just over 100 years later Constantine the Great, albeit late in his life, took Christianity as his religion and it should be noted that this was just after he had spent some of his final years in Britain – did his time among the people of Britain convince him of the faith? Given, therefore, that the Britons were acknowledged as the first Christian nation, it was reasonable for those committed Britons to believe that in 410 the Romans were finished as a nation, and that as Rome itself had fallen, they were now the last bastion of the Christian faith. Moving forward in time, the problems that the Britons were facing were compounded when the small raids by the Scotti and Picts were eclipsed by the sweeping tide of Germanic tribes that began moving into the east of the country. It would require someone that could not only unite the various warring factions of the Britons but also instil in them sufficient strength and purpose to stem the advance of the Saxon tribes. By fighting with a unique unit, different to anything the Saxons had, and by portraying himself as the champion of both Britons and Christians, even displaying the banner of Christ, Arthur was able to bring the people together in a common cause that encapsulated the two vital elements that mattered to the Britons at that time: survival and righteousness.

It is the author's opinion that the reason Arthur was able to achieve these successive victories is because he used the sea as his main means of transportation, using ships to transport his most valued men, his hearth troops or knights. Arthur only used routes across country when it was necessary to bring the Saxons to battle, a short and crucial campaign always starting from a place where his ships could dock and he could assemble with the local forces that had come by land. This also allowed him to retreat to safe islands or coastal places almost inaccessible by land at this time, certainly places well beyond the reach of the Saxons and a place of sanctuary at need, Tintagel, Bardsey and Anglesey, and perhaps the Scilly Isles, being perfect examples. If we examine all of the places associated with Arthur then they are all close to, or are places that have, harbours. Many of them are Roman harbours which would have still been sound to use at this time. Over twenty such sites existed in Arthur's time, stretching around the western coast of Britain from Bitterne, opposite the Isle of Wight, all the way to Bowness near modern-day Carlisle. The large Roman settlements of Gloucester, Caerleon and Chester are included as they all had access to their protected tidal harbours from sheltered river estuaries. Indeed, Welsh mythology does name one of the two ships which Arthur is said to have had as *Prydwen*. For such a small force that could be carried in one ship of the time, with a maximum of say 120 men aboard, to win so many battles seems unprecedented, but there are examples from history where a small, determined force, enthusiastic, highly motivated and well led, can achieve great things in a small timeframe. Yet an elite fighting force would be capable in those times of such small armies to make a marked impression on a battle if they were decidedly superior to everyone else that they were fighting. Remember that Vortigern thought that three ships of Saxons (armed with just spears and shields) could make a big difference to his fighting strength against the Picts and Scotti, so what could some armoured men with strong war-horses achieve?

The only thing that could have made Arthur's force so powerful was if he had troops that were better equipped than any other individual force around at the

Lugg Vale seen from Croft Ambrey Hillfort, a Border valley route well used by marching armies and connected with Arthur.

time. Those men would need to be better armed, better protected and trained to fight as a unit, and above all dedicated and confident in their leader. Being well fed and healthy with a known haven to retreat to that was secure enough for them to lick their wounds and prepare for the next battle would have been of great benefit. Arthur may well have commanded a force which was made up of the last surviving descendants of a Sarmatian force that had been stationed at Chester under the Romans. If not the descendants, then maybe they had obtained the armour and weapons of that departed force, giving him a cavalry unit capable of knocking out the enemy, who would have had no answer to this type of troops. The one military arm that is always poorly represented in Dark Age warfare is cavalry. The Picts, themselves thought to be descended from the Scythian horse armies, as we have seen above, and the Normans at the end of the period were the only two nations to use the horse in sufficient numbers to produce a balanced army. If, therefore, the core of Arthur's army was well-armed, well-protected and well-disciplined cavalry, then these 'knights' would, when used on the right terrain, be able to smash through any foot force that was not formed into a dense and solid shieldwall against them. Any lightly armed foot troops caught in loose formation would be simply mown down and completely shattered by a full-blown charge, and any lighter troops following up would be able to mop up any wounded survivors. If there was a small unit of light cavalry following on behind, then their speed and manoeuvrability would allow them to complete the victory by pursuing their enemies, who would be trying to escape on foot, the Saxons at this stage having no cavalry of their own. Arthur has become synonymous with having knights at his round table; there were no knights as such but there would have been armoured heavy cavalry as they were widely used in the armies of the Middle East and Persia, so armoured men would have been familiar. When the stories of Arthur were finally written for a medieval world to marvel at, knights would have been the name for an armoured Christian man on horseback. It is very easy for a modern meaning to be placed upon something older because the word is of 'now' and not 'then' and the word of now has to be used by the person writing now for the reader to understand their meaning.

Arthur, by tradition, is connected with the isle of Avalon, which some historians have linked to Glastonbury and the massive tor that dominated the landscape and was surrounded by waves of reeds that covered the wetlands and so gave the tor the appearance of being a great island, making an isle of apples to fit the legend. If Arthur was a cavalry commander that needed to move swiftly, then he would not want to be pinned down in a wetland area from which the only escape route would mean negotiating long lines of treacherous paths with water surrounding him on every side and the whinny of a horse liable to betray his presence at any moment. Any such location would hamstring his most potent force and the Somerset levels are not within striking distance of any of the twelve battles with which he is connected. If we accept the evidence of Arthur moving the length and breadth of western Britain, is it not much more likely that he would make use of an island, as far as possible from the eastern shore? So how much more likely is the island of Bardsey on the North Wales coast, just off the Llyn Peninsula? Bardsey is mid-way between all of the surviving British kingdoms at this time, from Dumnonia in the south to Cumbria and Strathclyde in the north. Bardsey today is still some two-thirds of a square mile in area, around 400 acres, sufficient to provide food for a small group of people, with its flat arable land protected by a large hill. In the Dark Ages the island was larger than it is now, having been reduced by rising sea levels to its present size, and during the fifth century it is reputed to have been a refuge for persecuted Christians. A small monastery was built there, to be succeeded in 516 by an abbey, St Marys, built by Saint Cadfan, who came from Brittany. For many centuries the Welsh bards praised the island's virtue and it was important for 'the burial of all the bravest and best in the land'; was not Arthur one of their best and bravest in the land? In later medieval times, three trips to Bardsey were considered to be the equivalent for the soul as one trip to Rome and Bardsey is said to have no less than 20,000 saints buried on the island. There are two important links to the Arthurian legends; the first is that on the island there flourishes an apple tree the like of which cannot be found in any other place in the whole world – Bardsey is truly the island of the apple. The second is that many earth structures have been identified, some going back to pre-Roman times, but there are also two areas of round huts and rectangular buildings dating from the Dark Age period, both in sheltered areas of the island, supporting claims that it was a well-used Dark Age site. The microclimate is unique here and wind and tides can combine to make the island inaccessible for many days at a time, but also to protect it from the worse of the cold weather, making it able to extend its growing season. What better place for a leader of men to rest and recuperate under the care of a Christian community than Bardsey?

There is no mention of Arthur in the ASC, but this was an Anglo-Saxon record of events and as can be seen, at certain times the record goes quiet. There is scant information about events or people other than Saxons and when they lose a battle there is little mention of the victors. The Saxons confirm how they win things, not how they lose them, and this is particularly evident in the early years of the chronicle. Unsurprisingly given the above information, the strongest evidence for Arthur comes from the Welsh bards and the Welsh monk Nennius and a people united and defended by an iconic figure are far more likely to record him than any others; by the same reasoning, the Saxons are unlikely to write of a man who out-manoeuvred them and defeated them at every turn. From 501 to 547 there are only eleven inclusive entries within the ASC, no exhalant victories are reported and there are just two references to killings: one is a British king, Natanleod, in 508, who apparently led an army of 5,000 men, although there was no talk of a battle; the other, an earlier entry from 501, claims that a Saxon called Port killed a high ranking British man at Portsmouth, where Port had arrived with two Saxon ships. There are no glowing reports of conquest and no talk of defeats but these years would match the timescale of Arthur's battles, the last and most crucial of the twelve being Mount Badon.

516 Mount Badon – Mid-Glamorgan

This is the twelfth and most important battle in the list given to us by Nennius, which for good measure Gildas has also recorded in his hand, and Gildas describes it in the following three words, 'Obsessio montis badonici', suggesting that this battle lasted longer than a day, which is supported by the *Annales Cambriae* record for the year 516: 'The Battle of Badon in which Arthur carried the Cross of Our Lord Jesus Christ on his shoulders for three days and three nights, and the British were victorious.' Unlike the Welsh Annals, however, Gildas does not name Arthur; he names Ambrosius Aurelianus, who first appears in British history much earlier, as a leader of a separate British powerbase which was opposed to Vortigern and was linked to associated tribes in Brittany. This use of the same name may simply indicate a family line, with the name travelling down from father to son. It is difficult to see any of these British leaders as anything more than tyrannical warlords, each doing their best to both defend the remaining British people and further their own fortune at the same time, and those that were successful would have gained popular support. Or, as some historians think, were these names such as 'Vortigern' honorary titles, a name to represent their exalted position as speaking for Britain in matters of state where representation was called for, perhaps, for example, when dealing with the Church in Rome?

Once more we are faced with conflicting claimants to a battlesite. Mount Badon is linked with Badbury Rings in Dorset and Badbury near Swindon, where Liddington Castle lies, and these are the two main claimants. Both of these English sites are hillforts, which fits with the description of a three-day battle. It would seem logical that the Britons either broke into, or broke out from, a hillfort to take the victory, most likely breaking out with the advantage of surprise, height and impetus that a descent of a gentle hill into the enemy's ranks would bring. It is more likely, however, that as this was the last battle of the twelve and therefore the most crucial one of the campaign, it would either be fought at the Saxon door or at the British one. Therefore, as all of the other battles in these campaigns were fought on western Britain, it is in South Wales, close to Arthur's own territory, that Mount Badon was surely fought? The description of a three-day battle clearly implies that it was fought at a hillfort or outside a defended settlement, and if the British were defending then they were clearly outnumbered by their Saxon opponents, otherwise the Saxons would not have been confident enough to besiege the British in their own refuge, so far from the Saxon homelands away to the east. We also know that the Saxons were the aggressors, with the battles being fought in the west of Britain, and that clearly the Britons had decided to fight a defensive strategy. This is a sound military strategy when the terrain of your home is far more beneficial to defence than going into the enemy's territory, which is more open and more suited to their greater numbers of men.

It is likely that the Saxons had come right into the centre of the British lands to try and finish Arthur and his men once and for all, hoping that his death would divide the British kings as before, and so allow the Saxons to then defeat the petty kingdoms piecemeal. Alternatively, Arthur may have deliberately drawn the Saxons into his territory so as to try and finish off the Saxon hierarchy while they were stretched and had a long distance to travel back, so that any stragglers could be picked off, thus completing a total victory. If Arthur could win this great victory it would prove to the other kings that he was worthy of being the true leader of all the Britons and so buy them all time to regroup in order to take the war to the Saxons in the future and so retake some of their lost lands. We do not know whether the Saxons arrived by land, a difficult march from their homelands leaving them with a long, thin and

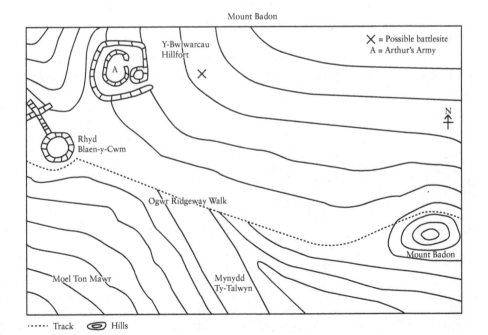

Mount Badon

Y-Bwlwarcau Hillfort

X = Possible battlesite
A = Arthur's Army

A

N

Rhyd Blaen-y-Cwm

Ogwr Ridgeway Walk

Mount Badon

Moel Ton Mawr

Mynydd Ty-Talwyn

······ Track   Hills

exposed line of supply, or, as is more likely, whether they came by sea, perhaps having monitored Arthur's movements and then gathered a fleet in order to pursue Arthur to his homeland; the Saxons had been raiders by sea until they began to settle in Kent and the Scotti may well have been prepared to rent them ships for such an enterprise as the Scotti still raided the Welsh coast. Given all of the above then the most likely site for Arthur's defence would be one of the hillforts scattered across the thousand-foot-high hills that lie south of Maesteg and north of Porthcawl, with the River Usk estuary an appropriate landing area and one that Arthur himself had used.

The case for the site being at Y Bwlwarcau is put forward by Gilbert, Wilson and Blackett in their book *The Holy Kingdom*, published by Bantam Press, and their arguments are very convincing. The information fits with what is written, and the topography also fits; even the names of the fields, 'field of the white tents' and Maescadlawr itself, 'field of the battle area', could hardly be more compelling. In addition, the numerous remains of long-abandoned earthworks and many scattered burial cairns and tumuli further support the case for this site as numerous small earthworks fit with a short siege, the three-day battle. How, then, can we explain Nennius's claim that '940 men fell on one day at a single onset of Arthur; and no-one killed them but he alone, and in all the battles he came out victorious'? What we surely have here is a literal meaning used to emphasise the power of one man. What is more likely is that for once, when the battle of Mount Badon was fought, the ambitious warlords and the petty princes who had been constantly vying to gain absolute control of the remaining British lands themselves put their faith behind one overall commander, the man who had been 'chosen'. Arthur had proved in the previous battles that he knew how to beat the Saxons and it was the planning of one man that achieved the victory and which led to the deaths of the majority of the Saxon army, not by his own hand, but by his decision making and the

Y Bwlwarcau Hillfort, the likely encampment for Arthur before the Battle of Mount Badon.

tactics that he deployed. Given the few facts that we have, it is likely that for two days the Saxons attacked the Britons in their defensive enclosures. After two days of this siege, Arthur then prepared his men for a dawn charge, which would be downhill into the Saxon camp, the field of the white tents. If an army was caught unawares, half asleep, perhaps unarmoured, by a force of mounted charging men then it is possible that they would be completely destroyed.

All the classic military tactics are there: a downhill surprise attack with mounted men against a disordered group of men, half asleep and half armoured. If they were unweaponed due to the element of surprise, then it would be nothing short of a massacre. It is the very fact that we have a number of casualties, 940, that allows us to gauge something of the size of the armies that fought here. The earthworks themselves are quite small and yes, 1,000 men could shelter in there and fight for a number of days, but they could not withstand an indefinite siege; there would be insufficient room to store the food and water required. If events did unfold as the author envisages, then it may be that as the majority of the Saxon force was destroyed, perhaps they had as few as 1,000 men and that just sixty escaped into the morning gloom, that mist that would have hidden the British charge and deadened their horses' hooves until they were almost upon their enemy, but would also have allowed a few quick thinking Saxons to escape from the wrath of the British hero and his armoured entourage. The number of casualties could be false, could be exaggerated to show Arthur as a hero, but if that were the case would not the dead be in their thousands to make Arthur look more incredible? When we have little enough to go on, we have to use what we are given and such a number, given due consideration, does look feasible. We know that armies were generally small in number. This would make any small, elite force of warriors, such as Arthur's mounted men, an even more potent force in a battle. It also confirms the details for Mount Badon: a force of around 1,000 Saxons is sufficient to besiege a smaller force of Britons trapped in a hillfort which at first glance does not look too imposing. This is not one of the major massive series of earthworked hill such as Maiden Castle or South Cadbury, which the Saxons would not have dared to attack, but instead a low hillfort on a gentle range of hills, and it would have been enough to entice the eager Saxons in. Once the Saxons were encamped below, Arthur let them attack, and he drew them into a false sense of security so that he could then fight on his terms once he had gauged their strength. Those terms were at dawn on the third day, when Arthur opened the trapdoor and rode out to destroy the Saxon host in their camp.

If, from what brief knowledge we have of Arthur, we accept that he was a shrewd tactician and a brilliant general then the place he chose for his twelfth battle and the way he destroyed the Saxons epitomises both of these great qualities. As can be seen from the map, the hillfort is constructed in such a way as to provide the occupiers with an excellent defensive position: a complicated set of earthworks with rolling but damp ground around it, including some springs that would supply the defenders with fresh water. But with springs come areas of boggy ground that can harass and slow an enemy approach, especially if they advance in a solid formation. Such a well-positioned hillfort was capable of being held even when the defenders were outnumbered by the enemy, and the interlocking entrances provide killing zones for the defenders that are more reminiscent of the construction of later medieval castles. Some of the Iron Age hillforts did have elaborate interlinked earthworks with different sections, some of which were on different levels, and some even had false entries to confuse would-be attackers. Any Saxons that did break in to Y Bwlwarcau would have found another set of earthworks to scale, so one can appreciate that if this did happen then after two days of fighting the Saxons, not having been able to capture the hillfort, would have been demoralised and may well have suffered heavy casualties from their assaults. What better time for a counter attack than when you have thwarted your opponent for two days so that you can catch them cold and completely unawares on the morning of the third day, when they are at their most vulnerable?

So with the Saxons now crushed and the chance for peace to return to the western half of Britain, Arthur had laid the foundations that would allow the Britons to continue to work together on the rebuilding of the defences for their western kingdoms without the continual threat of war to distract them. Then, with their defences secure, the Britons would be able to march out east and commence a campaign to reclaim Britain for the Britons. We do not know how far any of these longer term aims were fulfilled. We do know that after 517 the Saxon advance was halted because the ASC records very little between the years 517 and 547. There are just eight entries for thirty years; three battles are recorded, all of which (surprise, surprise) the Saxons win, including one on the Isle of Wight and two of unknown location. In addition, three eclipses

Mynydd Baddon, where the Saxons camped 3 miles north of Bridgend and were destroyed by Arthur.

are also recorded and finally we are told that in 547 Ida became the leader of Northumbria, the first Saxon power, it seems, to grow after the defeats to the Britons; most significantly, Northumbria is the furthest Saxon kingdom from South Wales. Clearly, by the lack of information in the ASC, the Britons had stopped the Saxon advance for a generation, unless there were other battles and events which were not recorded in any form, either orally or in writing. What Arthur also archived was a Christian legacy, a loyalty that would have appealed to both the Church and the people. Within that force that Arthur created, there would have had to have been a core of seasoned warriors who were strong enough to last through battle after battle at a time in history where battle casualties would almost inevitably account for the greater part of the army each time they fought; and somehow, through twelve battles, Arthur maintained enough men to ensure victory each time. This core was most likely the leaders and their sons from the other British realms who were glad to be part of a force that was turning the tide. Their exploits would look good to each other and to their people, who would have been desperate to stem the advancing Saxon tide. Above all, perhaps, it is this achievement of unity among the Britons that was immortalised in the minds of the poets who were the first to hear, or maybe even see, something of what Arthur achieved. So it was that this ideal was then passed down from generation to generation so that the virtues of Christianity and the kinship of men banding together as brothers to beat a common foe would be exalted and copied by those who would come after. Such virtues would indeed reflect Christian ideals at this time: triumph over the pagans by a unified people, led by a Christian 'king', who was 'elected' by his people; if this is indeed how it happened, then little wonder that poets wrote about it and bards told of it for centuries to come.

537 Camlann – Gwynedd

How cruel, then, are the Fates? Barely had the dust settled on the wars with the Saxons than there occurred an event that would literally shake the world for a generation, and it was an event over which no-one had any control at all. On the other side of the world a huge volcano, Krakatoa, erupted and threw so much debris into the atmosphere that it would create a nuclear winter for the next few years, blighting crops across the globe and blocking out the sun, which would lead to starvation, death and plague across every civilisation of the world. This is explained in great detail by David Keys in his book *Catastrophe*. The evidence for such an event is overwhelming, and here are a few of the salient points which support Key's theory. Mr M. Baillie, a Professor of Paleoecology at Queens University, Belfast, Northern Ireland, is a leading authority on dendrology. This is the study of the growth of tree rings and how they can be interpreted to show if the climate allowed a tree to flourish or not at a given time, providing data on the climate, rainfall and so forth. As all tree rings are unique, like a fingerprint, but common across a single growth year, a continuous record has been accumulated of global tree patterns going back to 3,000 years BCE.

Mr Baillie has been able to show that in those 5,000 years there were just five bad time periods where 'major environmental shocks' affected the planet, and the last of these five was from the years 536 to 545, commencing just a year before the Battle of Camlann. In Ireland the Gaelic Irish Annals record failure in the bread harvest through the years 536 to 539, while contemporary Chinese sources record snow in August and severe crop failures in the same years. A dense, dry fog was reported from China across the Middle East and into Europe, whereas in South America drought was a major problem. Finally, in the Annales Cambriae there is written, 'Gueith camlann inqua Arthur & medraut corruerunt et mortalitas in brittannia et in hibernia fuit.' This translates to 'The strife of Camlann in which Arthur and Medraut [Mordred] perished, and there was plague in Britain and Ireland.' This one sentence tells us many things. Firstly, this was not one of the battles against the Saxons because it is not listed along with the other twelve. Secondly, it is not a victory as it is not recorded as such for either side, so both forces must have been fought to a standstill and then the survivors withdrew to bury their comrades, possibly at their own respective tumuli close to the battle given the state of the country at the time. Also, both leaders must have been killed or severely wounded in the battle as no-one else of note is mentioned. In addition, because no enemies are listed and there is no exaltation, this has to point to a civil war, where the parties are known to one another and their deaths are all the more painful to report. Finally, the reason for such a calamitous civil war is plain to see: there was plague in Britain and Ireland and the need for men to be able to feed the people of their small kingdom was greater than the need to stand together, and so all starve and fall together. It

The deceptive River Dovey in the Camlann Valley.

was the basic need to survive that drove a wedge between the previously allied kingdoms. So having fought for a generation alongside one another to defeat their enemies, the climate changed dramatically, food became scarce, disease and death were rife and now each prince or state among the Britons had to choose, either Arthur or Medraut. Such a dilemma would have been terrible for all concerned; for some reason no agreement of any sort could be reached and the British kingdoms were plunged into a civil war.

The word Camlann translates from the Welsh to simply mean 'crooked glen' or 'crooked bank'. There are several places vying to claim Camlann as their location, not least because the horror that is commercialisation could follow; one only has to visit Tintagel in Cornwall to see the mercenary use made of the name of Arthur. Queen Camel in Somerset, which is very close geographically to the enormous Iron Age hillfort of Cadbury and which was occupied in the Dark Ages (both before and after Arthur would have died), falls into the right time frame and location to be Arthur's Camelot. Then there is Camelford in Cornwall, and the famous 'slaughter bridge', which has been shown archaeologically to be have been fought over in the Dark Ages, but that battle was fought as late as 823, when the Cornish Britons grappled with the Saxons of Wessex as the latter were trying to complete their western expansion. Then there is the most likely candidate and also the only valley named Camlann, which is in the heart of the Welsh mountains: a valley which has ancient burial mounds, tumuli, at either end consistent with a battle having been fought there. This location makes great sense both geographically, as valleys meet there from all points of the compass, and also tragically as it is deep within what would have been British territory and far away from the prying eyes of Saxons who have welcomed the chance to destroy whichever force triumphed from such a battle. Had this battle been fought in or near Saxon territory, they could have waited and picked off the winner with their fresh forces and it would have been gleefully recorded in the ASC. What a valley Camlann is; it is drained by the River Dovey as the river makes its way out of the mountains and south-west to the sea. The river here is mesmeric; she is a meandering beauty that flows as gentle as a silk scarf wrapped around the spurs of the mountains that she bisects, her pools are deep and the water clear but too deep to cross, so deceptively deep that she could lure you in and you would disappear to the bottom. Then she is a girl, scurrying over the shingle of a broad ford, so shallow that you can cross in seconds, your feet barely wet, laughing and teasing those that watch her as she skips across the pebbles. Then she screams and cries with pain as she cuts her way through a gorge some fifty feet deep, grinding her way through the rock as she has done for centuries, leaving deep round holes like a dozen eyes of a water god to catch the splashing water in, while all the time she rushes by, polishing the rock as smooth as glass, and all this variety in just a few short miles.

The valley floor is just as varied; spring lines on the sides of the valley 100 feet above the valley floor feed fields with so much water that they are a marsh on a sloping hillside. There are smooth pastures without any mark to signify a change so that without warning you come to a vertical drop, an unsuspected wall of 50 feet (16 metres) and a disaster to any army unaware of its presence; the land drops like a step built for a giant. Nowhere is the valley floor very wide, meaning that an army would have no choice but to fight if it was cornered, and in some places the valley is narrow enough to shoot an arrow across it. The valley is clearly marked on the Ordnance Survey Map at

The main ford across the River Dovey and the likely site of the Battle of Camlann.

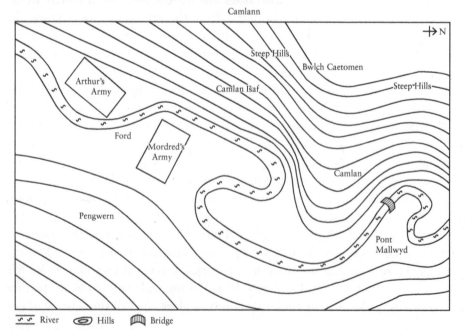

852,112, where the name Camlan Isaf sits, and 'Isaf' when translated can mean any of the following: 'lowest, basest, humblest, most depressed', not words to describe the clear beauty of the scenery within the valley. So do these words somehow refer to Medraut, where the lowest, perhaps basest of men, turned in greed upon his own kin to try and gain an advantage in a world that was being torn apart by famine, plague and pestilence? If two great leaders were at war and they had to pick a place that would be known to all to settle their dispute, then Camlann could be such a place because it could not be mistaken for any other. One can only imagine what kind of battle took place here as the two sides met knowing that it was a winner-takes-all battle. It is most likely that Arthur would have come from the sea, thereby still using his tried and tested methods of warfare, but this is twenty-one years (a generation) since the triumph of Mount Badon and Arthur would have been much older. Having landed, he would have marched along the Dovey Valley while Medraut would have come from some mountain stronghold, marching along the route of the river to meet the aged hero. The most likely place for the battle would be close to the ford; by blocking this crossing, whoever got there first could choose their terrain. It seems from the brief account that the battle was to the death, in this case of both the generals involved. Being from the same realm, both armies would have been similar, probably evenly matched, making the battle evenly balanced, and when two sides both need to win one can imagine that no side asked or received quarter. The two tumuli at either end of the valley may indicate the burial places of some of those involved. If there is any truth in legend then Arthur was mortally wounded after killing Medraut and was taken back to his beloved Isle of Avalon to die and be buried; the location of Camlann makes such a final journey feasible and immortalises Bardsey.

For the Saxons as well as for the Britons, the horror of the worldwide catastrophe meant that for a second generation the two sides were at a

Dyrham battlesite, showing the earthworks where the Britons were crushed in 577.

stalemate. The Saxons, however, recovered more quickly and slowly began their westward advance once their population had recovered sufficiently to allow them to build an army to commence campaigning again. Once the Saxons were mobilised the story was the same as before Arthur appeared, the Britons were slowly pushed further and further back until at the Battle of Dyrham in 577 the resistance of the Britons was finally broken and the Saxons had reached their goal, the Severn Estuary; now the majority of what would become England was under their control. Once more, the Britons were restricted to their western kingdoms, among which Wales was again the most secure.

CHAPTER 6

The Dark Age Invasions
578–1066

Wales in the Dark Ages

Following the annihilation of the last field army the Britons could muster, Wales was left isolated and that isolation would grow over the next few centuries as the Welsh people continued their Christian and agrarian way of life, developing their laws and language apart from their associated kingdoms of Cornwall, Cumbria and Strathclyde. It was just as well that Wales endured to keep alive the memory of their forebears because both Cumbria and Strathclyde would be eventually be swallowed up by the expansion of the northern Saxon kingdom of Northumbria. No power would succeed in conquering Wales but it was only with difficulty that she was able to resist the Saxon advance. The communities at this time were small and were more like small clans that the large tribal units that had existed under the Celts. The kindred family or *tud* was the key bonding structure as regards family and all were answerable to the noble that owned the land and all, whether tenant or slave, were ultimately answerable to that lord. That observance, together with an adherence to the ways of Christianity and the attendance of church, united the people and for most of the population, including the nobility, it was still about survival and not expansion. Wales, as ever, would be on the defensive against outside invaders and not looking to expand.

For the warriors of Wales, warfare came in different forms during this period; sadly for the Welsh people, the commonest type of conflict was at home, where the princedoms fought almost continually, one among the other, to have mastery over all the others. The Welsh were used to coastal raids and they were repeatedly asked to defend their homes and churches against the Scotti, who raided from across the Irish Sea. The Saxons also had their eyes on Wales and as Mercia's power grew, her armies gradually pushed back the Kingdom of Powys, whose lands are thought to have originally stretched as far as Wroxeter; having pushed the Welsh back, Mercia then probed into Wales and although there were battles, none are clear, but this is typical for this period of Welsh history, where conflict is recorded but with scant detail. Despite the might of Mercia,

Picts

Picts

Britain in 600

▬▬ Extent of Saxon expansion

Britons   Bernicia

Scotti

Rheged

Northumbria

Deira

Mid
Angles

East
Anglia

Welsh
Britons

Mercia

Hwicce

East
Saxons

West
Saxons

South
Saxons

Kent

Britons

Britain in 700

The Saxon kingdoms

the terrain and the solid Welsh tactics of defending endured and none of their territory was lost to the Saxons. Indeed, at times some of the Welsh princes allied with the Saxons and Welshmen were to be found far from home, fighting in Northumbria and in the east of Britain. Occasionally a Welsh force would go on its own raid, marching far into Saxon territory and returning with cattle which, once stolen, were driven back to their mountain strongholds.

After almost 200 years of warfare along the border between the Welsh and the Saxons, Offa of Mercia either repaired or reconstructed the great dyke that would separate the two countries with the object of keeping the Welsh in, and hardly had this barrier been built than the Saxons had to look to the east and the Welsh once more to the coast as a new raiding menace had arrived: the Vikings. These pagan warriors were to dominate the next 250 years of British history as their raids intensified and they gradually forged for themselves a kingdom in England which covered 50 per cent of the country before eventually, in 1016, the Danish Cnut would sit as the 'English' king. The Vikings caused havoc wherever they landed and Ynys Môn was often attacked, being more vulnerable than the rest of Wales as it was a fertile island with numerous landing places. Wales was now coming under increasing attack from Viking raiders, particularly Danish raids in the period between 950 and 1000. Caradoc of Llancarfan tells

Offa's Dyke is still a recognisable ditch and rampart in many places.

of a great raid to Anglesey where Godfrey Haroldson captured 2,000 captives in 987 and only the intervention of the King of Gwynedd, Maredudd ab Owain, prevented his people being taken into slavery and that was by paying Haroldson a large ransom. In spite of the many skirmishes and battles fought in Wales against the Vikings, there are a few which are detailed enough to allow investigation. However, right on the old border in Mid Wales between Powys and Mercia, a battle did occur which has given an incredibly detailed insight into warfare during this period and illustrates just how far a Viking army could penetrate inland after a century of raids, something questioned for many years with regard to the feasibility of the Vikings operating with boats so far from the sea. However, archaeological evidence from Eastern Europe has clearly shown how the Vikings traded all the way to Byzantium (modern Istanbul) by using the river systems wherever possible and pushing their boats across land when necessary to connect between waterways; the shallow draught of the boats made them easy to push upon rollers across the terrain.

893 Buttington (Welshpool) – Powys

Buttington today is a very small hamlet situated on the wide plain of the Severn Valley, some 4 miles inside the Welsh border, and it lies close to the modern course of the River Severn. There is an inn and a church and a small number of houses and farms and, recently, a small industrial estate. The market town of Welshpool is a further mile to the west and the remains of the important Dark Age monument of Offa's Dyke run close by. With regard to the majority of Dark Age battle sites, modern historians have little or no written evidence to enable them to identify one location from another; this, when coupled with the lack of archaeological evidence available for those battles fought more than 1,000 years ago, makes an exact identification of a battle site even harder. Given the literary evidence available from cross referencing the entry for the year 893 in the ASC, together with the archaeological evidence from the *Archaeologia Cambrenesis*, it is clear that this hamlet of Buttington is the exact site of a Dark Age battle and as such it makes Buttington a gem among all battlesites in both Wales and Britain. This is what the ASC says:

> When the King had turned west with the army towards Exeter, as I have said before, and the Danish army had laid siege to the borough, they went to their ships when he arrived there. When he [the king] was occupied against the army there in the west, and the [other] two Danish armies were assembled at Shoebury in Essex, and had made a fortress there, they went both together up along the Thames, and a great reinforcement came to them both from the East Angles and the Northumbrians. They then went up along the Thames until they reached

the Severn, then up along the Severn. Then Ealdorman Ethelred and Ealdorman Aethelhelm and Ealdorman Aethelnoth and the King's thegns who then were at home at the fortresses assembled from every borough east of the Parret, and both west and east of the Selwood, and also north of the Thames and west of the Severn, and also some portion of the Welsh people. When they were all assembled, they overtook the Danish army at Buttington, on the bank of the Severn, and besieged it on every side in a fortress. Then when they had encamped for many weeks on the two sides of the river, and the King was occupied in the west in Devon against the naval force, the besieged were oppressed by famine, and had eaten the greater part of their horses and the rest had died of starvation. Then they came out against the men who were encamped on the east side of the river, and fought against them, and the Christians had the victory. And the King's thegn Ordheah and also many other King's thegns were killed and very great slaughter of the Danes was made, and the part that escaped were saved by flight.

In 893, King Alfred the Great, ruler of Wessex, was preoccupied with a Danish invasion in the south-west of England. This is supported by evidence elsewhere in the most important written source for the period, the ASC, where the entry for 893 states that two Danish fleets with a combined force of 140 ships was making for Exeter. At this time, another Danish force, apparently made up from four different armies, was making its way up the River Thames and then up the River Severn until it was overtaken by English and Welsh forces at Buttington, near Welshpool. Accordingly, King Alfred sent three ealdormen to gather what men they could to tackle this new threat, which had appeared so surprisingly far inland. An ealdorman was an appointed and sometimes hereditary title carried by a man who, in conjunction with the sheriff, was responsible for the administration of a shire. Their importance in military terms is that they were also responsible for commanding the armed force of their shire, the levy or fyrd, on behalf of the king whenever, and to wherever, the monarch so commanded.

At Buttington the Danes either occupied an existing fort or earthwork or constructed a defensive position of their own. From the east came an English army and a similarly sized Welsh force appeared on the west bank opposite them; although the Saxons and the Welsh were often at war, the appearance of a Viking force meant that old differences were put aside for the moment as the Vikings were in this instance the enemies of all. This position meant that effectively the heathens were surrounded and they were then besieged in this state for some weeks. This was an impossible position for the Danes; they had no way of escape without conflict and very little chance of their supplies being replenished by any kind of relief force. Accordingly, with their food supplies gone and their numbers and fitness declining, they were left with no alternative but to try and fight their way out. To head west would be suicidal; they would have needed to cross the Severn and fight a Welsh army with the advantage of ground and with an English army at their heels. The only logical way was therefore east and back down the Severn valley, but straight into the arms of the waiting English troops. This meant that the Danes would only have been facing one enemy, as the Welsh army would probably have been forced to remain isolated on the far bank of the Severn as it seems unlikely that there was any means of crossing the Severn quickly; for the Vikings to have arrived there at all meant that the River Severn had been in a swollen state to allow the Viking ships to progress so far inland.

It is the author's belief that this Danish army made its way to Buttington by water. The Danes, in common with other Vikings, were master boat builders and built a variety of differently sized ships based on their requirements. All Danish ships were of shallow draught and capable of moving fast, even when rowed against wind and tide while carrying not only men but also horses and supplies. These ships were capable of carrying anything from a dozen to 100 men, and when on long voyages the men on the ships would work in shifts, half of the men resting while the others rowed; this meant that the ships could be kept moving at all times. When returning downriver, the river would carry them and their booty, meaning that the majority of the crew could rest before their return home, whether that was a base on the British mainland or a distant fjord in Scandinavia. The Severn is known to have been navigable as far as Poolquay, just 2 miles north-east of Welshpool, until the last century. Wroxeter, located 5 miles west of modern Shrewsbury, was the key Roman town in Shropshire; in the second century AD it was serviced by Roman craft making their way up the Severn. Indeed, the stone from which the church at Wroxeter is constructed carries marks indicating that the stones were once part of the Roman quay that served the 200-acre site of the Roman and then British city.

One can imagine the scene. The Danes have rowed against the flow of the river for several days, perhaps raiding on their way and resting up at night well away from any signs of human activity. Then they come to a wide-open valley with hills far away on either side. Unknown to them, the rain on the Welsh mountains has swollen the two rivers that meet west of Shrewsbury, the Vyrnwy and the Severn, causing them to burst their banks and flood the valley. The Severn would be the weaker of the two currents at this point and also the much wider valley. Noting this fact, the Danes pushed on, unaware that the course they are now taking is simply across flooded marshes and is not a normal riverbed or inland lake. The flooding of this valley for much of the autumn and winter of 2013/14 illustrated how the valley would have looked to any Viking crew: a wide, still inland pool with a river's course meandering through it but with much of the flow to either side sluggish or even stationery. As an evening approached, the Danes spy an old earthwork close to a great dyke that has been on their port side at times for the last few miles. They gather their boats together and use the mound as a base for the night. The Danish warriors are

alerted in the night by those on watch, who have seen torches about a mile to
the west on the other side of the water. Alarmingly, further torches are seen a
little later on, but this time they are on the eastern side of the river, from the
direction of the hills that the Danes passed earlier in the day. The Danish camp
stirs into life, and as dawn begins to break, those on watch are horrified to see
that the river has overnight retreated some twenty yards to the west, and it is
still visibly falling. The Danish ships, which had been half in and half out of
the water, are now resting in tall sodden reeds and grasses atop a field of mud.

With the full light of day, the harsh reality of their situation dawns upon the
Danes: this was not a lake but a river in spate. Their ships are stuck on sodden
ground now, some distance from the river, a distance that will increase unless
more rains come and the river rises again. There is a Welsh army standing on
the west bank of the river. Although the Welsh are out of missile range at the
moment, if the Danes try and drag their ships to the river they will have to do so
in the face of prolonged attack from the arrows, slingstones and javelins of the
Welshmen. Meanwhile, to the east an English army is forming up on the lower
slopes of the long mountain ridge behind them. The Danes are surrounded, a
long way from their homes and a lifetime away from any assistance. At this
point the Danish leaders must have held a conference to discuss their options.
Do they defend their position, while they wait for the river to rise again, and
so escape between both armies without having to fight, simply running the
risk of a few casualties from missiles? Or do they risk an all-out attack before

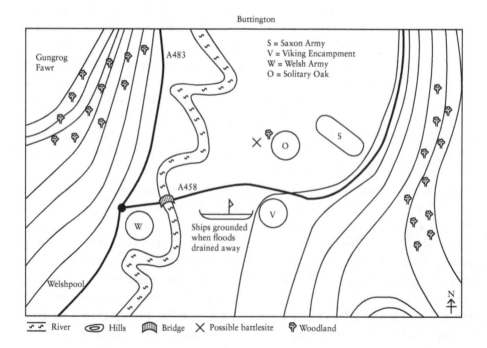

more English and Welsh troops may arrive? The ASC states that they were 'encamped for many weeks', so one can safely assume that the Danes decided to consolidate their force, perhaps rationalising the ships into the minimum number required to get home and breaking up some of the others. This would provide them with the materials to construct a rudimentary palisade around their camp as well as providing fuel for fires to cook and light their camp by night. As is the way with Britain, the rain does not fall to order and now, though the Vikings probably prayed to their gods every day, no rains fell in sufficient quantity to raise the river level to anywhere near its former height. As the time passes and still no rains come, it is possible that some of the Danes start to suffer from disease, hunger or wounds suffered in earlier battles and the Danes continued to rationalise their resources. This must have been a desperate time for the Danes, trapped and incapable of doing anything save watching the sky for rain, sharpening their weapons for the fight that must surely come if the rains do not, with their belts getting tighter and their bodies weaker as food supplies dwindle. Eventually, the situation becomes so desperate that the Danes decide that they have to try and break out. By now, the weather has probably got much warmer, drying out the land around their remaining boats and indicating that perhaps summer is near at hand and that the likelihood of any more heavy rains has passed until the autumn. Almost all of their food is gone, but the Danes need strength to fight their way out. Their only source of fresh food is their horses, so in desperation they kill enough of them to feed the remaining men; perhaps, as only one horse head was found in the burial pits, one horse was sufficient to feed the whole force. They plan to break out in the last light of evening after they have rested all day; this will give them a chance to run through the English lines and then scatter into the darkness of night in an 'every man for himself' situation. Accordingly, they have one last meal together, calling one last time on their gods to assist them before they prepare for battle. No doubt they sang songs and told victory tales from their past to keep their morale high for the fight to come.

Faced with only one course of action, the Danes break out of their encampment and assault the English lines. Danish armies only ever contained a few horsemen so perhaps one or two of these led the charge to try and punch a hole through the English lines, closely followed by the bulk of the Danish force. It is possible that a number of escape routes were all put into action at the same time and that some of the Danes dragged a number of the smallest boats to the river to try and escape that way while the rest of their army held the English host at bay. The darkness would have helped to protect the Danes as they advanced towards the Welsh army, who would undoubtedly have watched the battle unfold before them across the valley as much as light allowed and they would have no doubt thrown their missiles at any target that presented itself. The fighting is evidently fierce as a named king's thegn, Ordheah, is killed along with many other English thegns.

At this time a thegn was a landowner with an income of more than four hides per year, whereas to become a king's thegn would mean that the landowner had an income of more than forty hides per year. There is still much debate as to what area a hide covered. A hide is defined as the land necessary to keep one family for a year, and varies on interpretation between 30 and 120 acres. It is likely that at least a few of the Danes would have escaped, but clearly the battle is won by 'the Christians' (the Saxon English) and there is 'a very great slaughter of the Danes'. Eventually, when the metal noises of battle fade away and there are no more cries of pain or curses on the wind, calm would have descended. Clearly at this point there are no Danes left fighting and perhaps the Saxons lit torches to explore the battlesite, but more likely they would have waited until morning, when they could search the battlefield properly, strip their opponents' bodies and take their weapons, armour and anything else of value. If the English had any mounted troops they might then have undertaken some kind of pursuit to try and hunt down those few Danes that had succeeded in escaping, for they knew which way they would be heading. The two key questions to all battles are: where were they fought and how many men were involved? With Buttington, we know the site and we even have a clue to the size of the armies involved. From the AC we know that exactly 400 skulls and associated bones were found in the three burial pits discovered under the churchyard, but were all of these Danish dead? We know from the *Anglo-Saxon Chronicle* that some Danes escaped 'by flight', but the word 'slaughter' suggests that the majority of the Danes were killed. With this in mind, it seems likely that the Danish army was no more than 500 strong, which would make the size of the fleet between ten and fifteen ships depending on their capacity. The action of the Danes can also provide a clue as to the size of the English army. The Danes adopted a defensive position, which would suggest that their army was significantly smaller than the English. Had the Danish force been anywhere near equal in size to the English then they would have attacked at once rather than risking more English troops arriving, giving the English the advantage in numbers. At first glance the Welsh army is even more difficult to gauge, but as it chose not to try and interfere in the battle, choosing instead to adopt a holding position on the far bank of the Severn, then it would suggest that the army was smaller than the English, and therefore possibly smaller than the Danish force as well. The advantage of their position was sufficient for the Welsh to ensure that the Danes could progress no further west but it also indicates that the Welsh army was not large enough to consider crossing the river once it had returned to its normal level to attack the Danes.

Despite extensive research, no one from the local secular community has been able to complete the full history of All Saints' Church at Buttington. Legend has it that a church was built on the mound to commemorate this victory over the Danes, but there is no evidence as yet to support that, though the yew tree which stands close to the church has been dated to 893. The current church is

The River Severn in spate, seen from Buttington church; the river can spread to over a mile wide in places.

believed to be of seventeenth-century construction, on the site of a much earlier medieval base. All Saints' Church today still sits upon a small mound, with a deep ditch running along its eastern edge, and roads on its western and northern edges. These all lie below the level of the church mound and form exactly the kind of site that a force would select as a protected position. One can only speculate as to what was here before the church was built and before the Danes arrived. Given the amount of Roman and Celtic remains in the area and its close proximity to Offa's Dyke, perhaps the Danes occupied what was already a prepared, if long abandoned, small defensive encampment, maybe the site of a watchtower constructed by the Mercians to allow signalling to continue along the length of the dyke. In 1838, while digging foundations for a new schoolroom at the south-west corner of Buttington churchyard, the Reverend Richard Dawkins made a remarkable discovery. He uncovered three pits: the largest contained 200 skulls and the other two pits each contained 100 skulls. The sides of each pit were lined with human arm and leg bones. All the teeth within the skulls were perfect, suggesting that the men were in the prime of life. Some of the bones and skulls showed signs of violent death, as some of the skulls had been fractured. Horse bones and teeth were also found in the pits. All of these bones were collected and reinterred on the north side of the churchyard, save for many of the teeth, which were sold off by the workmen who were performing the reburial. It was believed at the time that a dead man's tooth was a cure for toothache, and the workmen received between 6 pence and 1 shilling for each tooth. The Reverend Dawkins later wrote about his discovery in the journal *Archaeologia Cambrensis* Volume 28, 1873, pp. 214–215. Whether these burial pits were made at the time of the battle or were created subsequently when the site became consecrated, is at present unknown, but in his article, Dawkins speculated that the latter is probably the most likely.

So why was the battle fought here? We know that the English pursued the Danes for between 160 and 200 miles, depending on the route taken, from the Thames all the way to the Welsh border; what we do not know is whether they marched on foot or rowed upriver. The author has lived long enough within the confines of this part of the Severn valley to see the dramatic moods that the River Severn can portray. Despite the controls of the Clywedog Dam, the river still regularly bursts its banks, causing chaos to the modern transportation system by flooding road and rail routes, sometimes causing their closure. The Severn, which is in places only a few metres wide, can flood the valley to the width of a mile following just 48 hours of rain. Imagine how much greater the rise and fall of the river would be in the days before the Clywedog Dam was built; in those times, much of the valley would be nothing more than soft marsh land. Importantly, when the river does flood, much of the side water is sluggish, as calm as a lake. It would be perfect for craft to move on, particularly when the land was not enclosed with hedges and walls and punctuated by scattered farm buildings, as it is today.

Conclusions

Buttington is a very significant Dark Age battle because when all the evidence is put together the location can be pinpointed to within a fairly small area, certainly less than a square mile, and that is most rare; one can never say 'the

Above left: Buttington church mound, the likely site of the Viking camp in 893.

Above right: Buttington church and the yew that commemorates the battle.

battle definitely happened in this field', but with Buttington we can say it was one of these few fields. It is also one of those rare occasions in the history of the Viking incursions when the English slaughtered their Danish opponents. Much has been made of the defensive tactics developed by Alfred the Great in the 880s. According to David Smurthwaite in his book *The Complete Guide to the Battlefields of Britain*, it was these tactics that enabled him to force the Vikings to either accept Danelaw or return home in the year 896. Buttington is not mentioned in Smurthwaite's book, but surely if 896 was the key year for the Vikings to admit that they had had enough of warfare in England and Wales for a time, the news of the battle of Buttington in 893 filtering through to the majority of Viking leaders over time would have played a significant part in influencing them to rethink their strategy? The Vikings realised that they could not afford to sustain a war against the English if they were going to suffer such complete defeats as they had done on the upper reaches of the River Severn. The Dark Ages span over 600 years of European history and they are called 'Dark' simply because there is a lack of written evidence and a lack of archaeological evidence to clarify what took place in those turbulent years between 409 and 1066. To the historian, therefore, Buttington is a most valuable site because here the main written source for this period, the *Anglo-Saxon Chronicle*, is supported by the discovery of the hundreds of bodies that were systematically buried so close to the battle site. Buttington typifies a lost Welsh battlesite: there are no

The most likely site for the Battle of Buttington in 893.

information boards on site and there is no plaque to the battle; for the visitor there is a car park available, provided a few years ago to serve the church.

Although many princes tried to elevate their princedom to be sole master of Wales, the very same terrain which for so long defied the Romans and the Mercians also defied those princes trying to make themselves King of the Cymry. Such complete control could only be achieved, as had been shown before by the Romans, if the ruling power had a series of strong, interconnected forts or castles. During the Dark Age and into the medieval period, this could only be achieved across Wales if someone mastered the other princedoms through marriage or alliance rather than simply by victory in war. The first man to rule almost all of Wales was Rhodri Mawr (Rhodri the Great), who was the King of Gwynedd during the ninth century and who succeeded in expanding his power base to rule both Ceredigion and Powys. Throughout this time, the coast of Wales was continually raided by Vikings; St David's Cathedral was attacked numerous times. The problem for all would-be Welsh leaders was to unite the country so that it could work together to mobilise and defeat such incursions into its territory, but no-one was able to provide that unity. Upon his death, Rhodri's realms were divided between his two sons, but they did nothing to continue the process towards unity. This fell to Hywel Dda, which means Hywel the Good on account of his great moot, the Whitland, at which the Welsh laws were formulated into an accepted code for all Welshmen. He also extended his control to most of Wales by the year of 942, forging a large principality called Deheubarth that covered the greater part of south and west Wales. He also pursued a peaceful 'foreign' policy with the English, which, given that both peoples were still suffering Viking raids, was a shrewd policy to undertake. Sadly for Wales, after Hywel's death in 949 his sons could not maintain their father's influence and Gwynedd once more broke away from the rest of the principalities.

The increase in the number of Viking raids that now terrorised the Welsh coastal fringes from 950 seems to have redirected the Welsh warriors to look to their own defence rather than looking to unite their kingdoms and it was not until the early eleventh century that Llywelyn ap Seisyll once more united Gwynedd and Deheubarth. Llywelyn ap Seisyll's wife, Angharad, was in fact the daughter of Maredudd, Maredudd being the grandson of Hywel Dda who (as we mentioned above) was forced to pay a ransom for the return of some of his own people. It is not certain how much of Wales Maredudd ruled at the height of the Viking raids but Llywelyn ap Seisyll took control of Gwynedd in 1018 when he defeated Aeddan, who was the Prince of Gwynedd, though it seems that Aeddan had taken the throne by force and not by succession. Either way, Llywelyn ap Seisyll was taking no chances about the future and he killed Aeddan and his four sons. Llywelyn ap Seisyll was then challenged by Rhain (also spelt Reyn), the Irish ruler of Dyfed, who claimed he was the heir to the throne of Gwynedd and insisted that Maredudd was his father.

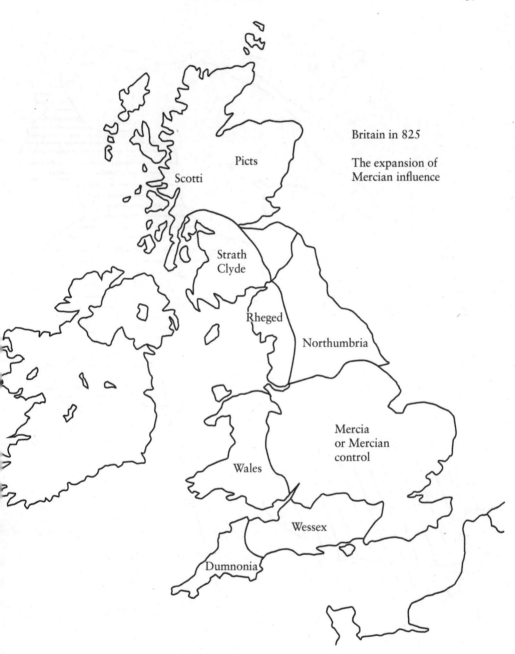

Picts

Scotti

Strath
Clyde

Rheged

Northumbria

Wales

Mercia
or Mercian
control

Wessex

Dumnonia

Britain in 825

The expansion of
Mercian influence

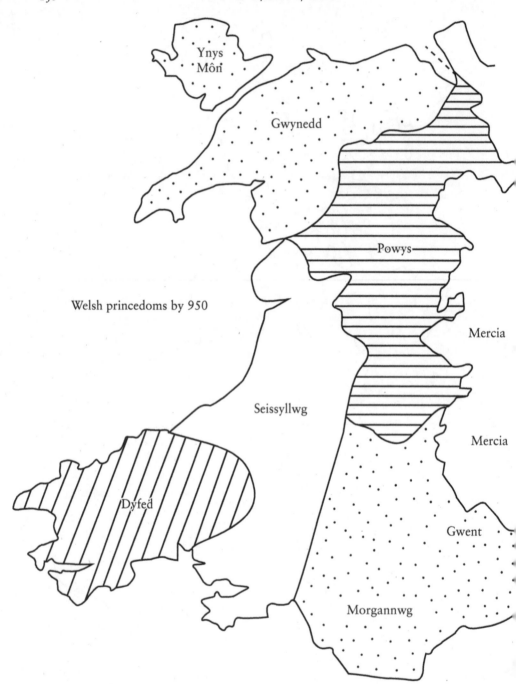

Ynys
Môn

Gwynedd

Powys

Welsh princedoms by 950

Mercia

Seissyllwg

Mercia

Dyfed

Gwent

Morgannwg

1022 Abergwyli – Carmarthenshire

Rhain's claim was accepted by the men of Dyfed, which concerned Llywelyn ap Seisyll sufficiently for him to march south to deal with Rhain's claim. It is possible that Rhain was an Irish warlord, some of whose family had settled in Wales in the preceding centuries, as this was not an uncommon occurrence. But conversely, there were also Welsh nobility who at times took refuge in Ireland and would then return to claim their titles. As we know, the majority of the armies in the Dark Ages were very small, often less than 1,000 men, and as no numbers are available from Caradoc of Llancarfan's account we must assume that these two armies were quite small. Llywelyn ap Seisyll is most likely to have used one of the two Roman roads that met just east of Carmarthen, where Rhain was like to be. So Llywelyn ap Seisyll might have marched west from Llandeilo but, given that he was more likely to be in the centre of his kingdom, he probably marched south from Llandovery, which would have allowed him to make use of an old hillfort on Merlin's Hill, just 3 miles east of Carmarthen and commanding a view over the open plain below him, including the conference of the rivers Gwili and Tywi and the Roman roads. The hills just to the north of the Tywi form a long ridge here, an archetypal defensive position and one that any army would not have ignored. Rhain, marching out from Carmarthen, would have seen Llywelyn ap Seisyll and his men and no doubt, as Rhain advanced towards them, Llywelyn ap Seisyll would have advanced to the lower slopes of the ridge, just north of Abergwyli itself, so as to entice Rhain to attack him.

Pen-y-gadair hill, where Llywelyn ap Sesissyl waited for Rhain Yscot.

The ridge at Abergwyli, down which Llywelyn's Welsh army charged Rhain's Irish force.

Llywelyn ap Seisyll's army would have consisted of a few experienced heavily armed men who would have been his personal retinue, his most loyal and strongest fighters, and the rest would be a roughly equal mix of bowmen and spearmen, few of whom would be wearing armour. Rhain's force would have been very similar as he too would have had a small unit of loyal and well-armed hearth troops, as they were known. With them, he would have had mostly bowmen and some javelinmen from his southern Welsh princedom, but with his Irish connections he may well have had some units of mercenary Scotti with him, who could have given him some spearmen and possibly some axemen as well. Overall there would have been little difference between the two armies and this is borne out by the account in the *Brut*, which says that 'there was a general slaughter on both sides'. Llywelyn ap Seisyll had waited for his opponent to attack, and he did so after the usual stirring speeches to his men, after which there would have been a short exchange of the few missiles that each side had before Rhain charged home. After the battle had raged for some time, the *Brut* states that Rhain 'retreated in a fox-like manner'. The problem for Rhain and his men was that retreat was difficult and the *Brut* says that the carnage and pursuit that followed the victory lasted all the way to Mercia, with Llywelyn ap Seisyll destroying and pillaging every place. This is clearly unlikely as, firstly, laying waste to such a vast area would have taken a much greater army and a considerable amount of time, as it was 100 miles to Mercia. Secondly, it would alienate the very people that Llywelyn wanted to rule.

The *Annales Cambriae* state that Rhain died in the battle, and this would seem more likely for as Llywelyn ap Seisyll's men advanced, they would be pushing Rhain's army back into an area bordered on three sides by water formed by a great bend of the River Tywi and the inflowing River Gwili. With Llywelyn ap Seisyll's army blocking the only exit from this water sided

Troops trapped against the River Tywi stood little chance of survival.

Abergwyli battlefield, where Rhain's army was destroyed by LLywelyn ap Sesissyl.

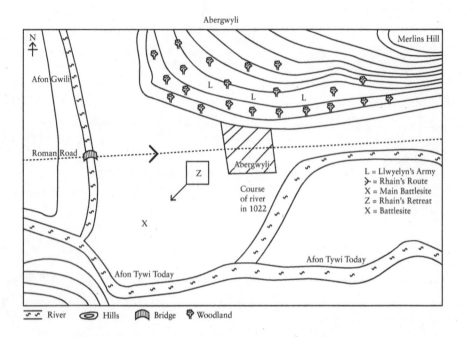

trap, one can imagine some men fighting to the death while others decided to chance their luck and tried to cross one of the rivers and so escape. The battle was over and Llywelyn ap Seisyll, with a complete victory, had regained all of South Wales; according again to the *Brut*, his reign was one of prosperity – hardly someone who would therefore slaughter everything in his path once the battle was won and his enemy slain. Sadly, he died a year later in 1023, but this brought his eldest son Gruffydd ap Llywelyn to prominence at the young age of sixteen. In many ways, children of sixteen today are far more advanced than those children of sixteen born fifty years ago, such are the leaps in technology in the intervening generations. There are the same differences between a boy of sixteen in 1023 and a boy of sixteen now: then, a boy was taught to fight, hunt, stalk and live off the land; it is all relevant to the time that one is born into. Henry V was just sixteen when he led the left wing of his father Henry IV's army at the Battle of Shrewsbury. There is some confusion as to the commencement of Gruffydd's reign and his ability to rule, as some of his father's kingdoms seem to have slipped away from his control. In 1023 Iago ab Idwal ap Meurig began to rule Gwynedd and Gruffydd seems to be out of the picture for a while before re-emerging when he regained Powys. By the 1030s Gruffydd was galvanised into action, and on seeing yet another rebellion in Gwynedd, by the subsequent assassination of Iago and the exile of Iago's son to Ireland, Gruffydd used his own forces to recover the princedom. Gruffydd had now restabilised the situation which his father had held and was king of both Gwynedd and Powys.

1039 Rhyd y Groes – Powys

Having united many of the Welsh people behind him, Gruffydd wanted to prove that he was the man capable of leading his people in defending their rights and their lands. Gruffydd decided that the best way to take the minds of his fellow princes and those of his people away from their internal struggles was to get them all to look outside of Wales, so he chose to take war across the border and into England. Once more, Caradoc of Llancarfan in his *Brut* tells how Gruffydd 'pursued the Saxons and other nations ... and overcame them in a multitude of battles'. Not all of these encounters would have been battles as such; many would have been small sieges and attacks on isolated settlements as he picked targets along the border that could easily be captured. By always attacking within striking distance of home, he was never far from safety, thereby copying exactly the same tactics as the Silures and Caratacus had used so many centuries before him. One does not have to look far to understand why a Mercian army rode towards Wales in 1039; either they had heard of unrest in Wales and decided to take advantage of it for themselves, or Gruffydd had started attacking border settlements as soon as his kingdom was united behind him so as to draw the Mercians towards him – in the case of this battle, it seems more like the latter.

Rhyd y Groes means the ford of the cross and the only place in the Mid Wales area where those two things combine is just 5 miles south of Welshpool, and it is a place that everyone would know because the ford was used all the time as a meeting place so that parleys could be held there. The ford meant that a whole series of structures were built to guard the crossing of the river, as we shall see in more detail when we look at the Battle of Montgomery in a later chapter. The ford still exists, near Montgomery, at Rhydwhyman, the destination point of the Roman road that heads west out of Shrewsbury, and just a few miles before the ford as one head towards Wales two Roman roads cross at the place still called today Rhyd y Groes; a small wooded valley lies there, a stream-cut valley in the middle of a long ridge that runs east–west along the northern edge of the valley, while the southern edge of the valley has the deceptively dangerous River Camlad running along it before another line of hills rises to the south. This is no narrow valley like the Dee, where the Alleluia Victory took place; this is a valley almost a mile wide, but if it had been raining as it so often does, and if the ground was wet and the river in flood, then it would have been a bad place to get caught by an unexpected attack.

There is only one way in which a Welsh army could have defeated a full Mercian army that was marching fully prepared for a campaign, and that was to catch the Saxons completely unaware by means of an ambush. The Saxon/ Mercian army would have consisted of a lot of infantry with spears and a number of small units with bows, javelins, slings and axes. Their best troops

Above left: Rhyd y Groes, now a staggered crossroads for road safety.

Above right: The hidden valley which the Welsh army used at Rhyd y Groes now shelters a caravan holiday park.

would have been the *huscarls*, who were the personal retinue of the commander, Eadwine, and these may have been on horses for more rapid movement, though it is unlikely that the whole army was travelling on horses, otherwise a Welsh ambush into so open a space would not have been so effective. Many of the valleys in Wales were still well forested in this period and although some valleys had been cleared for agriculture, many small river and stream cuttings would have still been choked with dense foliage. The Welsh army, dressed in clothes of natural colours made from home-spun wools and home-made dyes, would have blended in well with a deciduous forest. Being mostly without armour, keeping quiet before an attack would not have been difficult for the Welsh, as only Gruffudd and his loyal hearth men would have had armour and it is likely that their horses were well hidden elsewhere, high up on the ridge, ready for an escape and well out of Saxon earshot. The rest of the Welsh army would be once again a mixture of spearmen and bowmen supported by a few skirmishers with a variety of other missile weapons, javelins and slingstones.

The small valley that today is home to the Rhyd y Groes caravan park is the most likely place on the northern ridge where the Welsh army would have hidden; this thin, narrow valley is only a few hundred yards from where the Roman roads cross and that was probably the place that the army had agreed to pause to allow the rear of the column to catch up with the front so that they could rest before continuing, or perhaps decide to rest for the night. If the Mercians had set off from Shrewsbury in the morning then it would have been getting late in the day by the time that they reached Rhyd y Groes, as the journey is around 20 miles. Sadly, we have no numbers for the men involved on either side, but we know that at other battles involving Gruffydd he fielded armies of around 1,000 men, so one can imagine that the Welsh army (as this

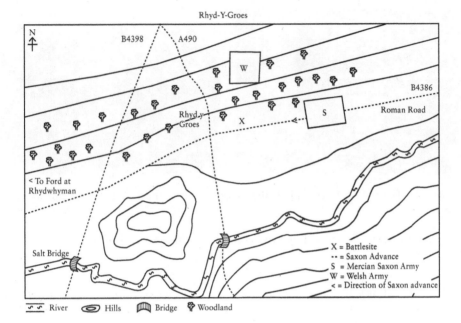

was Gruffydd's first campaign into unknown territory) was not that strong, as he would not have had the reputation he would later enjoy so that men would flock to him. Taking that into account, and the nature of his attack, let us assume that Gruffydd had around 500 to 600 men. In contrast, Eadwine had no doubt heard reports of this Welsh prince who had defeated his rivals and was massing his forces near the border; Eadwine may have had reports of recent assaults on Saxon manors or farms, and his army was probably a thousand men.

It is most likely that the Welsh attacked just as the head of Eadwine's column reached the crossroads and his men were strong out in a line, carrying their weapons not for fighting but as comfortably as they could; perhaps the setting sun was in the Saxons' eyes or dusk was just beginning to fall. Without warning, across the long line of troops that stretches all along the road, a host of arrows fall, many finding their mark as they are so long a target that the short-range bows of the Welsh at this time cannot miss. Within seconds, other missiles fly into the line before the Welshmen armed with their long spears charge in, hitting the long line of men in the flank as those Saxons are just beginning to come to terms with their plight and turning to face their assailants.

The initial impact would have pushed many of the Saxons away from the Welsh and down towards the River Camlad, which is in itself a small river, but its channel is cut through an alluvium plain: its banks are soft and crumble easily and they are normally at least 6, sometimes 10, feet above the water level. It is too wide to jump and the water is brown and thick with all the silt

Above left: The sodden battlefield of Rhyd y Groes, where the Saxons under Eadwine were killed.

Above right: River Camlad at Rhyd y Groes, where many Saxons drowned.

and sand running in it, so you cannot tell the depth, and the bottom is like quicksand, thick and oozy; the Camlad is no river to be pushed towards when you are losing a battle! In the ensuing slaughter, as the Mercians and their mercenaries or allies were pushed south across the valley, Eadwine himself was killed. This was a complete Welsh victory and although on Welsh soil, for the first time in almost a millennium a Welsh general was taking the fight to the invader instead of being permanently on the defensive.

Some idea of the complexity of Dark Age and medieval politics and alliances can be gathered from the structure of an 'English' army between 885 and 1066. The crown of England during these turbulent years was worn by Anglo-Saxons, then Danes (Vikings), then the Anglo-Saxons again and then finally the Norman head of William I. The composition of an army in this time until William's victory was based on a core of Anglo-Saxon huscarls (king's bodyguards) and the traditional spear carrying fyrd, a form of well-trained militia that was the nearest equivalent of the standing army of today. However, the rest of the army could be made up of Normans, Vikings, Welsh or Scotti and this army could be fighting against other armies that contained different factions from the same countries as one princedom or rival kingdom tried to eliminate another.

Flushed with success, Gruffydd then attacked Dyfed, which had been lost to Hywel ab Edwin, and defeated him at the Battle of Pencader in 1041. It is recorded that after his exile Hywel returned with a Viking force but was again defeated, and this time Gruffydd killed Hywel in another hard-fought battle. Whenever chance allowed, Gruffydd ap Llywelyn harried the Saxon lands along Offa's Dyke; so successful were his campaigns that the 'agricultural land around Oswestry had reverted to forest' while the 'Wye's southern bank lay empty'. These quotes taken from the Doomsday book show the extent to which the Welsh incursions had driven away the previous local population; however, they had not replaced them with any of their own people. While Gruffydd ap Llywelyn was triumphing to the east of Wales, Gruffydd ap Rhydderch of Gwent retook Deheubarth in 1047 and proclaimed himself king. This was achieved by a victory in a battle between the huscarls or hearth troops of each claimant, with Gruffydd ap Llywelyn losing 140 of his best men in the action. Despite Gruffydd ap Llywelyn's efforts, he could not oust Gruffydd ap Rhydderch, who held on to his newly won kingdom until 1055, when Gruffydd ap Llywelyn finally defeated Gruffydd ap Rhydderch in battle and recaptured the lost princedom of Deheubarth. Gruffydd ap Llywelyn now allied himself with a Saxon, Aelfgar, who was the son of Earl Leofric of Mercia. Mercia was once the great Saxon state but had been replaced by Wessex and Aelfgar had since had his earldom of East Anglia taken by Harold Godwinson (later King Harold) and his brothers.

With his rear now secure, Gruffydd ap Llywelyn could once more advance east and this combined Saxon-Welsh force marched in the same year on Hereford, which was defend by the Earl of Hereford, Ralph. Each side had around 1,000 men in their ranks and the Welsh and their Saxon allies waited for the defenders to march out to meet them, probably west of Hereford, where the Roman road would have been the easiest way to march on the city. Ralph had many Normans in his ranks and they decided to fight in the Norman style, and against the well organised and defensively minded Gruffydd ap Llywelyn, they charged as cavalry. The battle was an absolute disaster and the *Brut*, Florence of Worcester, and the ASC all record that Ralph and his men retreated as soon as the 'Britons' assaulted them and they were able to 'run away because of their horses' (ASC). Clearly the Norman horses were not that fast, or the retreat began after 'a severely hard battle' (ASC), for they lost around 50 per cent of their force with apparently none of the Britons (Welsh-Saxons) being killed. Clearly some of the defenders would have been killed, but the appalling imbalance suggests that Ralph got his tactics completely wrong and he would forever be known as Ralph the Timid following the defeat. Worse was to come: the Britons then attacked the city itself, where the garrison were so lax as to have been caught eating their lunch! There was nothing to stop Llywelyn's men, and the Minster, the castle and the town were completely destroyed. Earl Harold Godwinson was given the task of redressing the balance and he quickly arrived to oversee the refortification of the City of Hereford. As part of the reconciliation process, Aelfgar was restored to his earldom so that a peace treaty among the Saxon nobility could be concluded. Harold, however, would not forgive Gruffydd ap Llywelyn and bided his time for revenge. Gruffydd ap Llywelyn now consolidated his position within Wales and succeeded in seizing the areas of Morgannwg and Gwent, along with other territories along the border with England, and he won a further victory over another English army, this time at Glasbury, near Hay-on-Wye, in 1056.

Gruffydd ap Llywelyn was now able to claim sovereignty over the whole of Wales and to be king thereof. It seems that even Edward the Confessor was prepared to recognise Gruffydd and from 1057 until his death in 1063, Gruffudd ap Llywelyn was King of Wales; for the one and only time in its history, Wales was united behind one man. Aelfgar died in 1062 and this gave Harold the opportunity he had been waiting for. Around Christmas 1062, Harold, with the king's approval, marched into Wales and attacked Gruffydd's court at Rhuddlan. Gruffydd escaped with a few of his men in the one ship that got away; all the other ships were destroyed. Harold was now aided by his brother Tostig and they led armies into both North Wales and South Wales before meeting up in the north, somewhere near Snowdon, where Gruffydd was hiding; it is believed Gruffydd was killed by his own men. The *Ulster Chronicles* state that it was Cynan ap Iago who killed Gruffydd, gaining revenge for his father's death some twenty-five years earlier; to show to Harold that the king was dead, Gruffydd's head and the figurehead of his ship were sent to Harold. Cynan had had his revenge and Harold now had his, laying waste to much of the country and its people, and no men were left alive to bear arms again against the 'English'; as Gerald of Wales put it, Harold 'left no-one that pisseth against a wall'. Following Gruffydd's death, Harold now married his widow, Ealdgyth, and the short-lived realm of Wales was once more divided back into her former smaller kingdoms. Bleddyn ap Cynfyn and his brother Rhiwallon came to an agreement whereby in return for peace, Harold would be given the rule of Gwynedd and Powys. Harold's power would not last long: three years in Wales and a few months on the throne of England.

With Harold's defeat at Battle, near Hastings, in 1066, England came under the rule of Normans and their first taste of warfare would be the sacking and burning of Shrewsbury in 1069 as the Welsh and Saxons under Edric the Wild gave the Normans a flavour of what to expect when they rode west and risked crossing the great dyke that had for so long been the dividing line between Welsh and Saxon. The arrival of the Normans would see strange new alliances as old enemies switched allegiances and the foes for so long now found themselves oppressed by Normans from France and Flemings from the Netherlands.

CHAPTER 7

The Norman Invasions
1067–1216

Background

At the Battle of Senlac Hill, remembered today as the Battle of Hastings, Saxon Britain was conquered by William I and his army (blessed by the Pope) of Normans, Bretons and mercenary knights. In a relatively short number of years, rather like the Romans before them, the Normans had conquered most of England, including suppressing a number of rebellions in East Anglia, Northumberland and Shropshire, but again like the Romans, they had not yet started to think about conquering Wales; that would come in good time. The Normans were the first people since the Romans to invade with a 'complete' army, a balanced force that blended heavy and light troops with mounted knights and missile troops, and this is one of the reasons why their invasion of Britain was completed so quickly and was the most successful since the Romans. Once their foothold was established, achieved by beating the armies sent against them, the Normans again copied the Roman strategy by building small settlements right in the heart of the main areas of resistance. The Romans had built forts and ultimately towns; the Normans built small castles called motte and baileys, where a conical mound (motte) was positioned at the side of an open, flat space (bailey), all of which was enclosed by a wooden palisade. The motte would have been topped with a wooden tower, and over the next four centuries, according to need and location, some of these would stay as wooden walls while others would be developed into solid stone castles. The motte and bailey was the residence of the local aristocrat and in time, through the simple economics of supply and demand, many of the mottes developed into the centres of villages and then towns. There are still hundreds of these motte and baileys scattered all across England and Wales, some isolated and abandoned earthworks while others still sit in the heart of a town. Those mottes in towns sometimes still stand and the locations within the town represent their former role; Oswestry, for example, still has a fine motte below which is the Bailey Head, where a twice-weekly market still flourishes and is itself served by Bailey Street. Having thus secured England with a policy of containment through fortresses, the Normans began to explore the mountainous territory to the west, though from the action at Hereford in 1055 and the fact that Welsh troops had already fought as mercenaries under William I against the Scots, the Welsh were not unknown to these 'French' invaders.

It must be noted that when the Normans began their campaigns in 1081, it was only eighteen years since the prime of Welsh manhood had been massacred by the Saxons and therefore the population had not yet recovered and a new generation of fighting men had not matured. Those few fighting men that were available would have been no real threat to the organisational strength and experience of the Normans, and so it proved: by 1094 almost all of Wales was under the control of King William II of England, his father having died in 1087 in Rouen. The whole of this period in which the new French kings of England tried to control their Welsh neighbours would be dominated by a series of alliances and disputes between the Norman nobles and the king they claimed to represent and the princes of the Welsh kingdoms; add to that mix Flemings who settled in Pembroke and armies of Irish (as the Scotti were now termed) and there is no wonder that there was no peace in Wales. Some Normans allied with the Welsh through marriage, while despite their appalling treatment at the hands of some of the Normans, some Welsh still allied with Normans in the hope of ultimately returning to power. The Normans were gratuitously cruel to the Welsh, who were in turn as barbaric to the Normans when they caught them: blinding, castration and mutilation were widespread punishments. As quickly as castles were built, they were attacked, supplies were ambushed and bridges destroyed. Gradually, the Norman yoke spread across the fertile agricultural lands but many of the mountainous areas were left alone: they simply were not worth the risk. At this time, the area in Cheshire, Shropshire and Herefordshire along the Welsh border acquired a new name. 'The Welsh Marches' is a term that has varied with time; in the early medieval period it related to lands that were governed by members of the nobility on behalf of the king, but the lords were given specific legal rights and because of those special powers they were to a certain extent autonomous as long as there were no rebellions. The Marcher Lords, though beholden to the king, were almost independent of the monarchy and at times, as we shall see, some Marcher Lords even took up arms against their king.

1098 Priestholm (Anglesey Sound) – Isle of Anglesey

After 1094 there was something of a Welsh revival but two Marcher Lords, the earls of Chester and Shrewsbury, were tasked with stamping out this Welsh fervour and they mounted an expedition, which marched along the traditional invasion route for North Wales, the Roman road from Chester to Anglesey (Ynys Môn). Given the recent Welsh resurgence, which had been helped by mercenary troops from Ireland, the two earls, Hugh d'Avranches (Earl of Chester) and Hugh de Montgomery (Earl of Shrewsbury), would have set out with a sizeable force, probably not less than 1,000 men. The Welsh, true to form, harassed the column of men but retreated before it, eventually retiring to Anglesey, where they hoped that a mercenary Irish-Viking force would assist them. The pockets of the Marcher Lords ran deep and they paid the Irish-Vikings to row them across to the island so that they could get to the Welsh who were hiding there. Somehow, some of the Welsh leaders escaped by boat to Ireland themselves, leaving the island to be ravaged by the Normans, which they did with glee; one of the lesser atrocities was the kennelling of their dogs in a church at Llandyfrydog. While the Normans were enjoying their orgy of destruction, a new Viking fleet (now the fourth army to arrive) appeared off Priestholm (or Puffin Island, or Ynys Seirol) and attacked and defeated the Irish-Viking force in possession, leaving themselves the new masters of the eastern end of Anglesey. The Viking *Orkneyinga Saga* describes 'a great battle in Anglesey-sound' and this is consistent with the gentle beaches and fields which come down to the sea between modern day Beaumaris and Puffin Island, so that the most likely place for the encounter that followed was the sloping fields between Aber Lleiniog and the shore, which is confirmed in the *Brut*.

The target for the Viking force may well have been the priory at Penmon, which the Normans were now in a position to defend. The accounts of the battle by Gerald in his history and by Caradoc in the *Brut* differ but piecing

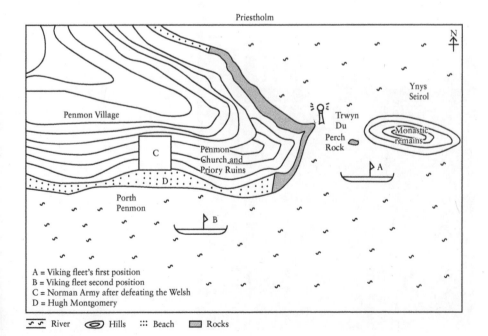

Priestholm

N

Penmon Village

Ynys
Seirol

Trwyn
Du

Perch
Rock

Monastic
remains

C

Penmon
Church and
Priory Ruins

A

D

Porth
Penmon

B

A = Viking fleet's first position
B = Viking fleet second position
C = Norman Army after defeating the Welsh
D = Hugh Montgomery

〜〜 River   Hills   ⋮⋮ Beach   ▨ Rocks

Anglesey Sound, looking south-west down the Menai Straits.

Puffin Island (Priestholm or Ynys Seiriol), where the Vikings waited to see who triumphed.

Remains of Penmon Priory, one of the oldest religious sites in Wales.

The beach between Penmon and Lleiniog where Hugh of Montgomery challenged Magnus Barefoot and was shot with an arrow.

them both together, it seems that the battle started with the Vikings at sea shooting arrows at the Normans, who stood on ground just off the beach. Hugh de Montgomery, not content with what presumably he saw as cowardice among the enemy, rode down the beach and into the sea, challenging the Vikings to come and fight. The Vikings were perhaps outnumbered as they decided to remain on their ships but the general, Magnus Barefoot, and another marksman both targeted their bows at Hugh de Montgomery, who had the nickname of Hugh the Proud, as he stood defiant in the surf. Despite his helmet and his long coat of chainmail, which is reported to have come to his knees, the arrows found their mark and after one had hit him on the nose-guard, a second one penetrated his eye socket and 'flew afterwards through the head'. Whether the Vikings then came ashore and fought with the Normans is not clear, but all the reports say that it was not until low tide that the body could be recovered.

Magnus sailed back to Scotland, while Hugh d'Avranches decided that the Welsh and the Vikings could keep Anglesey for themselves to fight over and the Norman force withdrew back to the Mid Wales borders. As far as it is possible to tell, this skirmish involving Magnus Barefoot was the last time that a Viking fleet or raid was involved in military action as a solo force; some Irish-Norse were still employed as mercenaries at times. The coastal fringe at the eastern end of Anglesey is still very rural and one can imagine the fleet of Viking ships hoving to and shooting at the Norman troops massed upon the shore. Penmon Priory and the associated sites, including St Seiriol's Well, after whom Priestholm (or Ynys Seiriol) is named, are well worth visiting as the well dates back to the earliest Christian times on the island in the sixth century. Penmon Church contains some original stone crosses, while just a short distance further on the views across to Priestholm are quite surreal as the distances become deceptive. After the Normans' embarrassment at Priestholm, Hugh d'Avranches, Earl of Chester, was as good as his word and kept away from Anglesey while the Welsh, who had been set back by the Norman defeat, regrouped. In the southern half of Wales it was the same: a standoff as the Normans consolidated their position and built more castles while the Welsh controlled the more remote countryside but were not strong enough to break the grip that the motte and bailey castles gave the Normans over the surrounding areas; the Welsh were as yet not strong enough by themselves to attack these wooden and earth fortresses with any chance of success.

1116 Aberystwyth – Ceredigion

On the coast of west Wales, the situation between the Normans and the Welsh was no different to any other parts of the kingdom: castles were built as bastions of the Norman way of life, and to support them, Saxon and French immigrants were brought in to farm the land and tend the livestock so that the area would prosper. In 1113 Gruffydd ap Rhys, Prince of Deheubarth, visited Gruffudd ap Cynan, the Prince of Gwynedd, at his family seat at Aberffraw on Ynys Môn. For all the civil wars between the Welsh princes, there was still honour and Gruffudd ap Cynan still owed an honour debt to the House of Dinefwr as Gruffydd's ay Rhys's father, Rhys ap Tewdwr, had aided Gruffudd ap Cynan in his own bid to reclaim the lands of Gwynedd in 1081. While at Aberffraw, Gruffydd ap Rhys met Gwenllian, the beautiful youngest daughter of Gruffudd ap Cynan. The lady Gwenllian was by all accounts strikingly pretty and there was an instant attraction between the two young people. After a brief courtship, the couple eloped and from then on Gwenllian joined Gruffydd ap Rhys on all of his military campaigns, learning the ways of a warrior.

At times of unrest, these castle communities were isolated while the countryside, which was dominated by the Welsh, would rise up in rebellion. In 1115 Gruffydd ap Rhys became the leader of a large force of men termed 'lunatics' according to the *Brut*. In early 1116 this vagabond force began attacking the immigrant Saxons and laid waste to Swansea, Llandovery and Carmarthen before heading north through the mountains. They then reached and stormed the small castle of Penweddig, just north of Aberystwyth, which belonged to a castellan named Razon; the garrison of Penweddig was slaughtered, with news reaching Razon at his own motte and bailey castle at Tanycastell, by Rhydyfelin, just 2 miles south of the modern centre of Aberystwyth. In shock at the ease with which Penweddig had been destroyed, Razon was not going to risk his own fortress being so easily overrun and he sent for reinforcements from Ystrad Meurig castle, some 10 miles towards Tregaron. On hearing what had happened so close to them, the garrison at Ystrad Meurig under Gilbert (Razon's overlord) sent back some reinforcements marching north-west overnight to assist their comrades. Meanwhile, the Welsh army of

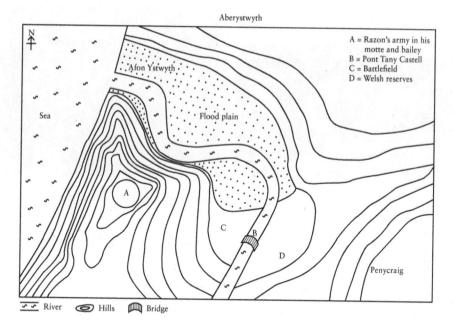

Aberystwyth

A = Razon's army in his
motte and bailey
B = Pont Tany Castell
C = Battlefield
D = Welsh reserves

Gruffudd camped alongside the River Rheidol at Glascrug, Gruffudd letting his men rest and feast on the cattle and provisions that they had plundered from all of the places they could, including from the Church of St Padarn at Llanbadarn.

The next day the Welsh army abandoned their camp and the *Brut* gives a detailed account of the sorry sight as they straggled across the valley and advanced on Razon's castle; they looked nothing more than a rabble 'without ensigns ... without counsel ... without a commander'. The whole force hesitated on the east side of the River Ystwyth, seeing the high walls of the fortress (presumably wooden walls at this time); they hesitated to advance further and apparently stood around looking for a means of breaching the walls that lay across the bridge and above the fields beyond. Razon, the Norman-French commander, sent some archers down to try and lure the Welshmen across the bridge and into those fields below the motte. These loosely dispersed archers shot their arrows across the River Ystwyth and galvanised the Welsh into action. It seems that the Welsh army did not have many bowmen, because if they had, they would have simply entered into a fire-fight with the Normans and outshot them. Instead, the Welsh spearmen took the bait and charged across the bridge, while the archers, on seeing the Welsh coming, simply ran back to the shelter of the castle.

Razon's guile had worked and down from the castle rode a group of his heavily armoured Norman knights, who charged into the advancing Welshmen. As we saw when we discussed the battle of Hereford, Norman knights charging into 15-foot-long spears does not always favour the horsemen

Above left: Aberystwyth's Norman motte and bailey castle, 2 miles south of the modern town.

Above right: Pont Tanycastell; the Welsh crossed a wooden bridge here to attack the Norman castle.

and the Normans did not have things all their own way. At least one of the knights was unhorsed and only saved from death by his chainmail, which gave sufficient time for his colleagues to rescue him and literally drag him back to the Norman ranks. Seeing the Normans retreating, some of the Welsh followed up their success; others, more wary, hung back by the bridge. Razon knew that the battle was on a knife edge but seeing the Welsh force now split in two, he sent out the rest of his knights and also his foot soldiers and told them to keep close order. The Normans charged again and this time the dispersed Welsh spearmen could not defend themselves against the onslaught and they fell back towards their colleagues. The whole Welsh force dispersed, fleeing in all directions as the Normans pursued the stragglers as they fled for their lives; it was a crushing Norman victory. Gruffudd ap Rhys fled into hiding and, like many Welsh princes, he learned to bide his time for the chance of revenge; Henry I put a bounty on Gruffudd's head but he was not betrayed. Gruffudd must have replayed the short rebellion in his mind over and over again as he tried to stay one step ahead of the Normans, intent on stamping their authority across the country. He would have been pleased with how much they achieved but also aggrieved by how apathy and indiscipline had cost him the battle at Aberystwyth; importantly, Gruffudd would have learned from the defeat, ready for the next time. The land, although almost all in agricultural use, is in private hands and the castle ruins atop the hill are not accessible; however, the shape of the motte and bailey and the prominence of the hill are both still clearly visible and it is a well-chosen defensive position for a castle, with the River Ystwyth running around the two sides of a naturally steep hill. The river and the fields around it in which the battle would have taken place are all visible, in spite of a few buildings and roads which have been developed.

Above left: Aberystwyth: the site of the Norman charge into the disordered Welsh spearmen in 1116.

Above right: The fields opposite the Pont Tanycastell where the Welsh spearmen waited before charging over the bridge.

By the early 1110s both the Welsh and the Normans were more interested in peace than conflict and King Henry I had more pressing issues in France to concern him than who ruled Wales; needing men for his campaigns on the Continent, he allowed Gruffudd ap Rhys to rule an area of Wales, the Cantref Mawr. This small area of south central Wales was important in medieval times as the location of the main seat for the princes of Deheubarth at Dinefwr. With this accord in place, a relatively stable situation developed though there was still the odd outbreak of violence in south-east Wales. Despite the agreement with Henry I, further Norman pressure was put upon Gruffudd and his lands, and after he and Gwenllian had both led counter strikes against the Normans from their forest strongholds, they fled in desperation to Ireland in 1127, from which Gwenllian's family had originated; and they took their family with them for safety.

When Henry I failed before his death to fully resolve the matter as to who would be his successor, he lit a fuse that exploded with such effect in 1135 that it would have repercussions for the next twenty years across England and France, but the war for the English crown would be fought in Britain. So bad would things become that the nineteen-year period of King Stephens's reign would be known as the time of 'anarchy', and it was said that the country was ruined and all undone and darkened with such terrible deeds that men said openly that 'Christ and his angels slept'. The problem for the Norman barons was that they did not want to be ruled by a woman and Henry had failed to get sworn oaths from his knights that they would uphold his decision. Henry had had three legitimate children; the eldest was a girl named Matilda who lived to be sixty-five, but her two brothers both died before their father. The eldest boy, William, died tragically at sea when aged just seventeen in 1120 and the other died shortly after birth. Henry I also had twenty-four illegitimate children, including nine more sons, but his second wife failed to produce any heirs. On Henry's death, Matilda, the appointed heir, was in Anjou; and so while the English barons decided whether to oppose Matilda and support Stephen but in so doing go against Henry's wishes, the Welsh saw an opportunity to break out in a fresh rebellion.

1136 Maes Gwenllian – Carmarthenshire

It is not certain when Gruffudd ap Rhys and Gwenllian returned to Wales but they were certainly active immediately after the news of Henry I's death had filtered through to Wales. Across southern Wales, the Welsh rose as one, and before the Normans were fully aware of the situation around 500 Fleming and Saxon settlers were slain between Swansea and Loughor. Gruffudd ap Rhys went with their eldest and youngest sons to see Gruffudd ap Cynan with a plan to raise the whole of Wales in rebellion; Gwenllian stayed in Deheubarth with her two middle sons, who were eighteen and sixteen, while her husband was in Gwynedd seeking the great alliance. While Gruffudd was away, Maurice of London and other Norman lords led a series of raids against Deheubarth, and such was the ferocity of these attacks that Gwenllian felt that the time for avoiding battle was past; she hesitated as to whether to wait for her husband or to go on the offensive alone. Her captains were loyal to the family and amid widespread rumours that the Normans were about to begin another offensive (possibly falsely planted to draw the Welsh forces out from their forest and mountain stronghold) Gwenllian led her army out to make war on the Normans and relieve the pressure on her own lands. With her forces gathered, Gwenllian donned her own armour and marched south. By rural, less conspicuous routes they made for the Norman motte and bailey alongside the River Gwendreath Fach.

Kidwelly Castle, protected by the Gwendreath Fach.

Maes Gwenllian seen from Kidwelly Castle; the Welsh formed up on the ridge in the distance.

There is little doubt where the battle was fought as the field of Maes Gwenllian has been named since time out of mind, but the way in which the armies were deployed is not documented. Maurice of London was determined to wipe out Gwenllian; it is most likely that he had gathered a strong force together for that purpose. Peter Newton, in his book *Gwenllian*, maintains that the Welsh were ambushed from the hills to the east, Mynyddygarreg, which dominate the site. Yet this seems unlikely; firstly, knowing the Welsh and their guerrilla tactics, it would seem unlikely that Gwenllian would have ignored the heights and in fact it is far more likely that they took those heights to view the surrounding countryside and the layout of any Norman camps outside of Kidwelly castle, to the south-west of Mynyddygarreg. Secondly, such steep hills would be no advantage for mounted Norman knights to charge down; in fact, it would be near suicidal. It is far more likely that the Welsh, on approaching Kidwelly, saw the Norman camps, gauged that they were outnumbered and knowing that battle was inevitable, took up a strong defensive position just to the north and the east of the field of Maes Gwenllian, at the base of the ridge below Glanhiraeth. There are no details as to the numbers involved but given where the battle was fought and the appalling outcome for the Welsh, with hundreds of men slain, it would appear that victory was due to the overwhelming numbers of Normans, who had planned for such a day, and being better equipped, routed the Welsh.

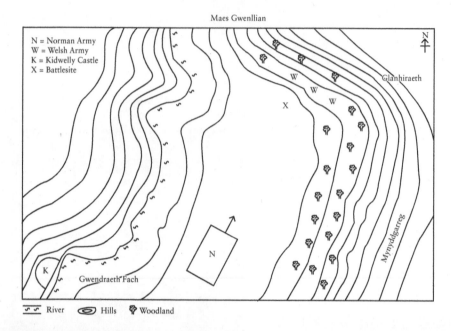

Mynydd y Garreg, the ridge behind Maes Gwenllian where the Welsh waited for the Norman army.

Maes Gwenllian Battlefield, where the beautiful Princess of Wales died.

Some say that Gwenllian died in the battle with her son Morgan; others say that she was summarily beheaded at Kidwelly castle along with her other son, Maelgwyn. What is certain is that the name of Gwenllian would inspire the Welsh to greater determination to avenge her death. If she was beheaded, then whether or not she said the words 'Remember ME' just before she was executed does not matter; the important thing is that people have, and at Kidwelly Castle a memorial stands to a valiant true shield-maiden and Welsh warrior princess. The fields north-east of Kidwelly in which the Welsh army was destroyed are still gently rolling pastures and although the lanes are narrow, there are places to pull in and view the site. At the extensive ruins of Kidwelly Castle, there is a monument to Gwenllian, the site being in the care of Cadw, and the magnificence of the castle is still evident in the height and magnificence of the towers and battlements preserved for visitors to experience. Cadw is the Welsh government's historic environment service, which works like English Heritage to protect and make accessible historical and important environmental sites in Wales; it is named Cadw from the Welsh word meaning 'to keep' or 'to protect'.

1136 Crug Mawr (Crugmore/Cardigan) October – Ceredigion

The shock at the news of Gwenllian's death slowly echoed around Wales, with people apparently flocking to see the field where the bodies were left to rot as carrion for the crows where people wept presumably not only for the souls of the departed but also for their own fate to come. The first portion of revenge for Maes Gwenllian was extracted when Richard FitzGilbert was ambushed and murdered at Coed Grwyne, when he was on route from Abergavenny to Brecon. Owain and Cadwaladr, both sons of Gruffudd of Cynan of Gwynedd, gathered a large host and invaded Ceredigion, capturing five Norman castles including Aberystwyth, which had resisted capture just twenty years earlier. There is some confusion as to whether the men of Gwynedd returned home to distribute their ill-gotten gains of wealth and arms among their men before returning again to Aberystwyth to meet up with Gruffudd ap Rhys and his forces or whether they stayed and distributed them where they were. A sudden retreat and a planned return later was never the best way of keeping an army motivated, as often the men would leave once they got close to home with sufficient payment and they would then wait until the next uprising, when their original payment had run out, before rejoining a campaign. It is far more likely that they stayed on the field and stayed strong by being together, which would explain the size of the army that they were able to build. According the *Brut*, when Gruffudd Ap Rhys arrived the total strength of the army was '6,000 fine infantry and 2,100 cavalry in armour'. As *Cassell's Battlefields* states, such a force with so many men in armour would be most unlikely, given that 'the whole knight service of

England at the time was only 5,000 men'. A more accurate appraisal of these numbers would be that when the three men and their forces were united they had a large force, the population now having well recovered from the ravages of Harold's atrocities some three generations earlier. In addition, the land had been repopulated by Saxons ousted from their own homes in England and some of these may well have joined the rebellious Welsh ranks rather than be slaves under the Norman yoke. In addition, the Welsh armies did at times use horses to move quickly through the hills, though they did not necessarily ride them into battle. Having just captured a whole series of castles, the three Welsh generals would have had a considerable supply of arms and equipment to share among the men, and it is not unreasonable to suppose that those with armour were given horses to bear them while the lighter armed men marched alongside them. Fresh from their victory at Aberystwyth, the Welsh army of around 8,000 men marched south towards Cardigan, where Robert FitzStephen and

Crug Mawr, the conical hill, viewed from the east.

Crug Mawr viewed from the south, with the likely battlefield site in the foreground.

Crug Mawr

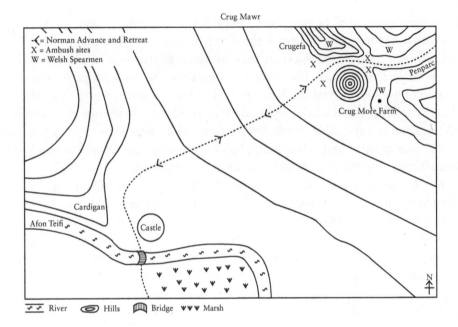

= Norman Advance and Retreat
X = Ambush sites
W = Welsh Spearmen

Crugefa
Crug More Farm
Penparc
Cardigan
Afon Teifi
Castle

N

〰️ River ◎ Hills 🏛 Bridge ▾▾▾ Marsh

also Maurice FitzGerald, Lord of Lanstephan, were preparing their own army, having gathered forces from across the whole of South Wales.

The Normans numbered around 3,000, a fair number of whom, probably 50 per cent, would have been armoured; many of them, say at least 500, would have been mounted. Like all Norman forces of the time, it would have been a balanced army with crossbowmen and spearmen on foot, knights on horseback and supported by lighter troops with spears, javelins, bows and slings. It seems for once that the Norman scouts failed to report that the Welsh army was so close; perhaps this indicates just how widespread the Welsh uprising was, and that there were no Norman patrols within the Ceredigion area. When ready, the Norman host marched north out of Cardigan to go and see what damage the Welsh host had caused to their north, no doubt thinking that they would deal with Gwenllian's husband the way that they had dealt with her. The Welsh army, being mainly from North Wales, would have been predominantly spearmen supported by javelinmen, bowmen and perhaps some Irish mercenaries given that Gruffudd ap Rhys had recently returned from there. The site of the battle was 'Crug Mawr, the big hill, on our left, soon after riding out of Cardigan' (Gerald), and today the road still passes between two large hills; the one on the right as the Normans approached would have been Banc-y-Warren, to the rear of which lies Crugmore farm. As you are looking at these hills today from the south-west (i.e. from Cardigan and the Norman viewpoint), they look a little forbidding, but they are not unduly high and there are no visible forts or earthworks. Such is the shape of the hills that a Welsh force could easily have been concealed behind them, with perhaps a token force to draw the expectant Normans in. Whether there was a fort on the left or west side of the hills is a matter of conjecture now as much of that end of the line of hills has been quarried away. The author did visit the site back in 2007 and there was certainly one curved ditch around what looked like a motte, but whether these were as a result of quarrying or they were actual remains of a one-time fortification is impossible to tell. Suffice to say that with an army of 8,000 men under your control and a better equipped army of 3,000 coming towards you, Crug Mawr was the perfect place to ambush your enemy.

The *Gesta Stephani* (an anonymous twelfth-century record of the reign of King Stephen) states that the 'Welsh divided themselves into three terrible bands, well ordered and soldierly'. If an army of Welsh spearmen was to be effective against experienced Norman soldiers then they had to be well drilled and well formed, so this contemporary account would seem accurate (though it may also have been a form of propaganda to account for the subsequent developments in the battle) as the Normans were worsted. The Welsh, who had clearly learned from their earlier encounters with these bitter foes, would have planted a small portion of their army, say 2,000 spearmen, to block the road north. Their missile troops would have waited, hidden on the reverse slope of the hills, and the other two banks of spearmen would have hidden behind the hills on either side of the road. None of these hidden Welsh forces needed to appear until the first of the Normans were engaged with the spearmen to their front, after which the Welsh trap could be sprung; the Normans engaged to their front could not escape save by fighting. What happened next is agreed by all the chronicles on the battle. After some ferocious fighting, the Norman forces were eventually overpowered, put to flight and pursued as far as the River Teifi in the valley below, from where they had come. As always happens when an army is in flight, panic took over and as the fleeing Normans tried to cross the bridge it apparently broke under the weight, plunging all upon it into the eddying river below. Other Normans would have tried to swim or wade across; the combined result was carnage as hundreds drowned in the river, so many that the river was clogged with the bodies of both men and horses. The town was no refuge as the Welsh attacked and burnt it to the ground; only the solid stone walls of the castle, which were defended by Robert FitzMartin, were able to hold out.

The battlesite is still for the most part easy to see, being open fields, though they are all in private hands. The hills still dominate the landscape, especially as they are bisected by the modern A487. This major victory at the end of a successful Welsh campaign put the area of Ceredigion, which had once been a part of Deheubarth, under Gwynedd control. The Welsh princes would now fall out with themselves once more as each side wanted its share of the glory and to be outright ruler. That was a pity for a united Wales, as were the deaths in 1137 of both Gruffydd ap Rhys and Gruffydd ap Cynan. Had the Welsh princes stayed together,

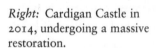

Right: Cardigan Castle in 2014, undergoing a massive restoration.

Below: Cardigan's bridge over the Afon Teifu; the bridge collapsed in 1136, drowning many.

with the chaos across the border in England as Stephen and Matilda now fought out a brutal, atrocity laden war with each other for the English crown, the Welsh may have been able to assert themselves and produce a Norman-free, united Wales once and for all. Stephen was a weak king and had such troubles of his own that Wales was mostly left to its own devices; so the local Normans continued their probing campaigns as before and restored Norman rule to most of those places ravaged in the south the previous year. For most of Stephen's reign, the Welsh in North and Mid Wales succeeded in taking the struggle to the Normans, with Owain ap Gruffudd picking up the mantle of his father. Gruffudd ap Cynan's long reign had, with the aid of others, made the principality of Gwynedd the most influential state in Wales. His base was on Anglesey and, with the threat of Viking raids now gone, the island was a strong defensive position, as far removed from the Normans as anyone could get. When, in 1120, Gruffydd ap Cynan had become too old to lead Gwynedd's forces, Owain and his brothers Cadwallon and Cadwaladr had donned armour in his place. Cadwallon, as the eldest, was heir but he had been killed in battle against the men of Powys in 1132, leaving Owain to inherit Gwynedd in 1137. Initially, Owain shared the lands with his brother, but, as is so often the case, the two surviving brothers could not always agree and disharmony dogged their leadership. In 1143 Owain stripped Cadwaladr of his lands for his part in the murder of Anarawd ap Gruffydd of Deheubarth. From 1143 Owain basically ruled alone and took advantage of the civil war in England between King Stephen and the Empress Matilda. Owain succeeded in expanding Gwynedd's boundaries further east and south than ever before as he captured the stronghold of Mold in 1146 and later went on to capture Rhuddlan before sending scouting parties into Powys. Cadwaladr was finally driven into exile in 1155, when, ironically, he fled to the new king, Henry II, and having found favour with him was given lands in Shropshire.

1157 Ewloe (Coleshill) – Flintshire

Henry II came to the throne in 1154 on the strength of an agreement between his predecessor Stephen and his mother Matilda; as the Norman line had now been ruling England for almost 100 years this is a suitable time to call the Anglo-Norman monarch's armies 'English'. While Wales had been busy in rebellion, Scotland had also taken advantage of the chaos in England to steal large tracts of northern England, but Henry II quickly reached an agreement with Malcolm, the King of Scotland, and all of the lands were returned. After this, Henry II immediately began strengthening all of his castles and the defences of any existing castles within the newly returned lands. Content that his policies were coming to fruition in the rest of his lands, Henry II then turned his attention to Wales, seeking to redress the balance of power and recapture key strongholds. Aided by the Prince of Powys, Madog ap Maredudd, Henry II made his base at Chester, ready for an invasion along the normal route into North Wales along the coast plain, with additional troops supplied by the most northern Marcher Lord, Earl Ranulf of Chester. Owain, aware of Henry II's movements, had amassed an immense host (*Brut*) and the Welsh lay in ambush along the line of hills that run parallel to the Dee Estuary, between Hawarden and Coleshill via Ewloe. As there is a succession of excellent places along the route from which Owain could have chosen his point of attack, the matter is at first glance confusing. Henry II clearly knew of Owain's presence as he had received reports informing him that Owain was reinforcing the earthworks and ditches associated with Wat's Dyke (the northern end of Offa's Dyke) so as to strengthen the border of Gwynedd. Clearly this was something that Henry II was not prepared to tolerate; it was one thing to have the Welsh invade and plunder, but to start constructing and reinforcing an older border was simply not acceptable. Sources seem to agree that Henry II split his force into two columns, one taking the direct route towards Owain and thereby risking the chance of an ambush while the other force, led by Henry II himself and some of his barons, went west of Owain's T-shaped upland deployment (posted on the heights) with the idea of attacking Owain from the west so that Henry II could ambush Owain's waiting ambushers.

When one examines the topography, this must have meant that the two columns separated not long after leaving Chester; to undertake a division into two columns when they could be seen from the hills they were approaching would have been naïve. With their plans laid, the two columns advanced on either side of the Warren Mountain (a low hill) and the Penarlag (Hawarden) hill, all of which would have been wooded; once split, the armies would have quickly lost sight of each other. The size of the armies is again a matter for conjecture: Henry II, planning a long campaign, would not have risked marching so far and to a potential siege at Rhuddlan without a considerable force. Owain, so far from home on Anglesey, must also have had a fair sized force to be able to split it into two and cause Henry II's column so many casualties. It is not unreasonable to suppose that Henry II had around 5,000 men split into two equal columns, while Owain must have had at least 4,000 to prepare for action the way he had done. While Henry II's army would be the balanced mixture of spearmen, bowmen, armoured foot and armoured knights in both columns, Owain was likely to have kept all of his spearmen for the open ground near the coast and sent his javelinmen and bowmen to perform the ambush.

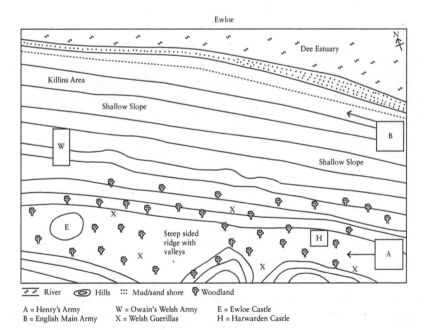

A = Henry's Army   W = Owain's Welsh Army   E = Ewloe Castle
B = English Main Army   X = Welsh Guerillas   H = Harwarden Castle

Above left: Dense foliage in deep-sided valleys at Hawarden, perfect for Welsh ambushes.

Above right: Birds wheeling around the ruins of Hawarden Castle.

In spite of his precautions, Henry II's own column was surprised by the Welsh, 'lurking in pathless mountain defiles and swamps, as their custom is', and a bitter battle ensued. This was most likely to have been the land below the remains of Hawarden Castle, around which the ground is still naturally undulating, with small rivers, rolling hills and streams in narrow cuttings. If a running battle was fought along this undulating ridge, this would explain what happened next, as somehow Henry II managed to fight his way through the rough terrain and emerge behind Owain's lines, and that was despite suffering heavy losses, including the death of some barons and desertions from respected knights. This sudden appearance of Henry on Owain's right rear, coupled with the approach of the coastal column to his left front, and spying Henry II's fleet also approaching along the estuary, convinced Owain that it was time to depart: 'He left the place and retreated' (*Brut*).Using the author's methods of working back from the end of the battle, it would seem that the final actions occurred between Ewloe Castle and the modern settlement of Shotton to the north of it. This gentle, north sloping ridge would be the perfect place for Owain to watch the coastal road below, for until the seventeenth century the Dee Estuary at high tide reached as far as the northern edge of the roadway, meaning any advancing force could be trapped there, by the sea at high tide and by quicksands at low tide. Owain had felt assured that his advance force hidden at the base of the 'T' at Hawarden would be able to take care of itself in the difficult terrain and the dense woodland that grew there and to a certain extent it did, killing many and almost killing Henry II himself; even though Henry II emerged from the fight, his army had been badly mauled. The old Stamford Way is in parts a ridgeway and connects with both Hawarden and Ewloe castles, and this may have been the way Henry's column initially climbed the ridge and so into the Welsh advance guard. Interestingly, just below where

Owain's left flank would have stood is an old lane called Killins Lane; it may only be a coincidence, but as the fleeing Welsh and the advancing English would have fought down the slope towards the Dee Estuary, the pathway would have crossed the southernmost edge of a battlesite. The author has tried, as yet unsuccessfully, to find the derivation of this name and for how long the lane and the area around Killins Farm have been so named. Much of the site for this running battle is still accessible and the area around Hawarden Castle and Ewloe Castle are particularly interesting, with many earthworks and the dense woodland providing a feeling that time has stood still in some of these sodden valleys and the steep hillsides that surround them. There is convenient parking at both sites, which allows the visitor time to walk both ends of this running battle and appreciate how tired Henry II's men must have been, marching and fighting for several miles along the high ground with so many dips and climbs to traverse. Coleshill seems too far removed to be the actual site, given all of the available evidence.

With the Welsh retreating apace, Henry II consolidated his battered forces but pushed on along the coast to besiege Rhuddlan, where Henry II's fleet had been told to rendezvous. However, the fleet, understanding that the Welsh were slowly retreating ahead of Henry II's army, anticipated that the Gwynedd stronghold of Anglesey would be scantily guarded with so many men away on campaign and they decided to attack. Led by Henry FitzRoy, the English attacked but their landing was repulsed and FitzRoy himself was killed. Despite Owain's success in the Ewloe woods and the safe retraction of his men, Henry succeeded in resecuring Rhuddlan and the two men agreed a peace in which Owain surrendered the lands of Rhuddlan and Tegeingl back to the Earl of

Above left: The ridge between Hawarden and Ewloe Castle, across which Henry II fought before encountering Owain Fawr.

Above right: Sloping ridge from Ewloe Castle to Killins Lane at Coleshill (Flint), where Owain's men were deployed.

Chester and agreed to render 'homage and fealty' to Henry. Once more there was an uneasy peace along the Welsh border as the balance of power slowly fluctuated on the Scales of Fate.

1165 Crogen August – Powys

The balance of power shifted in Wales in 1160 when Madog ap Maredudd, the Prince of Powys, who had so opposed Owain died, and swiftly Owain moved to take advantage and retook some territory in the east of Wales from Powys. In 1163 he formed an alliance with Rhys ap Gruffydd, who was now the Prince of Deheubarth, so that together they could challenge English rule. Once the news reached Henry II that he faced the age-old problem of a Welsh revolt, he made plans for a major invasion and gathered a large force at Oswestry in early 1165. With everything ready, King Henry II once more set out to invade Gwynedd but instead of the usual coastal route from Chester, he decided to try a different route along the River Ceiriog Valley, over the Berwyn Mountains and then down into Corwen before heading north into central Gwynedd. This route – which leads to Llanarmon Dyffryn Ceiriog, where St Garmon's Church sits (see the Alleluia Victory) – is a most scenic one and the views are stunning as the paths climb towards the mountains some 2,500 feet (800 metres) high. While this is a beautiful journey for a modern-day tourist, it was hardly a safe route for an army on campaign, starting off in a narrow valley with dense woodland and then rising up to a mountain plateau with little shelter from bad weather. This was a route that could be used by lightly armed Welshmen using the tracks and pathways that they had known and used for generations, but narrow paths, sometimes at precipitous heights, were not for heavily clad knights. Realising how narrow the valley was and how difficult and dangerous advancing through such terrain would be, Henry took 2,000 axemen with him who had orders to widen the path ahead of the force so as to make the journey easier. To allow the axemen to work uninterrupted, they in turn were protected by an advance guard of pikemen, a shrewd move by the king given that the North Welsh attacked with long spears as their weapon of choice. Given these large numbers of additional troops, Henry II's total force must have been close to 5,000 or even 6,000 men. The main part of the army would, as for Coleshill, have been balanced and armed for dealing with an undisciplined Welsh rabble, if they had been fighting on rolling English pasture land that is. Owain's force would not have needed to have been large for the campaign that he intended to fight, probably no more than 2,000 men, and those would have largely consisted of light troops, archers and javelinmen, who could move more swiftly than the English. The Welsh force would have been broken up into small groups which would have been strategically placed along the route at the places where the English force would be most vulnerable. After an attack,

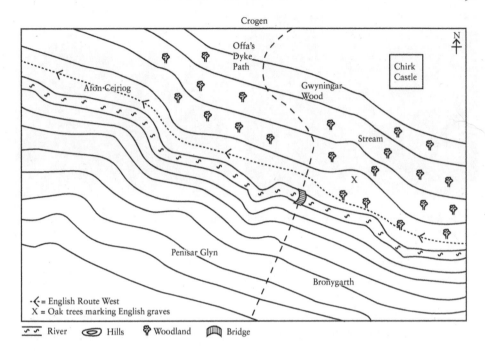

Crogen

Offa's Dyke Path

Chirk Castle

Afon-Ceiriog

Gwyningar Wood

Stream

X

Penisar Glyn

Bronygarth

⤺= English Route West
X = Oak trees marking English graves

〰 River   ◎ Hills   🌳 Woodland   🌉 Bridge

a runner from the first force could move up the valley and report to the next force as to what had transpired and how far the English were away. Therefore the Welsh force could keep attacking and disappearing back into the woods, and so harry the heavily laden English army for the whole length of the valley, their progress slow due to the widening and clearing of the route by the axemen.

The narrowness of the Ceiriog Valley, hemmed in by steep-sided hills and dense with deciduous forest and a wide but shallow river meandering through the bottom, meant that there was little room for the English army to deploy and bring sufficient men into action every time the Welsh attacked. The first and most important attack was less than a day's ride from Oswestry and took place near the hamlet of Crogen. One can imagine that if the going was slow, with the axemen having to clear the way, it could have already been getting dark by the time the first 8 miles had been travelled and the English army came to the place where Offa's Dyke crosses the River Ceiriog, a notable landmark for a Welsh force to rendezvous and, being one of the narrowest parts of the valley, the perfect place for an ambush.

The Welsh chose their targets carefully and one can envisage them sitting hidden in the dense undergrowth, watching the axemen and the pikemen pass and waiting for the king's entourage to arrive. With a hail of arrows, javelins and stones, the horsemen below would have been sitting ducks for the Welshmen above them. Henry himself would have been wounded, if not killed outright, save for the fact that a knight, Hugh de St Clare, who was the

Above left: Crogen's narrow valley floor between the River Ceiriog and the steep mountain sides.

Above right: One of the mighty oaks that marks the graves of the English dead.

Constable of Colchester Castle, sacrificed his own life by throwing himself in front of a shaft that had been meant for King Henry II; this was presumably a spear or javelin shaft as St Clare would not have been able to move quickly enough to block an arrow's flight. In the panic that begins after such an attack, men and horses would naturally move away from the point of attack, but this would have driven the knights toward the fast flowing River Ceiriog and the danger of drowning in heavy armour, even in quite shallow water. Crogen is the perfect place for an ambush: the valley floor is only 100 yards or so across and the river takes up another 10 metres and the sides of the valley are steep and wooded, offering protection to the ambushers if the victims of the ambush are able to return fire. The casualties on the Welsh side were very few, while the English lost a number of knights, who were buried on the battle site, very close to the Offa's Dyke Path, in an area still known as the 'Gap of the Graves'. This was the first and most telling of the Welsh attacks and the only one reported by name, but the Welsh continued to harry the English army all the way to the mountains. Once Henry II's army had climbed up onto the Berwyn Plateau, the Welsh had disappeared like the morning mist that rises from the mountains. Having suffered some days of running ambushes, the English then had to endure an extended period of wet weather that slowed their march across the sodden and marshy ground. The king had made a grave tactical error and had been defeated by a combination of the atrocious wet summer and the superior tactics of Owain and his alliance of Welsh princes, all of whom provided troops for the united Welsh force. Henry retreated and did not try and invade Gwynedd again, while Owain was free to continue his campaigns, which included recapturing Rhuddlan castle in 1167, after a siege of three months. The bridge at Crogen bears a plaque which has recently been placed there to commemorate the battle and there is a series of information boards which tell the history of the time; the burial ground is marked by some enormous oaks trees including 'The Great Oak of the Gate of the Dead'. The site is not far from Chirk Castle and is also on the Offa's Dyke Path, so it is not difficult to visit on foot as part of another walk. There is very little room to park a vehicle here, the only convenient place being in front of the cottages by the bridge. Henry II was both embarrassed and enraged at the failure of his successive campaigns into Wales, and in retaliation he ordered that all Welsh hostages held in the area were taken to him at Shrewsbury; there, he personally oversaw the mutilation of twenty-two prisoners, two of whom are reported to have been Owain's sons. Having extracted some revenge for his humiliation, the king apparently returned to his French court in Anjou; if he could not beat the Welsh, then he could at least beat their harsh climate by escaping abroad.

After the death of Owain in 1170, Rhys ap Gruffudd, the ruler of Deheubarth, proclaimed himself Prince of Wales and became the dominant force in the country until his death in 1197. Rhys wanted neither war with England nor war within Wales and worked hard to secure a period of peace, and in 1171 he made peace with King Henry, for which he was granted the right to keep possession of all of his recent conquests. He was also named as the king's chief minister for Wales, with the title of Justiciar. Rhys succeeding in maintaining these peaceful relations with King Henry until the king died in 1189, despite his sons Maelgwn and Gruffydd feuding with each other, which would continue after Rhys's own death as they fought over the succession to be Prince of Wales. Rhys seems to have seen the death of Henry II as relieving him of his obligations to the monarchy and when Richard I refused to see Rhys at Oxford (to where he had been persuaded to travel by Prince John) in order to make peace, the Welsh prince returned to Wales and attacked more Norman settlements, campaigning

Above left: Crogen bridge over the River Ceiriog; some of the English undoubtedly got pushed back into the river and drowned.

Above right: Memorial plaque to Crogen, 1165, on Crogen bridge.

almost until the time of his death in 1197, when he was sixty-five years of age. He died as a result of a great pestilence that gripped the land, killing many people. The disease is not recorded as one of the outbreaks of the bubonic plague, but clearly some virulent virus was at work because the 'tempest killed innumerable people and many of the nobility and many princes, and spared none' (*Brut*); Rhys was buried at St David's Cathedral.

England under Richard I was dominated by the rule of Prince John, as for most of his reign Richard was either on route to and from Cyprus and the Holy Land or at war. Richard spent such little time in England that Prince John ruled for him until Richard was killed by an arrow while on campaign in France, at the Siege of Chaluz in 1197, and the crown went to John. John was the fourth and youngest of the brothers and he gained a crown it seems he was destined to inherit. John had ongoing debts to contend with that had been accumulated in the costs of Richard I's wars and his castle building in France; there was also the ransom which John had to pay in order to free Richard from the captivity of Leopold V, the Duke of Austria, who had captured the English king near Vienna in 1192, Richard eventually being released in 1194. The need to raise money to fund new campaigns and the loss of English lands to the French king, Philip II, increased the pressure on King John, whose whole reign was typified by plots and sometimes open rebellion, either in England or in France. The simmering discontent amid the nobility, particularly the northern barons of England, culminated in the Barons' War of 1215–16, which France joined by invading England in 1216, Phillip II sending an army under his son Prince Louis to claim the throne. John died in 1216 and the country was ruled by William Marshal, who was declared the Protector of the young Prince Henry, who was at the time just nine years old. Despite John's death, the bitter civil war continued until Royalist victories in 1217 at Lincoln, Dover and Sandwich finally brought an end to the war. With peace returning to England, Prince Louis gave up his claim to the English throne and returned to France; it seems that the English barons preferred an English regent to a French king! The barons' great agreement, the Magna Carta, which King John had set his seal to in 1215, was resuscitated by William Marshal and reissued in an updated form in 1217 as a basis for future government.

Despite the years of turmoil, John had found time to visit Wales during almost every year of his reign and there was an uneasy balance of power held between the three powers of the Marcher Lords along the Anglo-Welsh border, the royal territories in Pembrokeshire and the independent Welsh lords of North Wales. King John needed stability somewhere in his kingdom and married his illegitimate daughter Joan to the Welsh prince Llywelyn the Great in 1205. A brief uprising by Llywelyn the Great in 1211 was swiftly countered by a large invasion force led by King John himself and once more peace returned. However, this peace was short lived; when the barons rose in revolt, Llywelyn was one of those who insisted that the Magna Carta was signed.

CHAPTER 8

The English Invasions
1216–1300

After John's death, Llywelyn the Great reinforced his powers in Wales at the Treaty of Worcester in 1218, whereby the young Henry III agreed to Llewelyn keeping his conquests, recognising the Principality of Wales that would endure until 1536, though at times it would grow through rebellion and other times almost lose what autonomy it did have under English oppression. Over the next sixteen years there was frequent hostility among all the major players as the Marcher Lords would test the strength of Llywelyn the Great, while he would test the strength of the king's forces in South Wales, where he would aid smaller Welsh territories that were under threat. All sides built castles to strengthen their defences and Llewelyn also looked to develop economic centres in an effort to bring more prosperity to his princedom; as J. E. Lloyd submits, Llywelyn was Prince of Wales in all but title. If provoked, Llywelyn showed that he could respond, as in 1223, when he invaded Shropshire and seized the castles of Kinnerley and Whittington near Oswestry, while William Marshall attacked and captured Carmarthen and Cardigan with an army assembled in Ireland. Later in the year, these petty, incessant wars were settled peacefully by an agreement signed between Henry III and Llywelyn the Great at Montgomery. In 1228, pressure was again heaped on Llywelyn the Great when Hubert de Burgh, who was one of the most powerful men in the kingdom as Justiciar of not only England but of Ireland as well, was appointed a lord and given the castle of Montgomery by Henry III. De Burgh instantly looked to encroach into Llywelyn's lands and in spite of his earlier agreement, signed ironically at Montgomery, the king raised an army to help De Burgh, who began to build a new castle within the *commote* (district) of Ceri. However, Llywelyn fought back and by October, and with the Welsh winter about to close upon them, the royal army was forced to retreat. Both the skill and strength of Llywelyn are illustrated in what happened next. Llywelyn had captured the Lord of Abergavenny, one William de Braose, in the Welsh counter-raids in Ceri; Henry was willing to dismantle the newly begun castle, but only if Llywelyn would pay reparations of £2,000 for the material and labour used; Llywelyn agreed but only if the king would pay £2,000 for the release of De Braose.

1231 Abermule – Powys

Despite the second intervention of King Henry III at Montgomery to restore peace in the area, Llywelyn the Great was still concerned about the power of Hubert de Burgh and his ruthlessness towards the Welsh people. De Burgh was still seething after the construction of his new castle had to be stopped as part of the king's peace with Llywelyn. Things came to a head when some of Llywelyn's men were captured by the garrison of Montgomery; they were first imprisoned and then beheaded. Llywelyn was furious and made up his mind that De Burgh and the English had to be taught a lesson that they could not continually break signed agreements on the division and governance of the land.

There is little information for what ensued but it is an important event because the battle and the subsequent peace brought to an end years of intermittent hostility. Llywelyn waited until his intelligence informed him that all of De Burgh's men were inside his castle; this had to be the case in order to enable his men to get close enough and for the plan to succeed; if any English patrols had spotted him and his army then that would have stopped the campaign before it had started. Llywelyn used a monk from Cwm Hîr Abbey to gain access to Montgomery Castle (no doubt in some casual way so as not to arouse suspicion), and let slip that he had seen Llywelyn and some hundreds of his men somewhere south of the River Severn and therefore on the Montgomery side of the river. This was too close for comfort for the castle as this meant that the Welsh could approach the town from over the hills to the south-west rather than across the ford at Rhydwhyman, where they could be seen approaching the town from the north. The Severn Valley would be no place to launch a Welsh ambush: the road was well used by all travellers as it was the main thoroughfare into Mid Wales; the likelihood of patrols would be greater, and so would the chance of being seen. The Severn River Valley floor was also quite wide and a natural place for an ambush, so close to Montgomery, did not present itself. The village of Llandyssil, which now nestles in a narrow steep sided valley just 2 miles south-west of Montgomery Castle, would seem the perfect place to launch an ambush: the valley dog-legs from east–west to north–south and is surrounded on all sides by hills rising steeply to over 500 feet, which were no doubt wooded in the thirteenth century. A few small streams run through this small valley and at times the ground can be boggy and soft.

A rough ridgeway then, the road is tarmacadamed today and this road makes its way down these hills, starting out at a high level close to the castle and well above Montgomery town and keeping to the side of a stream cut valley, it makes its way through the wide Llandyssil valley. This would be a much quicker route for the English to have taken than going all the way around via the ford at Rhydwhyman. From an English perspective, it also meant that they would encounter any Welsh force coming to attack

Montgomery Castle was at the centre of many English military campaigns.

The direct road west from Montgomery to Abermule.

The valley of Llandyssil, where Llywelyn would have mounted his ambush.

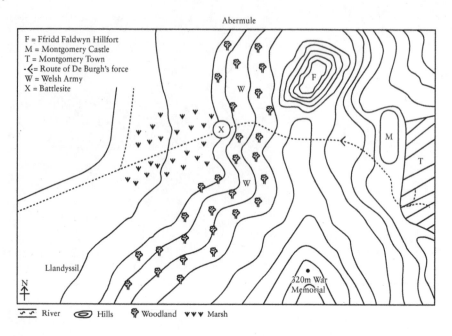

Abermule

F = Ffridd Faldwyn Hillfort
M = Montgomery Castle
T = Montgomery Town
-◀- = Route of De Burgh's force
W = Welsh Army
X = Battlesite

Llandyssil

320m War Memorial

N

〰〰 River   ◎ Hills   🌳 Woodland   ▾▾▾ Marsh

Montgomery. The organised pace at which De Burgh would have spurred his men to get ready for action can only be imagined: here was his chance to deal with the trouble maker once and for all, the Welsh upstart who was thwarting the Justiciar of not only England, but of Ireland as well, from expanding his lands. It seems that not long after the English rode out, they became trapped in marshy ground, upon which Llywelyn's men sprang out from their hiding places and attacked. A most violent battle ensued but the Welsh eventually gained a victory. The size of the forces would have been small, perhaps no more than a few hundred a side, which meant that while a part of Llywelyn's force was keeping the garrison busy in the valley, the rest of his force, probably several thousand, were free to attack and burn the town. Though some English escaped from the ambush, which presumably meant that most of De Burgh's force was mounted, the day was a complete Welsh victory. An all-mounted force would fit with De Burgh trying to move quickly to catch Llywelyn before the Welsh prince escaped, and also to the English being disordered by having to fight in marshy terrain. As it turned out, it was De Burgh who was lucky to escape, but a year later he was removed from office and was himself imprisoned over what was seen as his incompetence. Montgomery Castle crops up regularly in this military history of Wales and is well worth a visit; although in ruins, the masonry still stands tall and confirms the strength of the castle at the height of its importance. The countryside around Montgomery Castle is still agricultural and the valley to the south, wherein lies Llandyssil, is an irregular pattern of fields and farms; where the actual encounter took place is not certain, but the most likely site of the battle is at the foot of the hills, just 1½ miles from the castle. The castle has its own car park, but the battlesite itself, being open countryside, does not, though there are places where the visitor can pull in and observe the wooded steep slopes of the hills and the marshy valley bottom below, all of which was tailor-made for a Welsh ambush and well chosen by Llewelyn.

Following this successful attack, Llywelyn launched attacks on a whole series of towns, including Hay and Brecon, all of which were burned; Llywelyn's men then moved west to capture the castles of Neath and Kidwelly before rounding off the campaign by capturing Cardigan Castle once more. It was now King Henry III's turn to be furious and he launched a new invasion campaign that culminated in the construction of a new castle at Painscastle, between Builth Wells and Hay-on-Wye. Despite getting this castle built, the king was unable to gain any other advantage and looked to broker a peace deal. Eventually, after lengthy negotiations in 1234 at Myddle (a village 10 miles north of Shrewsbury), the Peace of Myddle was signed, whereby Llywelyn agreed to cease hostilities for two years as long as his lands were left in peace; as a part of the agreement, the Welsh prince was allowed to keep the towns and castles of Cardigan and Builth. The treaty was successful and renewed every year until Llywelyn died in 1140.

25 November 1233 Monmouth – Gwent

We have seen that there was almost continual unrest between the Welsh and the Welsh; the Welsh and the Saxons; then the Welsh and the Normans; and finally between the Welsh and the English. At the same time as all these wars were occurring, there were many outbreaks of civil war across England. These civil wars among the English rarely spilled over into the principality of Wales, but in the autumn of 1233 they did. Well, English against English is slightly untrue: it was an English lord against an English king, with French, Welsh, English and Flemish soldiers all involved. Richard Marshal was the second son of William Marshal, who as the Earl of Pembroke had been the Lord Protector during the minority of Henry III. Richard Marshal was also the leader of those barons opposed to the growth of King Henry's powers, and to make his position more unfavourable, Richard also opposed the growing number of foreign nobles at Henry III's court. In 1233 Henry held court at Gloucester; having been called to attend, Richard Marshal refused to go and in the presence of all there, Henry III pronounced Richard Marshal a traitor.

Richard Marshal withdrew to his own castle at Chepstow as King Henry III moved to Abergavenny with his army. Richard formed an alliance with Llywelyn the Great and his loyal supporter Owain ap Gruffudd, the latter being a grandson of Rhys of Deheubarth. Llywelyn kept away from the campaign but Owain took an active part, supplying troops to assist Richard Marshal. These combined forces of Owain and Marshal must have been quite large (compared to the king's own army), for when they seized Cardiff and then Newport and marched towards Abergavenny, the king retreated, leaving his enemies to capture Abergavenny and Grosmont. According to Roger of Wendover in his chronicle *Flores Historiarum*, Marshal and Owain, with just a few of their entourage, approached the town of Monmouth and the castle which lay beyond it to examine their defences and see if they were vulnerable to attack. It is not clear whether they mingled with the townsfolk to get close to the castle, or approached as knights on horseback, but apparently they were seen making their approach.

The castle had been put under the care of Baldwin III, the Count of Guînes, who was charged by Henry III with defending the town. It appears that Baldwin thought that Marshal and Owain were by themselves and so the count decided to attack at once, and it seems he turned out the whole garrison. Baldwin was of the French nobility and he would have had some mounted knights as part of his personal bodyguard, while the rest of this force was made up of Flemings (most likely his spearmen) and Poitevins (who would have been crossbowmen). The only way out of the castle was down through the town and over a bridge into the outer town, surrounded by some long ditch and palisade defences. Baldwin must have ridden almost half a mile by the time he reached Marshal and Owain, but from Roger's account all the men were mounted. Owain and Marshal cannot have seen Baldwin coming because at first they were clearly outnumbered: Marshal '…although engaged single-handed against twelve enemies, defended himself for a length of time' and at one point in the skirmish Marshal was unhorsed, so he unhorsed a Frenchman, took his horse from him and went back into the fray. Owain and

The ruins of Monmouth Castle above the River Monnow.

Monmouth's famous gated bridge over the River Monnow.

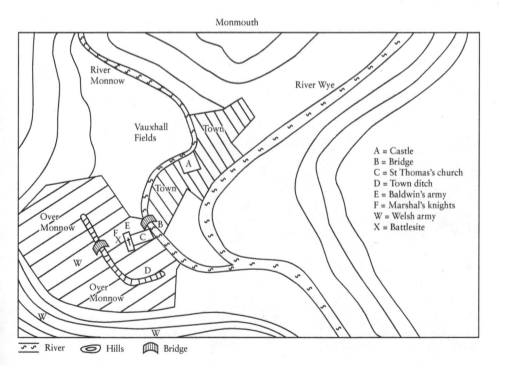

Monmouth

A = Castle
B = Bridge
C = St Thomas's church
D = Town ditch
E = Baldwin's army
F = Marshal's knights
W = Welsh army
X = Battlesite

Marshal's men were clearly within striking distance, for seeing their leaders under attack they advanced and joined in the action. Marshal's luck clearly could not hold out forever and Baldwin succeeded in somehow getting hold of him and dragged him towards the castle. A crossbowman, seeing his leader's predicament, shot a quarrel, which hit Baldwin in the chest, penetrating his armour, and he fell to the ground. The reinforcements that arrived to assist Owain and Marshal soon succeeded in driving the garrison back across the battlefield towards the castle. A bridge which is reported to have been in the 'neighbourhood' of the castle was found to be 'broken down', so the garrison could not escape the advancing forces and many of the men leaped into the river and tried to swim to safety, but Roger says that 'few of those who had sallied out from the castle returned safe'. The battle won, the victors made their way back to the safety of their own lands, and John of Monmouth, the lord of the castle, returned to take command. Baldwin survived in spite of his injury. Marshal travelled to Ireland and made peace with Henry III in 1234 but was later wounded in the Battle of the Curragh, and died shortly after. The traditional site of the battle has been Castle Field, which is to the west of Monmouth Castle and over the River Monnow from the castle and is known today as Vauxhall Fields. However, an order placed in 1234 for the timber from thirty oaks to repair the Church of St Thomas the Martyr, to the south-west of the town, suggests that the bridge adjacent to the church, the Monnow Bridge, was the one that was broken. The Monnow Bridge today is the picture-postcard stone bridge that still has its original gatehouse to guard against entry.

There are several puzzling items to be cleared up about this encounter. The garrison of such a castle would have been no more than 200 men, though Henry III did have news of the rebellion so he may well have strengthened it with mercenaries, so let us say 300 as a maximum number. It then seems

Monmouth's Town Ditch in Over Monnow.

The residential area of Over Monnow; the ridge where the Welsh hid lies behind.

that the whole garrison left the castle to deal with the threat below the town, as Roger informs us that few of the garrison returned after the rout. The combined force which Marshal and Owain commanded was in two parts: a small reconnaissance force, probably no more than twenty men so as not to attract too much attention, while the main force was several thousand strong, a large army capable of besieging large castles with, according to the *Brut*, engines of war for attacking castles. Owain and Marshal and their entourage would have been mounted knights, with chainmail and perhaps plate mail helmets; the rest of their troops would have been English heavy spearmen and heavy crossbowmen and the Welsh mostly light archers and javelinmen. This brings us to the location of these men, who were able to rapidly join the battle to aid Marshal and Owain once they were attacked. The area of Vauxhall Fields as the battlesite has two major issues. Firstly, there is no natural hill or ridge upon which the main besieging force might have hidden, ready to aid their commanders who had gone on ahead. Secondly, there is no record of any bridge having ever been built between the castle and Castle Fields (now Vauxhall Fields) until the modern footbridge. The author has checked with the current castle staff and curators, and to the best of their knowledge there was never a bridge, according to the records they have seen. If, however, one looks south-west of the castle, one comes to the River Monnow and then to the area of 'Over Monnow', a name surely suggesting that the town had spread in time beyond the river. Importantly, in the midst of this built-up area today is a ditch which is still known by the residents of the town as the 'town ditch'. It is a well preserved defensive ditch which would, when full of water and with a palisade on top of it, have made the outer defensive works of the town a formidable barrier if defended by the garrison. Although clearly visible, much of the ditch is overgrown and no doubt the original dyke on the inside was levelled when the houses were built.

The River Monnow winds between Vauxhall Fields and the castle, but there was never a bridge.

Both the River Monnow and the town ditch have a stone bridge today, but in 1233 they would almost have certainly been wooden. Most importantly, to complete the possibility of Over Monnow being the site of the battle, just half a mile from the town ditch rises the wooded ridge that contains St Dials Farm. This ridge, especially if wooded at the time of the battle, would be the preferred defensive position of a Welsh army. Given all of the evidence, it would appear that Over Monnow is the site. One can imagine the small reconnaissance force getting inside the outer defences between the ditch bridge and the Monnow Bridge, their men lying dispersed across the ridge with an ample height and field of vision to see what was happening below them. The garrison, getting news of their unwelcome visitors, charged from the castle, down the bailey and out over Monnow Bridge (clearly sound at this time) and the fight began. Owain and Marshal were heavily outnumbered until the main part of their army arrived and drove the garrison back to where the Monnow Bridge is now destroyed; but how and why in so short a time? Did the last few men of the garrison cut some vital ropes holding the bridge together so that it could be collapsed to save the town? Was it a drawbridge at the time and did the few men left on the castle side to operate the mechanism not lower it because they did not want to lose their own lives in the tide of Welsh soldiers that would surge into the town and take the castle? Did some Welsh soldiers come down the river in coracles and sabotage the bridge from underneath? All of these possibilities are plausible, taking all of the available information into account; there is precious little to go on, and there are no records available within the castle as to what may have happened in the battle. The visitor part of the castle has been refurbished and is now the home for the volunteer-run museum of the Royal Monmouthshire Royal Engineers (Militia), telling the history of the regiment from their inauguration in 1539, during the reign of Henry VIII, until the present day. A walk from the castle down through the town takes the visitor over the stone bridge and into Over Monnow, which is now a residential housing estate. However, the town ditch is clearly discernible and seems well preserved, if a little overgrown, in the centre of the street pattern. The whole skyline is dominated by the long, tree-covered ridge that runs behind the houses and one can envisage the Welshmen streaming down to aid their knights once the battle had begun.

Following the death of Llywelyn the Great in 1240, Dafydd ap Llywelyn succeeded him and was recognised as the rightful heir by Henry III, but when he had gathered an army the English king invaded, seeking to claim the lands from Dafydd that his father had so soundly defended. Until Dafydd's death in 1246, there was almost constant warfare as the English invaded time and again and the Welsh resistance was worn down. Dafydd tried to negotiate military

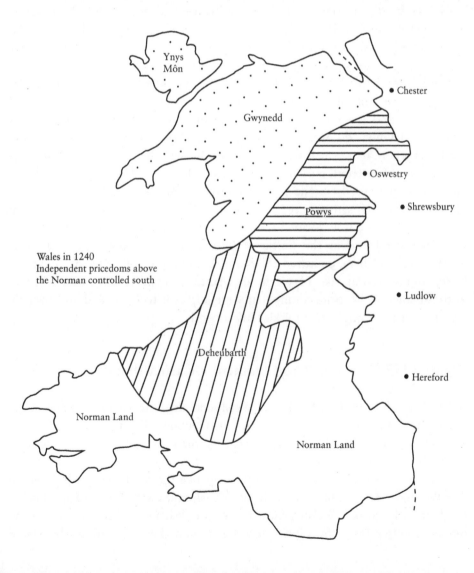

Wales in 1240
Independent pricedoms above
the Norman controlled south

alliances with the French and religious alliances with the Pope, but all of his efforts came to nothing. Dafydd's half-brother, Gruffydd, was imprisoned in the Tower of London as a hostage for Dafydd's compliance but Henry III was unable to use the blackmail for long, as Gruffydd died while trying to escape in 1244. This tragedy took some of the pressure from Dafydd's shoulders and he forged an alliance with other Welsh princes to attack the English. The Welsh made gains, taking back the castle of Mold, and when in August 1245 King Henry III again invaded Gwynedd, his army suffered a defeat in yet another narrow pass, ambushed by Dafydd's men somewhere close to Deganwy. Savage fighting continued around Deganwy until Henry, running short of supplies, was forced to agree a truce for the autumn and winter. The truce held but suddenly, in February 1246, Dafydd died. In the *Brut*, Caradoc named him the 'Shield of Wales'. Dafydd's marriage to Isabella de Braose had not produced an heir, so the two eldest sons of Dafydd's half-brother, Llywelyn ap Gruffudd and Owain ap Gruffydd, divided Gwynedd between them. These two men took the war to the English but attacks by the Marcher Lords pushed Welsh resources to the limit and at the Treaty of Woodstock in 1247 the two brothers conceded territory to the English in return for a guaranteed peace.

Llywelyn and Owain reluctantly went home to jointly rule their reduced kingdom of Gwynedd and to bide their time. However, this Welsh peace was shattered when, in 1254, Dafydd ap Gruffudd, who had come of age in 1252 (at the age of fourteen), paid homage to King Henry III. The king, pleased with the honour, promised Dafydd part of Gwynedd, much to the consternation of Llywelyn, who refused to accept this plan to further break up the princedom. Owain and Dafydd now formed an alliance against Llywelyn but their rebellion was short-lived and at the Battle of Bryn Derwin in June 1255, Llywelyn defeated his brothers, captured them and became the sole ruler of Gwynedd. Now, empowered at last, Llywelyn ap Gruffudd invaded and captured many of the smaller Welsh princedoms that were adjacent to Gwynedd and over the next two years brought them under his control.

2 June 1257 Cymerau (Coed Llathen) – Carmarthenshire

While Llywelyn ap Gruffudd had Welshmen flocking to his banner in the north, the same Prince of Gwynedd was also having influence in the south. The imposition of taxes on the barons had caused them to revolt against King John, and at times under King Henry III the same discontent manifested itself. When any king was at odds with his nobility, it opened the door for Welsh rebellion. The Welsh too felt the financial pain of English taxes and in 1256 Rhys Fychan (Fechan), who was a Welsh prince turned English tax collector, was thrown out of Dinefwr Caste by Llywelyn, even though they were distantly related.

Llywelyn ap Gruffudd was now in control of almost all of Wales and was pushing against the borders of the Marcher Lords' territory. Stephen Bauzan was the appointed County Sheriff and it was his obligation to restore Fychan to his post and to collect the unpaid taxes, by taking goods through plunder if necessary. A large English force was gathered at Carmarthen and set off for Llandeilo along the Roman road on the north side of the River Tywi; it was a strong force with renowned men-at-arms and many armoured horsemen, approximately numbering 4,000 in total. The Welsh force is quite hard to gauge, although given the general uprising it was probably several thousand strong, but may not have outnumbered the English army. The numbers mattered little for the style of campaign that the two Welsh commanders, Maredudd ap Owain and Maredudd ap Rhys, intended to fight. The Welsh would have been traditionally armed, with the vast majority of their force carrying bows and possibly a few slings and javelins. The more heavily armoured men would have been kept back for the final mêlée should that be necessary.

It seems that Rhys Fychan was playing a double game, a very dangerous tactic when torture and mutilation were commonplace, and for a traitor torture was a long and deliberately slow exercise designed to inflict maximum suffering before death. Fychan accompanied the English army to the outskirts of Llandeilo, where the force made camp away from Dinefwr Castle, probably on the valley floor, close to the river. The valley floor would have had ample space to accommodate such a large force and the level ground away from the hills offered some protection as they would have been out of bow range. Some of the flanks of the camp would also have been protected by the river and guards would have been posted. Fychan chose this time to leave the English camp and make his way to Dinefwr Castle, where he now declared his allegiance to Maredudd ap Rhys, the owner of the stronghold. While the Welsh had been content to let the English host march east, they now decided to soften

Dinefwr Castle; its predicament drew Bauzan's army out of Carmarthen.

up their enemy. The camp would have made a large target and apparently it was while they were camped that the English started to suffer casualties. It was mid-summer and the days were long, and with dawn Welsh arrows were shot into the camp from any woods and defiles that were in range of the English camp – the Tywi valley, like many in Wales at this time, would probably have been heavily forested in places. The English tolerated these intermittent attacks for some time and then decided that the safest thing was to return to Carmarthen. The journey home began slowly and at every place where the road was overshadowed by steep hills or woodland, the English army ran the gauntlet of missiles; it would mostly have been slingstones and arrows, but in some parts, javelins and short spears would have been within throwing range. With a force of 4,000 men spread out in a long column, the Welsh missile men could hardly fail to miss their targets. At an unknown wooded place named Coed Llathen (which was not near either Llandeilo or the River Cothi as these are not named), the Welsh attacked in strength.

The most likely site for this action is between Broad Oak and Caeaunewydd, which is in the area of Llangathen, as here the road runs for 2 miles with hills rising fairly steeply on either side but not precipitously; these are not the sides of a defile and so would allow attackers to descend, but would be hard going for men in armour to ascend if under attack. This major Welsh attack apparently took place around noon, the hottest part of the day, and when the English would have covered about 6 miles from their camp. The Welsh, emboldened by their ongoing success and now apparently outnumbering their enemy, came in among the mounted men, tipped them off their horses, and in the chaos killed and wounded many of them before making off towards Llandeilo with the baggage train, which included all of the spare horses and a quantity of weapons. As some knights escaped to continue on their way, it is most likely that this Welsh attack was targeted on the middle and rear of the column so as to split the force into two (divide and conquer), thereby allowing the Welsh force to escape with the valuable baggage while the front of the column continued towards what it probably now thought was the safety of Carmarthen. Sadly for the English, there was worse still to come as there were still several other places along the 10 miles before Carmarthen could be reached that were suitable for Welsh forces to hide in. The English would have been most vulnerable after the earlier major assault when crossing the River Cothi, which cuts north–south across the Roman road. A bridge spanned the river, but like all bridges at this time it would have been wooden and narrow.

A unit of Welsh spearmen would have been sufficient to hold the bridge, most likely supported by Welsh bowmen, who would have been able to shoot across the river, safe from English attack by being on the opposite bank. Mounted men would not have stood a chance in charging formed spears, and one can picture the scene as the battered and bloodied English column approached the bridge, only to find it held against them. Just as they were taking in the scene and Bauzan began considering his options, a volley of arrows would have thundered into them from the opposite bank, while from the low hills and woods to their right (northern) flank a Welsh host would have charged towards them. Unable to cross the river, the English would have looked to flee south which was now their only option alongside the River Cothi. A low ridge (with Abercothi place names) forces the Cothi to bend towards Carmarthen and beyond the ridge are

The bridge spanning the River Cothi, on the line of the original Roman road.

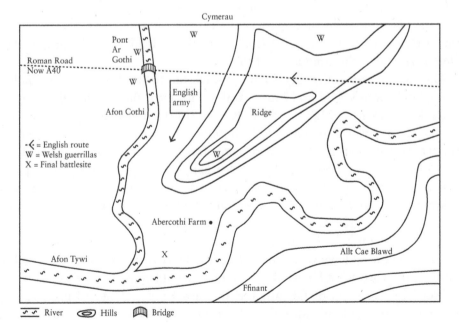

flat meadows, good ground for English knights if they are formed and ready for battle. The English, however, were not formed; they were being chased and harried and no doubt the Welsh, as the campaign had been so perfectly executed, had troops already stationed on the Abercothi ridge and their cries as they charged down the slope and onto the meadows would have been the death knells for the English. As the English force was almost completely destroyed, this last encounter must have been a bitter one, with the English trapped and completely destroyed, their commander Bauzan being killed in the final melee. This battle of Cymerau and/or Coed Llathen was really a running battle over two days and consisted of several intense encounters that took place along the Roman road, broken up with almost constant skirmishing in-between. Let us break down the two names. Cymerau translates as 'confluence' and as the final action comes, as we have shown above, in the Cothi-Twyi confluence, it all makes perfect sense, so we can safely say that the final action took place there. Coed Llathen is more difficult to locate; it literally translates as 'Wood' and 'Yard'. But prior to that final action, all of the casualties were caused on route. Perhaps the Llathen was meant and understood by the people of the time to mean 'in sections' – that the battle was fought in all the woods and in 'yards' as the English struggled along the road, being attacked at almost every step by a fresh Welsh onslaught. The *Brut* states that the 'barons, nobles and upwards of 2,000 of the army…were slain', and the campaign was a complete disaster for the English. All of the sites connected with this series of actions can be visited and many of them have hardly changed, as much of the river valley is still agricultural land; the scenery that accompanies the traveller while following the route is in places simply breathtakingly beautiful. There are no specific parking places near the final battlefield but there are some parking places near the bridge and a walk along the Cothi mimics the flight of the English as they were herded into the confluence of the rivers.

The Welsh, especially Llywelyn, pushed on to challenge more English strongholds across Mid and North Wales. However, the Welsh fell out again soon afterwards as Maredudd ap Rhys reaffirmed his allegiance to King Henry III. Llywelyn ap Gruffudd continued to push and test the English resolve as the English barons had again fallen out with their king and the eyes of the English were elsewhere. Eventually, over a two-year period, peace was agreed at the Treaty of Montgomery in 1267; Llywelyn ap Gruffudd was acknowledged as Prince of Wales, gaining Builth, Brecon and Gwerthrynion and also Whittington Castle, which his grandfather had captured back in the 1220s; finally, Llywelyn's brother, Dafydd, was also re-accepted into Gwynedd society. In return, Llywelyn swore homage to Henry III and the peace would last until 1272, when King Henry III's long reign would come to an end.

From the accession of Edward I as the new King of England in 1272, the relations between England and Wales once more deteriorated into conflict

Above left: Abercothi ridge, from which the final Welsh charge would have forced the English into the rivers.

Above right: Looking across the battlesite towards the confluence of the rivers Tywi and Cothi.

until, having laid his plans carefully, Edward declared war on Llywelyn in 1276. He led a storming English advance into Wales that led to the capture of Anglesey and most of the country's harvest. Many of the Welsh princes sued for peace and reluctantly Llywelyn accepted the Treaty of Aberconwy of 1277, which superseded the agreement made at Montgomery and drastically reduced Llywelyn's powers and his lands. By way of reconciliation, Edward met Llywelyn at Worcester and there he met Eleanor de Montfort, daughter of the baron Simon de Montfort who had led the great Barons' Rebellion that had ended with his death at Evesham in 1265. It seems that for once love conquered everything and Edward, seeing how things had evolved, gave permission for the couple to be married at Worcester Cathedral before they returned to Wales as Prince and Princess of Wales. Back in Wales, however, those Welsh princes who had been so quick to shun Llywelyn and bow down to Edward now began to regret their decision and over the next few years, as the demands of the English Exchequer grew, so did Welsh resentment. On Palm Sunday 1282, Dafydd ap Gruffudd attacked Hawarden Castle near Chester and later laid siege to Rhuddlan. The spark had once more lit a tinder-dry countryside and across Wales, princedoms revolted; Aberystwyth Castle was captured and burnt and Carreg Cennen Castle was also captured in south Wales. This was to be a time of personal tragedy for Llywelyn as he was not involved in the rebellion, but he wrote to the Archbishop of Canterbury, John Peckham, expressing his concern that the rebellion would be a disaster. Llywelyn, however, felt obliged to support his brother; at the same time his wife Eleanor died after giving birth to Princess Gwenllian. With the Welsh in arms, Edward invaded and history repeated itself as the King of England smashed through the ill-prepared Welsh armies. Llywelyn was offered a large estate in England if he would surrender Wales to Edward. Naturally, Llywelyn refused, saying that he would not abandon his people, whom his ancestors had protected 'since the days of Kamber son of Brutus' – basically since forever there had been Britons in Wales.

11 December 1282 Irfon Bride (Orewin Bridge) – Powys

With the gauntlet now thrown down, Llywelyn left his brother, Dafydd, to lead the defence of his homeland of Gwynedd and with his banner aloft he rode south to raise an army from the people of Mid Wales, before heading into South Wales to rally support there. Edward was determined that there would be no more Welsh resistance and he would put an end to 'the malice of the Welsh' (Cassell's). There is much confusion about what happened in this battle, but having walked the terrain, the accounts make sense if applied to the reasoning of generals in the field. All chroniclers broadly agree that the battle was fought outside of Builth Wells, just after Irfon Bridge, on the road going west towards Cilmeri. The confusion arises as to whether Llywelyn was killed during the battle, whether he was killed before the battle took place, or whether he died elsewhere of his wounds. Let us see if the jigsaw can be assembled so that a complete picture can be viewed as to what took place. The English were led by the Marcher Lord Edmund Mortimer, aided by Robert L'Estrange and John Giffard. They had an army of around 2,500 men and most of their troops would have been of three types, armoured knights and men-at-arms, spearmen and a mixture of crossbow and bowmen. The Welsh would have had their traditional mix of spearmen and bowmen; given the rallying cry of Llwyelyn he probably had a similar sized force to the English, but they would have been less well armoured than their English counterparts, though one source states that the Welsh had some 160 mounted men. The main chronicler for the battle was one Walter of Guisborough, who was writing around twenty years after the battle, though historians have questioned his reliability. All the other sources are much later and their accounts are of a much more straightforward medieval battle, ignoring much of Walter's information. When one reads Walter's account of the battlesite, it is extremely plausible, as the terrain matches the facts and accounts for both Llywelyn's death while separated from his men and for the sudden defeat of the Welsh from a position of strength.

At Builth Wells the mighty River Wye and the River Irfon meet, the latter already a good sized river, adding a considerable amount of water to the Wye. All around Builth Wells the rivers can only be crossed by bridges, so any crossing would be vital to an army. The sources agree that the Welsh were on a hill and that is easy to find: the road west from Builth Wells climbs steadily

Irfon Bridge today, the route taken by the main English column to attack the Welsh.

up a long slope, not steep but enough to slow an advancing army and difficult for armoured men on armoured horses to gather any speed for a charge. This hill sits above Irfon Bridge and without the bridge the English, who were based on the south side of the River Irfon, would never have been able to get near the Welsh forces; so as the road and the battle exist, so there must also have a bridge, probably a simple wooden one, close to if not exactly where the road bridge sits today. This hill is topped by a place marked as Caeau on the modern Ordnance Survey map of the area and this is where the Welsh waited. However, Llywelyn's scouts, who would have been watching the English movements across the river, reported back to Llywelyn that horsemen were heading west along a track on the other side of the river. These would be the men who Walter states had been told (by a Welsh traitor) that a ford existed several miles along the river which would allow the English knights to cross the River Irfon and so attack the Welsh from the rear. As Llywelyn was in command and would have had a strong horse as his mount, he set off west with another mounted man-at-arms to investigate these troop movements and to see if indeed a ford existed, because if it did then the Welsh would need to quickly redeploy upon his return.

The ford did exist, and still does today, and even after the wet winter of 2013/14 it was still fordable according to the flood depth markers, which showed just a two foot depth. Sadly for Llywelyn and his companion, some of the English mounted troops were already across the river by the time Llywelyn arrived, and seeing the two Welshmen ahead of them, and knowing that if they escaped they would raise the alarm, the English host swept forward. A company officer, one Stephen de Frankton from the Frankton settlements near Ellesmere, slew Llywelyn, his companion presumably suffering a similar fate at the hands of the English men-at-arms. While the English flanking movement advanced up the hill unseen between the ford and Cilmeri, the main body of the English army

Above left: The hills west of Builth Wells where the Welsh waited and fought the English without Llwyelyn ap Gruffudd.

Above right: The steep hill the English had to climb to get to the Welsh position.

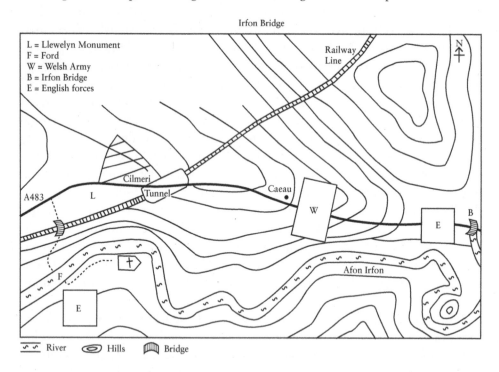

had crossed the Irfon Bridge to draw what they knew would be a hail of arrows from the waiting Welsh bowmen on the hills ahead of them. With a hillside position and a mixture of spearmen to defend and bowmen to attack, the Welsh army was in a strong position. This is borne out by all accounts, which state that the fighting was hard, though the Marcher archers slowly began to down their Welsh opponents. It was at this point that the English mounted men would have appeared on the rear of the Welsh position, following the ridgeway track from Cilmeri towards Irfon Bridge and Builth Wells. The land atop the small plateau is undulating rather than steep and perfect for a cavalry charge and one made into the flank or rear of an enemy engaged to the front would be overwhelming. Walter states that the turning point in the battle came when 'our cavalry charged up the hill above them, and having cut some down, drove off the rest at great speed'. The key thing then is that it was close to the ford where Llwyelyn met his death and where the flanking movement began a short time later against the Welsh position, which is not visible from the ford and vice versa, so that the Welsh did not know that their leader had been killed when the battle started. There seems to be a consensus that it was not until the head of Llywelyn had been washed and showed to the English command that he was recognised and this could account for some misapprehension that he had been killed in battle, or after the defeat.

The other key fact to remember about the later accounts of the demise of Llwyelyn is that they were written when Wales had been incorporated into the English realm and were under English law. Therefore, any account written then would have seemed brutal if it reported how the English had murdered a knight, and a Prince of Wales too, without even asking his name or offering him the right to trial by battle; effectively, it would have been describing a near execution. It would have read so much better, for those contemporary readers, if the brave Welsh prince had died in a corner of a field, fighting to the last alongside his men as his army went down courageously. Llywelyn's death was a hammer blow to the Welsh and Edward I's relentless drive to subdue the Welsh people for all time continued at a slow but inevitable pace.

The ford at Cilmeri where the English crossed to outflank the Welsh and by chance succeeded in killing Llywelyn ap Gruffudd.

Llwyelyn ap Gruffudd's monument at Cilmeri.

There is no parking near the battlesite so it must be reached on foot, either walking back from Cilmeri or up from Builth Wells. There is, however, a memorial with parking provided close to the site where Llywelyn's head was washed in a spring and not far from the ford, so that the stone memorial to the last of that line of Britons who had fought for independence for 1,230 years can be visited. Llywelyn's body was taken to Cwm Hir Abbey, a day's ride north of Builth Wells and set in one of the most isolated places in Britain. The site has a peace and serenity which allows one to appreciate the sanctity of the site. The grave lies amid the crumbling ruins of this once great citadel of Christian worship, which played such an important part in the history of Wales. For Llewelyn, it is a fitting tribute to the support that he gave to the abbey when he was alive.

Dafydd ap Gruffudd succeeded his brother but by early 1283 all of the remaining Welsh castles in Gwynedd were captured as Edward provided extra warm winter clothing for his men so they could see out the campaign without needing to retreat back to England and start again next year. The court of Wales was forced to flee into hiding in the mountains of Snowdonia, where Dafydd ap Gruffudd was finally captured in June 1283, betrayed by his own people according to the triumphant English.

Above left: Cwm Hir Abbey, in an isolated part of Mid Wales, where Llwyelyn ap Gruffudd is buried.

Above right: Llwyelyn ap Gruffudd's grave within the ruins of Cwm Hir Abbey, of which he had been a benefactor.

Dafydd has the unfortunate label of being the first named person to have been tried and executed for the crime of 'High Treason' against a monarch. King Edward ensured that Dafydd's death would be slow and agonising; Dafydd became the first prominent person in recorded history to have been hanged, drawn and quartered; such was his execution in early October 1283. Before Edward ascended the throne in 1272, he had already decided that the way to rule Wales was through strength in stone. The last successful people to rule Wales had been the Romans and they had controlled the country with a chain of forts; Edward would rule through a chain of castles. Between 1276 and 1295 he ordered the construction, or major repair, of seventeen castles. Under the Statute of Rhuddlan in 1284, the Kingdom of Gwynedd was dismembered and the land re-organised in an English model under which 'counties' were created; these were Anglesey, Caernarvonshire, Denbighshire, Flintshire and Merionethshire. Wales was now under English control and as such had to deliver men for her armies and navies and taxes for her exchequer. As unpopular as these impositions were, most nobility grumbled, it seems, but still supplied the men requested or paid the amount due. In 1287 Rhys ap Maredudd led a brief uprising and attacked English possessions in the Tywi valley, but he was also forced into hiding after 1288 and despite the remoteness of his retreats he still managed to lead a guerrilla war for another four years before being finally caught and then executed in 1292.

Wales after the Statute of Rhuddlan, 1284, showing castles ruled by English lords and extent of the Marcher Lord territories

5 March 1295 Maes Moydog – Powys

There was one final challenge to Edward's authority when, in 1294, Madog ap Llywelyn, who was a lesser member of the House of Aberffraw, led a brief but serious rebellion. At one point during the campaign, even Edward himself was besieged. The revolt came in response to a levy being placed upon the Welsh people by new royal administrators, who demanded yet more in taxes and troop levies. Madog was a cousin of Dafydd and Llwyelyn and proclaimed himself Prince of Wales as the next lawful successor to the royal Welsh line. The uprising spread with rapidity and the following castles were captured across Wales: Caernarfon; Hawarden; Ruthin; Denbigh; Morlais, and Kenfig; while Builth, Caerphilly, Criccieth, Flint, Rhuddlan and Harlech were all besieged.

Henry de Lacy, the Lord of Denbigh, and a small force was defeated outside the town of Denbigh when he attempted to retake his castle. Many smaller castles were also captured and undefended towns were burnt. Planning another winter campaign, Edward led an army, reputed to be of 30,000 men, into North Wales by the traditional route along the coast, though Edward found himself under siege in Conwy Castle over Christmas 1294, and it was into the new year before the Earl of Warwick and the navy could relieve the siege. Having relieved the siege and freed the king from his predicament, Warwick returned to Oswestry to await news of the elusive Madog and his army.

Word soon reached Warwick that Madog was in the vicinity. Warwick marched to Montgomery and then doglegged back over the hills towards Castle Caereinion and into the area of Moydog, where he found Madog's camp below. This hilly rural area lies west of Welshpool and is an upland valley, surrounded on all sides by high hills, a perfect place for an army to hide – unless you had been betrayed and someone told your enemy where you were. Warwick was able to fan his lighter armed men out around the tops of the hills so as to surround as much of the Welsh army below as possible. The size of Madog's army is not known, but casualties of over 700 are recorded and clearly some would have escaped, as Madog did himself, so around 1,000 is a fair estimate. The composition of the Welsh army is also not known but on this occasion it appears to have been all spearmen as Madog was unable to counter the missile attacks from Warwick's army. *Cassell's* quotes an actual number for the English army: 2,847 men, made up of 119 heavy cavalry, 2,715 Shropshire infantry and 13 specialist crossbowmen paid at the premium rate of 3 pence per day. According to Trevett's *Annales* the Welsh, seeing their predicament, formed up to receive the English attack with their spears pushed into the earth to stop the cavalry's attack.

Seeing the Welsh defensive schiltrons which Madog formed his men into, Warwick used his bowmen and crossbowmen to target the spearmen, who could not advance quickly for fear of breaking up their formation. Clearly, Madog had very few bowmen with him or they would have been mobilised to support their spearmen against this well-planned missile attack. Only when many of the Welsh spearmen had fallen did the English cavalry charge home, looking to exploit the gaps that had appeared in the Welsh spearwall. Warwick must have had his main force to the south-east of the site because many of the Welsh fled north and west, which took them to the rivers Vyrnwy and Banwy respectively. Both rivers were swollen by recent rains and many Welshmen drowned trying to escape across them, with the English knights in pursuit. The land today is still rolling fields and small areas of woodland, and is probably little changed from Madog's day and although there are no specific parking places, there are numerous convenient pull-ins for the visitor. Madog escaped with some of his men and baggage, but a smaller detachment of Warwick's army fought

Oswestry Castle motte is now a garden.

Montgomery Castle was an important English base from which many campaigns, fought in Wales, began, including Warwick's against Madog.

Warwick's night march from Montgomery would have taken him through Berriew.

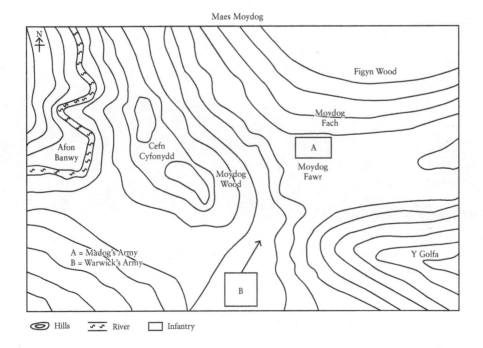

Maes Moydog

Figyn Wood

Moydog Fach

A

Afon Banwy

Cefn Cyfonydd

Moydog Fawr

Moydog Wood

A = Madog's Army
B = Warwick's Army

Y Golfa

B

Hills   River   Infantry

The hills which surround Moydog Valley would have been secured by Warwick's men.

Moydog Valley, where Warwick's men would have attacked Madog.

another engagement nearby, probably on the road to the north-west, which heads to Dolanog, then up and over the hills and into the Berwyn Mountains and the safety of the Welsh guerilla hideaways. A further 100 men were killed in this second engagement and Madog lost much of his baggage and plunder but somehow the rebel leader still managed to escape. Madog then spent some months as a fugitive until he surrendered to John de Havering, somewhere in Snowdonia, in the summer of 1295.

Surprisingly, given his treason, Madog was not executed but taken to London, where he was kept in the Tower until he died, possibly in 1312. Edward, incensed at the revolt, introduced more severe penalties for Welsh misdemeanours and levied more taxes, to pay for the damage done during this final rebellion against his castle building programme. It is little wonder, given the twelve centuries it took to conquer Wales, that today it still has more castles than any other country in the world, with over 500 recorded, and there are numerous small motte and baileys that were not converted from wood to stone, so the true figure may be even higher.

CHAPTER 9

The Great Welsh Rebellion 1400–15

Fourteenth Century

In contrast to the previous centuries of almost constant warfare, the fourteenth century was a period of almost unparalleled peace in Wales; yes there were rebellions, but they were few and far between. This period of calm is due to many factors, but from a military standpoint the key factor was that England was busy fighting elsewhere, and under the rules of governance Welsh troops were now a part of the English army. England fought a series of wars against the Scots, where there were three separate wars: 1296–1307, then 1313–27 and finally 1329–46. From 1337 England was at war with France and that war would last from 1337 to 1453, becoming known as the Hundred Years War, even though it lasted for longer. All of these campaigns took thousands of men away from their homes, and many of those soldiers came from Wales. It is little wonder then that there were few battles: there were not enough men within Wales for a noble to build an army from, even if there was any noble brave enough to take on the might of the English and their impregnable castles. In fact, most of the uprisings in the fourteenth century began as protests by the nobility of realms where the demand for recruits to pay military service to the Crown left few men at home to meet the agricultural needs and feed the population.

There was a small uprising in 1316 when Llywelyn Bren, resentful at the high taxes he had to pay, gathered a band of local rebels and put Caerphilly Castle under siege. They burnt the town and succeeded in surrounding the castle for six weeks before attempting to attack Cardiff. Having been thwarted, the Welsh army retreated north to a Welsh castle, Castell y Morgraig, but with a force of 2,000 men the Earl of Hereford, another of the powerful Marcher Lords, crushed the rebellion and after two years in prison in the Tower of London, Bren was returned to Cardiff, where he was hanged, drawn and quartered as a traitor.

In 1344, the Shire of Denbigh tried to extract yet more taxes from its oppressed people. At the May Day fayre in St Asaph a riot erupted when the English who had attended the fayre from Rhuddlan clashed with the local

Welsh townsfolk who, taking offence, chased the English out of the town before pursuing them to Rhuddlan. Encouraged by their success, the Welsh ransacked and pillaged the town before setting fire to it. From the castle the sorry sight of Rhuddlan greeted the English and they called upon the king to restore order. The rebellion, however, did not die down. John de Huntington, the Sheriff of Merioneth, was slain while holding court in, of course, the king's name, and all of the rolls which held the court records were stolen. The final act of violence was on 14 February 1345, when Henry de Shaldeforde, an attorney, and his men were ambushed by a Welsh force somewhere between Harlech and Caernarfon. As quickly as it had begun, the rebellion died away; it was more outbursts of frustration than a proper rebellion and although these isolated incidents sent small groups of Welshmen into hiding or to enlist as mercenaries to escape abroad, they did not enflame a population to widespread revolt. What these incidents did do is to ensure any Welsh villains that were caught received the maximum penalty under the law. For another generation there was generally peace in the Principality, but several times in the 1360s and 1370s Owain Lawgoch, whose full name was Owain ap Thomas ap Rhodri, planned invasions with French support to start a war in Wales to claim back the Principality for the Welsh. In 1369, Owain had set sail with a large fleet and a strong army before storms drove the French ships back to port and the invasion was abandoned. As with the Jacobites (nés Stuarts) 300 years later, the French were always happy to try and create a war on two fronts for the English and several other such invasions were planned. Owain was a formidable Welsh soldier who served not only in France but also in Alsace, Spain and Switzerland. He led a 'free company' (i.e. a mercenary regiment or band of men) composed entirely of Welshmen who fought for the French against the English in the Hundred Years War. Owain was the last politically active descendant of Llywelyn the Great and was rightly a claimant to the title of Prince of Gwynedd and Prince of Wales and was seen by the English monarchy as a serious threat. In 1377 the English planted a spy, a man named John Lamb, who was a Scot, to get close to and assassinate Owain. Over a period of a few months Lamb wormed his way into Owain's confidence, becoming his chamberlain, whereupon he stabbed the Welsh prince to death, receiving the sum of £20 for his deed, the equivalent today of somewhere between £5,000 and £10,000.

Owain Glyndŵr

One other important thing happened as far as Wales was concerned, sometime around the middle of the fourteenth century: a male baby was born in the year 1349, 1355 or 1359 – no-one seems totally sure; the BBC Wales History Website says 1359, so the author will stick with that date hereafter. If no-one is totally sure about the date of his birth, they are totally sure about his name: Owain Glyndŵr. Glyndŵr was born into the Anglo-Welsh gentry of the Welsh Marcher Lords, which gave Glyndŵr a distinct advantage as he was able to speak both English and Welsh and so could move on both sides of the border. Glyndŵr was also fortunate that he was born into a time of comparative peace in Wales: his father's lands were not under attack, there were no sides to choose for his family and he could grow with the unique opportunity to advance both his people and his king, Richard II. Glyndŵr was also descended from royalty on both sides of his family. His father, Gruffydd Fychan II, was a hereditary prince of Powys Fadog and also the Lord of Glyndyfrdwy, a beautiful upland area on the upper Dee Valley above Llangollen. This was a line of Welsh lords and princes who could trace their royal lineage back over 400 years and, most importantly, to a time before the Norman conquest of 1066, and these people were known as Uchelwyr. His mother was also of noble Welsh lineage; she was Elen (or Helen) Ferch Tomas Ap Llywelyn of Deheubarth (the Kingdom of the Southern Britons), which was a large triangular area of South Wales for which the three points of the triangle would be St David's, Aberystwyth and Swansea.

When Glyndŵr was just eleven years of age, in the year 1370, his father died and the young 'Owain ap Gruffydd' went to study under David Hanmer, living in his home as an apprentice, as was the norm in medieval times, probably until he was eighteen – a seven-year schooling. Hanmer was a rising lawyer who went on to be a Justice of the King's Bench, and it is believed that Glyndŵr, because of events later in his life, went on to study law at the Inns of Court. In 1383 Glyndŵr married Hanmer's daughter Margaret and set up his home at Sycharth, where he was squire for Sycharth and Glyndyfrdwy. In 1384 Glyndŵr had what is believed his first taste of military service, serving under the renowned Sir Gregory Sais, another Welshman, at Berwick-on-Tweed on the Scottish borders. Sais was an experienced commander who had fought in the Hundred Years War since at least the 1360s, if not before, where he held rank and possibly led a 'free company' of local Welsh and Cheshire men, both areas known for producing excellent longbowmen; Sais last fought in France at Calais in 1386. Glyndŵr was therefore schooled under a talented lawyer and an experienced soldier; all Glyndŵr needed now was to mix with English royalty. That chance came in the summer of 1385, when he was asked to serve Richard II in Scotland under the valiant John of Gaunt. During this campaign a rare heraldic clash occurred when it was discovered that two English knights were bearing exactly the same coat of arms, a blue shield with a yellow band (a 'Bend') across it. Such was the shock that after the campaign a court case had to be heard to allow Richard II to decide whether Grosvenor or Scrope could keep their current arms while an alternative was fashioned for the loser. Owain Glyndŵr, having been on the campaign, was one of the hundreds of witnesses and it allowed him to see the full conduct of a court and the way the law worked. Scrope, after a case lasting three years, was finally allowed to keep his arms, Grosvenor replacing the yellow 'Bend' with a yellow sheaf of grain, known as a 'Garb'.

Glyndŵr continued his military career in 1387 with some naval coastal defence experience when an invasion fleet of French, Spanish and Flemish ships was defeated. Glyndŵr served under Richard FitzAlan, who was the 11th Earl of Arundel and one of the most important men in the country, but this experience was cut short when Glyndŵr's father-in-law died and as executor he had to return to North Wales. Glyndŵr then seems to have settled for the life of a lesser Marcher noble and to have attended to the needs of his estates rather than matters of state. There is mention in the writings of the bard Lolo Goch, Welsh lord and poet, that Glyndŵr's home of Sycharth was a place of freedom where it was rare to see anything under 'latch or lock'. All of these events throughout Glyndŵr's early life show a man without incident, calm, it seems, in the way that he conducted himself and his business. We hear of nothing untoward as regards his character or his deeds, so we need to find what changed and drove this man to challenge all that he had been a part of without a blemish upon his character.

It was a wise move by Glyndŵr to keep away from London and the king, for 1387 had been a sad year for Glyndŵr and it became a sad year for England as once more there was growing discontent among the nobility of England, this time with the leadership of King Richard II. Five nobles, the 'Lords Appellant' (those who literally 'appealed to the king') challenged the way that the king governed and set in motion a chain of events that split the nobility into two factions: those who supported the king and those who opposed his rule. Henry Bolingbroke and the other four Lords Appellant defeated Richard's supporters at the Battle of Radcot Bridge in Oxfordshire and this led in the following year to the 'Merciless Parliament', where Richard's loyal ministers were convicted: some were executed and others who had already fled the country were sentenced to death in their absence. With the removal of his favourites, Richard had to tread carefully but he slowly reasserted his authority and made peaceful overtures to the French who, under Charles VI, were also looking for a peaceful end to the ongoing war. In 1397 Richard felt strong enough to turn the tables on his would-be rebels and had three of the Lord Appellants arrested: two were executed and one imprisoned. Later that year, during a dispute in Parliament between Henry Bolingbroke and Thomas de Mowbray, Richard took advantage and banished them both. Richard II suddenly felt much more secure and was once more able to reward his loyal followers; some, who had been recently elevated through the peerage, benefitted from the lands confiscated from the former lords whom Richard had just removed. As rebellion broke out in Ireland just four years after the Irish chiefs had submitted to Richard, he returned there with 8,000 men to reassert his authority over the island. The main antagonist and the main threat to Richard's crown, Henry Bolingbroke, still remained at large. In 1399 Bolingbroke's father, John of Gaunt, died; Richard determined that Bolingbroke would not succeed, disinherited him and changed his banishment from ten years to life. At the same time in France, Duke Louis of Orleans took control of the kingdom when Charles VI was certified as insane and unfit to rule. Louis instantly aided Bolingbroke to return to England, with armed men to support him; Bolingbroke was by now determined to take the throne. There was a better claimant to the throne than Bolingbroke; he was a Marcher Lord, Edmund Mortimer, the Earl of March, who was descended from Edward III's second son, Lionel of Antwerp. Against this stronger claim (Bolingbroke's father John of Gaunt had only been Edward's third son), Henry Bolingbroke claimed that he was a direct male heir to the throne, not through a broken female line like Mortimer. The country was rapidly approaching another armed conflict, but in an effort to avoid bloodshed Richard II and Bolingbroke met at Conwy, where Richard II had landed on his return from Ireland, in order to discuss their differences. What happened next is not totally clear but Richard was 'persuaded' to give up the Crown in favour of Bolingbroke, who was crowned as King Henry IV on 13 October 1399. Richard was removed from public life and was incarcerated in Pontefract Castle, where he died sometime in February 1400, probably of starvation so that there would be no marks upon the body, so that it could be seen that he had not been 'murdered' by someone's hand.

The usurping of the crown by Henry Bolingbroke, even prior to the knowledge that Richard was dead, was a development that some of England's nobility were far from happy with, so Henry IV's position was not universally accepted. Many Welsh people, for the first time, found themselves having to choose which English monarch to support and many felt that Richard II was their king. Still before the death of Richard, the first serious signs of rebellion occurred in Chester on 10 January 1400, when people rioted after the captain of Richard's personal archers, a Piers Legh, was publicly executed. When news eventually leaked out over the spring of 1400 that Richard II was dead, the atmosphere of tension along the Welsh–English border increased. The difference between these two kings is aptly illustrated by the issue that led Glyndŵr to choose sides as the country slipped closer towards civil war. Baron Grey of Ruthin and Owain Glyndŵr were neighbours and had long been so; equally long was Grey's reputation for being anti-Welsh. For some years there had been a dispute between these two lords over a piece of land. The matter had been set before King Richard II who, upon an examination of the facts, found in favour of Glyndŵr, who was convinced that the matter was closed. However, Grey was a close friend of Henry IV; Grey made a fresh appeal over the parcel of land and Henry IV found in favour of him. Glyndŵr himself now appealed, but the appeal was rejected without a hearing even being granted. It seemed to the law-abiding and God-fearing Glyndŵr that the harsh 'English' laws that were already designed to belittle the Welsh people were now pushed beyond fairness: there was no equality between a Welshman and Englishman under Henry's law. Grey took matters further and deliberately withheld a summons from Henry IV to Glyndŵr to provide troops for a campaign against Scotland; with no knowledge of the summons, Glyndŵr could not supply the troops requested, a summons he would have happily complied with had he have known about it for he was honour-bound to do so at the king's behest. By not supplying troops to Henry IV, the king considered the matter an act of treason, declaring Glyndŵr a traitor and that his lands were forfeit to the Crown. Henry IV, eager to stoke the fire already smouldering in his friend's belly, ordered Grey to deal with Glyndŵr himself. Grey seized the opportunity given him and decided to use force to secure Glyndŵr's arrest, going, it is stated, against promises made to the king to act with good grace. Glyndŵr had been set up and betrayed by the very system he had aspired to and worked within. He now had a simple choice, like so many Welshmen before him, either to stay and be taken and tried before what would be a biased court, and face execution as a traitor, or flee and fight.

Rebellion

On 16 September 1400, Glyndŵr was proclaimed Prince of Wales by the Dean of St Asaph in front of a small band of loyal followers, many from his own family and household; these included his eldest son, brothers and his brothers-in-law. The news of the rebellion spread much quicker than the news of Richard II's death had and it reached Glyndŵr's cousins the Tudors, who lived on Anglesey, both of whom had been captains of Welsh archer units in Richard II's armies. As the tide of rebellion rose, Glyndŵr rose with it and at the head of a small army they advanced in an arc, moving north from 17 September and then south-east before finally turning south. Ruthin was their first target and they quickly destroyed the town, Glyndŵr extracting sweet revenge for the falsehoods that Grey had laid upon him such a short time before. They then moved on to swiftly lay waste to Denbigh, Rhuddlan, Flint, Hawarden and Holt before moving on to completely destroy Oswestry on 22 September; just two days later the Welsh host had already sacked Welshpool and were making their return to the mountains to the west to complete their circle. However, they were unaware that they were being tracked by Hugh Burnell and a force of mounted men gathered from shire levies of Shropshire and Herefordshire, men loyal to the new king. On the second day after Oswestry, Burnell caught up with the fleeing raiders somewhere along the River Vyrnwy valley.

24 September 1400 Vyrnwy – Powys

This encounter is a true lost battlesite and although the title and date are known, the exact site of the encounter is not and there are several locations that

Owain Glyndŵr's motte and bailey home at Glyndyffrey.

A peacock guards the entrance to the ruins of Ruthin Castle, the original home of Grey, whose actions led to Glyndŵr's rebellion. The restored castle is now a hotel.

Alongside the River Vyrnwy, between Llansantffraid and Lanymynech, is not a place Glyndŵr would have let himself get caught.

are equally plausible along the length of the Vyrnwy Valley. The facts are brief but they do allow the researcher to extract an interpretation of what actually took place. Firstly, we need to consider Glyndŵr's position; he had marched in a curving arc which had taken in all of the English settlements, taking every piece of plunder his men could carry, and both his force and their equipment and wealth had grown on route. It is believed that the size of his force by 24 September had grown to around 400 men and all must have been mounted, both to move as fast as they had from town to town and to be capable of taking with them all of the plunder that they had been collecting; however, given their triumphant campaign thus far there would have been no shortage of horses from so many successful raids. The key thing to notice is that Glyndŵr had been working in a circle that was centred upon his own lands and he always kept his men within a day's riding of the mountains, which had so often been the sanctuary for fleeing Welshmen. In the history of the Welsh princes, they had always been able to disappear into the mountains and hide from their English pursuers, sometimes for years on end. There are caves in many of the mountain ranges of Wales, some natural and some old metal ore workings, and these were hidden to most people and seemingly known only to those that needed to protect their royal kin. Glyndŵr could not afford to stand still after he had burnt a town; he knew that all the available English forces would be out looking for him and his men and trying to prevent his next raid. Having been at Oswestry on 22 September, he would have been at Welshpool on the 23rd, leaving on the evening of the 23rd or the morning of the 24th. Historians, because of its title of 'Vyrnwy', have set the battle north of Welshpool, on the route back to Oswestry, but this would not make sense for the following two reasons. Firstly, to return towards a ransacked town just a couple of days after causing its ruin was to invite an encounter with an English force. Secondly, to march north, then west along the Vyrnwy River would not have been to any advantage. There is a perfectly good direct route north-west, which leads via Dolanog, where the River Vyrnwy could be met and then crossed to join a quicker and drier route up and over the hill of Yr Allt Boeth before descending into the main Vyrnwy Valley and the modern village of Llanwddyn. Much of the River Vyrnwy valley, between Llanwddyn and Dolanog, is narrow and winding with steep sides; there are few paths and the ground is far from suitable for either horses or an ambush. By taking the straight road to the Berwyns, Glyndŵr would not have spent long by the River Vyrnwy until he came to the modern village of Llanwddyn at the bottom of the main headwater's valley. This was so that he could come back as quickly as possible to his own lands and thereby keep his forces as far as possible from both Shrewsbury and Chester, where King Henry would most likely to have been massing his troops for an invasion into North or Mid Wales.

Let us now consider Burnell's position: like Glyndŵr, he must have had a mounted force that was able to move quickly in response to picking up the trail

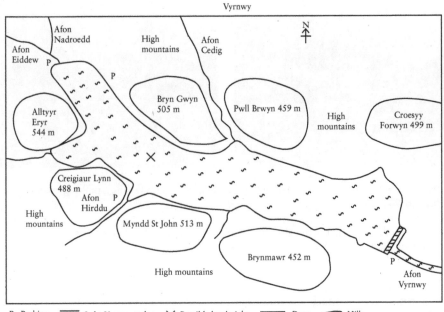

P Parking   ⌣⌣ Lake Vyrnwy today   ✕ Possible battlesight   ◤◤◤ Dam   ⬭ Hills

left by the passage of Glyndŵr's force. Having once located the rebels, Burnell would be looking to intercept them as quickly as possible, but not at danger to himself. Burnell would have also have wanted the glory of catching the rebel leader and gaining for himself if not a sizeable monetary reward then some rapid military advancement in recognition of his achievement.

If Glyndŵr knew that Burnell was following him then the Welsh would have laid an ambush for the English posse. If both armies were continually advancing then the only way that Burnell could attack the Welsh was by ambushing them when they were resting at the end of the day before night and the mountain mists drew in; give the terrain, there was no way he could pass Glyndŵr, who was taking the most direct route. Glyndŵr's men had not properly stopped for a rest for some seven days, as they raced on their rampage through the borderlands. Glyndŵr knew that he needed to get to a safe place, where they could distribute the plunder they had taken and make plans for the next rendezvous before the men could vanish back over the mountains to their homes, ready for the next campaign the following spring. It was late September already and the autumn rains would make campaigning difficult for anyone, but especially the English. The Welsh had achieved a great deal in a short space of time but their attacks were now over for a while; it was now time for the Welsh to hide and to harry the enemy as the English would surely come looking for them, especially for Glyndŵr, who would by now have a hefty price upon his head.

Above left: Numerous valleys converged in the original Vyrnwy Valley, making escape easier for hunted Welshmen.

Above right: Lake Vyrnwy; the drowned village of Llanwddyn lies below along with the likely site of the Battle of Vyrnwy.

The reference is made to the modern village of Llanwddyn because the original village, and with it the main head waters of the River Vyrnwy, are lost for all time with no chance of any on-the-ground research. All the main rivers that still feed the River Vyrnwy now feed the river via a large lake some 5 miles long. The original village of Llanwddyn lies 25 metres below Lake Vyrnwy, the lake having been formed when a dam was constructed in the 1880s to supply water to the fast growing city of Liverpool. However, the author has seen plans of the valley before the dam was constructed and believes that the events of 24 September can be pieced together as follows. After the attack on Welshpool, Glyndŵr and his men would have marched north-west, passing close to the Moydog valley, where Madog's army had been caught and slaughtered just over 100 years earlier. Glyndŵr would have then crossed the River Banwy, heading towards Dolanog and the Berwyn Mountains, and reached the upper Vyrnwy Valley late in the day. The Vyrnwy valley was partly glaciated, partly river cut, and along the first 5 miles of its length five short rivers merge to create the mightier river. This sheltered valley would have been the first place where the Welsh army would have felt comfortable enough to have relaxed, so far into the mountains, so close now to home and so well away from the prying English eyes that were searching for them. For the first time in his career Glyndŵr made a mistake; he did not set a guard, or if he did, it was insufficient for the task in hand. Perhaps Glyndŵr and his men were flushed with success and ale or both and felt so close to their homes that they felt free from the chance of discovery. For whatever reason, their guard was down, and at dawn the next morning, their camp was attacked. In the ensuing panic some men from both sides were killed, but clearly things did not go Burnell's way. Firstly, Glyndŵr and some of his men clearly escaped – Glyndŵr still had a mounted force of several hundred men in the spring of 1401. Secondly, Burnell had insufficient men to pursue the rebels any further so he must have lost casualties himself. Importantly for Burnell, he knew where the rebels had gone and he had news to impart when he reached the safety of Shrewsbury. Glyndŵr had now suffered his first setback and as he made his way back through the mountains, having completed his circle of destruction across the whole of north-east and east Wales, he was no doubt instilling in himself that he would not make the same mistake again.

The stunning views around Lake Vyrnwy make it worth a visit at any time of the year; as the whole site is a nature reserve, there are many different activities to be enjoyed, including canoeing. For anyone following the possible sites of the battle, there are numerous places to park a vehicle all the way around the lake and also below the dam itself, which is a classic piece of Victorian engineering. There are bikes to hire locally and there are many walks to be enjoyed, including some to waterfalls; the varied shape of the lake makes the whole valley beautiful from all angles.

Glyndŵr was lucky that he retreated when he did, for when Burnell arrived back in Shrewsbury on 26 September Henry IV was already there with a force gathered from twenty shires. Henry IV had been marching on Scotland, but on hearing of Glyndŵr's blistering campaign he turned south-west and marched to Shrewsbury, where he heard Burnell's news of his slender victory on the edge of the mountains. Henry IV led his army into North Wales, determined to stamp out the rebellion, though it is unclear what punishments he meted out in revenge; certainly, some Welsh nobles made their peace and bowed to the king. Although the route he took is not clear, it seems that his army was harassed constantly by both bad weather and persistent attacks from small bands of Welsh guerrillas. On 15 October, Henry IV returned empty-handed to Shrewsbury Castle, and

Above left: The head of Lake Vyrnwy, at the heart of the Berwyn Mountains.

Above right: Afon Eiddew, one of the main rivers that fed the valley and that now feeds the lake.

with the winter approaching the king knew that the campaigning season was over for the year, so he started planning the spring offensive for 1401 and gave command to Henry Percy, more commonly known as Hotspur, who was the legendary son of the Earl of Northumberland. The Percy family were the richest and most landed gentry in England and Hotspur's brief from his king was simple: bring Wales into line. Somehow the news of Glyndŵr's success spread across Wales and while Hotspur was heading south, rebellion was breaking out all over the Principality from Conwy to Cardiff and from Carmarthen to Chester; reports came in of bandits attacking any English settlements, and from people that were caught and tortured there was news of a new rallying call – 'Plant Owain', the children of Owain. The price on Owain Glyndŵr's head continued to rise. Hotspur's plan was to be conciliatory to the followers of the revolt but hard on the leaders and so in March 1401 he issued an amnesty to everyone except Glyndŵr and his two Tudor cousins; to a degree, the policy worked, for people began to pay their taxes and the attacks on English places diminished. Hotspur must have felt that everything was starting to go his way; that was, until the two Tudor brothers tricked their way into Conwy Castle on 1 April and captured the fortress from the English garrison. With forty men and provisions, they could hold out against a siege and although Hotspur had over 400 men, he knew such a siege would be long and difficult. In earnest, and in order to allow him to proceed with his campaign, Hotspur granted the Tudors their pardon. All Hotspur had to do now was catch their leader!

June 1401 Hyddgen – Ceredigion

As Hotspur's forces scoured the Welsh countryside looking for Glyndŵr, the famous general reported two skirmishes with the Welsh prince, one at a place recorded simply as 'M'. Whether these encounters were with Glyndŵr or not, there are no contemporary chroniclers to confirm those events or what followed at Hyddgen. What is clear is that whatever was happening in 1401 made Glyndŵr into a symbol of national unity; for the first and only time everyone got behind one man, one Prince of Wales. Rich and poor, learned and ignorant, men from every single corner of Wales were united; something had to have happened to spark that unity, because it was something that had never been there before. In June 1401 Glyndŵr and his still small number of men, perhaps between 200 and 400, were hiding in the high hills of central Wales, close to Plynlimon. Somehow, Glyndŵr's hiding place was located by a band of Flemings; most of the Flemings in Wales were settled along the southern coastal area, so they were a long way from their homes or garrison, and the name of their leader is unknown. One can only assume that these were a band of mercenaries, probably led by a mercenary captain who had been given free reign, possibly by Henry IV himself, to seek out the Welsh leader in his heartland. The Flemings would have been coming from the south, which fits with Hotspur attacking from the north, and the recorded accounts, although they are more than 100 years later, all confirm that the Flemings had 1,500 men.

Glyndŵr was a man of some military experience before the rebellion started, and even more so after nine months on campaign, and it is unlikely that he would have hidden both of his forces in one place. It is far more likely that he had split his force into two groups, with around 200 in each, and hidden them at different locations at either end of the mountains that rise through central Wales, one watching the roads south, the other the roads north. By the very nature of their size and structure, these small units of men were far more versatile than an army of thousands, which required housing and feeding every day. Glyndŵr's men could move easily across routes too high for normal armies and wagons to traverse and at night they could shelter in caves and in hides built from rough stone and hidden with fresh foliage so that unless someone was on top of it, no-one would even know there was anything there. This is possibly one reason why Hotspur and other English reports stated that Glyndŵr was in two separate places at the same time; maybe he had moved so quickly across the mountain paths that it did appear as if he had been in both places almost at the same time. However, there is a second possibility: it was not impossible for Glyndŵr to have someone impersonate him. His brother Tudor was almost identical to Owain, save for a wart that Owain had above one eyebrow; so by wearing similar livery, it was possible to create the illusion of being in two places at the same time. This also meant that Glyndŵr could keep the morale of his men high while at the same time spreading confusion among the English as to where he actually was. Some medieval kings in battle

Above left: Hyddgen looking south, the most likely way that the Flemings would have approached.

Above right: Hyddgen is a desolate, remote valley; ruined walls are choked in vegetation.

deliberately had men dressed in similar livery to confuse the opposition army as to who the real king was, a tactic employed by Henry IV himself at the Battle of Shrewsbury in 1403. This simple duplicity led some of Glyndŵr's enemies to believe him capable of performing magic by being able to be in two places at one time. There is nothing more wonderful for a desperate people than to believe that your leader, who is already charismatic, has supernatural powers. What happened next at Hyddgen was far from supernatural, though it would seem that natural powers may well have intervened.

The upland valley of Hyddgen is remote even today and the battlesite itself is to be found after a 3-mile walk, having parked at the end of the road after a 4-mile drive along a good C class road. The valley is split by two small rivers, which feed a constructed reservoir named Nant-y-Moch, and so fresh water would not have been a problem for a small army with stolen cattle, and no doubt wild deer and game surviving in the hills would have been caught and eaten. Hyddgen is just over 20 miles from Aberystwyth, but with half of that elevated it would have been at least a day's foot march from the coastal town. We have no definite information as the composition of either force. Glyndŵr's men almost certainly had ponies or horses, otherwise they could not strike quickly and escape, but none are mentioned. It was similar for the Flemings, but it is difficult to see how these mercenaries would have successfully located Glyndŵr without horses to carry the supplies they would have needed when searching remote uplands. It is not hard to work out how Glyndŵr's men would be armed; after their recent ransacking of a host of towns, they would be armed with the best of every weapon they had found, as well as some pieces of armour, and given the idle winter months, they would have been busy creating stocks of arrows and javelins ready for ambushes; no doubt many of their surplus

Above left: Tussocks of grass and deep, slimy peat pools cover the Hyddgen Valley, making walking off the path treacherous.

Above right: Alan checking the map for the site of the Glyndŵr stones.

Hyddgen

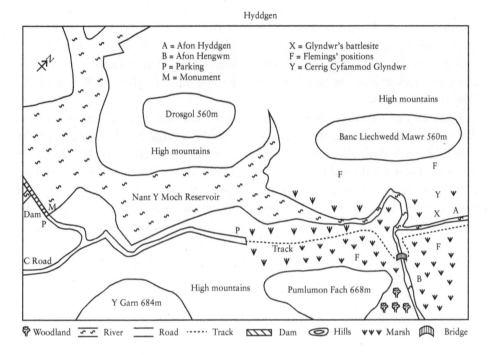

A = Afon Hyddgen
B = Afon Hengwm
P = Parking
M = Monument

X = Glyndwr's battlesite
F = Flemings' positions
Y = Cerrig Cyfammod Glyndwr

High mountains

Drosgol 560m

Banc Liechwedd Mawr 560m

High mountains

High mountains

Nant Y Moch Reservoir

Dam

Track

High mountains

Pumlumon Fach 668m

Y Garn 684m

🌳 Woodland 〰️ River ═══ Road ⋯⋯ Track ⬛⬛ Dam 🌀 Hills ▼▼▼ Marsh 🌉 Bridge

weapons were hidden in secret caches for future use. It is more difficult to determine how the Flemings were armed in this campaign, as they, when hired as mercenaries through the medieval period, were always spearmen so they may not have had any missile-armed men with them; perhaps they thought that their overwhelming numbers would be sufficient. The earliest account of the action comes from Gruffyd Hiraethog, who was a sixteenth-century bard, so he may have had handed down to him orally the stories surrounding Glyndŵr. Hiraethog states that the Flemings came to Hyddgant Mountain 'with the intention to seize Owain' and that 'no sooner did the English troops turn their backs, than 200 were slain' (Cassel's). Two later versions say that Glyndŵr, finding himself surrounded, fought his way out. A key thing to mention at this point is the terrain; even in hiking boots and with walking poles, any of the ground, once off a clear track, is difficult to move over. Much of the valley is a bog interspersed with outcrops of rock, so solid ground one minute quickly becomes an oozing pool the next; anyone visiting the valley should be properly attired. Some of the rocky outcrops could provide shelter with some form of wattled screen, which would be almost undetectable until one was right on it. There are derelict dry stone walled cottages, the ruins of which are now penetrated by trees, whose age is impossible to determine. The only sounds come from two sources: the almost constant chatter of thousands of birds, hidden from view save for the odd flash of a coloured wing, and from the occasional Royal Air Force fighters as pairs of them hurtle overhead with a sound like crackling thunder and a roar that for a few seconds silences the wild birds. It seems from the facts that Glyndŵr was clearly surrounded and outnumbered, but that he, and it seems most of his men, escaped with hardly any casualties among them; meanwhile, the Flemings, fighting on behalf of the English, lost 200 men.

There can be several explanations for this and some depend on the time of day that the battle was fought. The valley is like a large bowl and perhaps the Flemings, in surrounding the Welshmen, spread themselves too thinly along the surrounding hills and this allowed Glyndŵr's men, by forming a close-knit group, to charge through the cordon and escape; Glyndŵr's men would have known the solid ground, whereas the newly arrived Flemings would be advancing over difficult terrain where their spears would have been an aid to keeping on their feet, but not if they were attempting to fight. It certainly seems that the Flemings had few missile men, because as they had clearly surrounded the Welsh, if they had shot their crossbows into the closely knit group ahead of them and then closed in on the remainder, the Welsh would surely have been defeated. The other two key factors are linked: the time of day and the weather. So high up in the mountains, even in summer, as this battle was recorded as being fought in June, a cold night and a warm morning sun can lead to a thick morning mist. A wet day can lead to the clouds being so low at any time of the day that the whole landscape vanishes in the clinging wetness of the cloud. It is most likely that a combination of these conspired to cheat the Flemings of their prize and allow Glyndŵr to escape. If the normal process of a dawn ambush was planned then this would have also aided Glyndŵr, as his men would have been rested and the dawn in the summer is the most likely time for mist or fog to form almost instantaneously. According to all the sources, Glyndŵr succeeded in not only escaping but in killing 200 Flemings in the process, which means that every man of his struck down an enemy as they made their escape. For this to happen, it would seem most likely that Glyndŵr waited for exactly the right time, when all the elements were in his favour, to make his escape attempt, in order to both break the cordon and actually escape without being caught in the inevitable pursuit. Knowing the terrain when you are being slowly surrounded on all sides by an ever shrinking cordon is vital; using that knowledge just as the climate creates a mist from nowhere is genius and one can imagine the startled faces, as the Flemings, surrounding an area of around a square mile, suddenly see the whole landscape vanish before them followed by a host of muffled screams and cries which break the silence. There are some sources that state Glyndŵr succeeded in capturing the rest of the force, but this is extremely unlikely when the Flemings outnumbered the Welsh by a ratio of at least seven to one. Glyndŵr had escaped capture and inflicted his first defeat on a trained, if somewhat disorganised, enemy who should have done much better than they did. The clear winner overall was Glyndŵr, not because his victory demoralised the English but because it motivated the Welsh. The natives of Wales, who had been restless for so long without a leader, now believed in Glyndŵr and the rebellion spread.

There are a few places available to park close to and just past the reservoir, and the monument to the battle, erected in July 1977 to Glyndŵr's victory, can be found alongside the Nant-y-Moch reservoir. This monument is actually 3 miles short of the actual battlesite and a full visit requires a walk along designated paths and across the rivers to the place where the battle is commemorated by a large white stone in the west of the valley. According to some of the sources for the battle, it seems that there were two stones there originally, but only one was clearly visible when the author visited the valley in the spring of 2014. The walk is typical of an upland valley and although the paths for the most part are easy to discern, there are places that should be avoided to bypass deep pools and to cross the river. There are bridges and stepping stones to cross the rivers but off the paths and tracks the basic ground is very uneven, with rock outcrops, small pits and areas of marsh and bog; throughout this walk, extra care should be taken when crossing these natural obstacles.

King Henry IV, incensed at the failure of the Flemings to do his 'dirty work' for him, now once more called in the levies from many counties and gathered two forces at the Marcher centres of Hereford and Shrewsbury. While the king was combining his force into one large army at Worcester; meanwhile Glyndŵr once more attacked in the Welsh Borders. He completely destroyed the town of Montgomery and the castle before going on to again sack and burn Welshpool. He then turned south, attacking and looting many places including Hay-on-Wye, Bishop's Castle and Grosmont before returning into Mid Wales. With reports of Glyndŵr's attacks coming in from all over the Principality, the king decided to choose a different route into Wales but the result would be the same. Henry IV marched in a great circle via Brecon, Llandovery, Carmarthen,

One of the rocky outcrops making natural walls on the side of the Hyddgen valley.

The Hyddgen valley looking north; Cerrig Cyfammod Glyndŵr is the white stone mid-centre, left.

Aberystwyth and Builth Wells, leaving stronger garrisons at every town and castle he visited before he departed. Despite all of these endeavours and a change of route in the hope of capturing Glyndŵr unawares, he still did not succeed in even catching a sight of his enemy. Henry IV was furious by the time he reached Strata Florida Abbey, the home to so many graves and remains of earlier Welsh princes. Henry IV feared that Owain Glyndŵr, like the other Welsh princes before him, was being aided by the Church, some of whom were loyal to their Welsh kin. There is little wonder that some of the monasteries chose to aid the Welsh princes, given Henry IV's attitude and that of the English knights. After two days of drinking, Henry allowed his army to attack the abbey and the monks, destroying some of the abbey's structure, stealing the silver plate and even executing some of the monks for collaborating with the rebels; even groups of children were taken off in chains. The English were now some 70 miles from their nearest supply bases in Ludlow or Hereford and the further the king's army had advanced, the more opportunity the Welsh rebels had to get behind them and attack their supply convoys. Eventually, having drawn another blank in his quest for Glyndŵr, Henry IV ordered a return to England, where en route they would again feel the bite of the Welsh autumn weather; gales and torrential rain hampered their march, followed by flooding in which some of the army were lost before they reached the safety of Ludlow.

The year had been a successful one for Glyndŵr and ended with another success, when he held the English at the inconclusive Battle of Tuthill, just outside Caernarfon Castle, on 2 November 1401. The full details of the battle are not known but it seems that an English army, possibly under Hotspur, may have been attempting to break the Welsh siege of Caernarfon Castle. The battle is best remembered in Welsh legend for one simple but remarkable thing: Glyndŵr chose to fly a standard of a golden dragon on a white background, the traditional standard that Uther Pendragon had flown when the first Britons had fought the

Saxons to a standstill almost 1,000 years before and which had been passed on to Arthur, his son. This rallying call was Glyndŵr's final act of the year, calling on more Welshmen to rise and to free Wales from its oppressors. There are reports that 300 Welshmen died in the battle but no specific details of how these losses came about or what the English losses were. To Glyndŵr and his men it did not matter whether the weather was fair or foul and the Welsh carried on their incessant attacks on any vulnerable English troops or supply convoys.

The year 1402 started just as promisingly as 1401 had ended for Glyndŵr, as in January he attacked the land of his long-time enemy Grey of Ruthin, stealing many of his cattle; Glyndŵr was careful not to attack any property other than that belonging to Grey. This latest outrage added to the widespread concern among Henry IV's inner court circle that the revolt was now becoming a serious threat to the stability of the realm and that England herself could become embroiled in a war if the supporters of Richard II flocked to Glyndŵr's banner, especially in Cheshire, which had always been loyal to Richard II and was a key garrison for any invasion into North Wales. In North Wales, Hotspur was clearly making as little progress as the king had done through Powys and he believed that all the harsh laws were doing was driving support into Glyndŵr's ranks. The king and his councillors would have none of that kind of argument and, probably in response to the final insult of Grey's capture, Henry IV introduced a draconian set of rules known as the Penal Laws of 1402, which were actually three separate acts, passed by the English Parliament in early 1402 under the titles of the Wales Act, the Wales and Welshmen Act and the Welshmen Act. In total, these laws banned the Welsh people from: obtaining senior public office; bearing arms; defending a castle; defending their own house; buying property in English towns; and assembling in public. There were strict conditions, almost like a curfew, on when the Welsh people could be out during the evening and even the education of Welsh children was restricted. Worse still for the people who lived on the borders, Englishmen who married Welsh women also came under these laws and the two races could no longer intermarry. Such basic infringements on public life meant that no markets could be held for trade as this was an assembly and men could not carry a sword to defend themselves against any eventuality; these acts were designed to destroy daily life for the Welsh nation. These laws were the final straw for all Welshmen; the king had gone way too far and those that had been undecided about the rebellion now joined Glyndŵr's army in droves.

22 June 1402 Pilleth (Bryn Glas) – Powys

Glyndŵr himself had raised the spectre of political mythology into his leadership by the unfurling of the ancient banner; he was already thought of as some sort of warlock by his enemies, but his speed of movement while on campaign came from a mastery of the terrain, not from magic. In March 1402 a great comet was seen in the sky (not Halley's as it was well away from the Earth at this time on its repeating cycle), which the Welsh people took to be a sign that Glyndŵr would triumph; the other two great comet sightings had been in the year 0 when Christ was born, and when Uther and Arthur had fought and defeated the Saxons in the early sixth century (see Mount Badon). In April, Glyndŵr launched a direct assault on Grey's castle at Ruthin, where the noble had a considerable retinue of his own and some extra royal troops to strengthen the garrison; the assault was a ruse and seeing the Welsh skirmishers reluctant to retreat, Grey gathered all of his men together and charged the loitering Welshmen, who then fled into the nearby hills; Grey and his army followed, straight into the trap. It was a massacre: only seven of Grey's knights survived, all the rest were killed and Glyndŵr had complete revenge; the Welsh leader took Grey with him into hiding and demanded a ransom from King Henry IV for his friend's life. The victory at Ruthin merely added to the king's determination to crush the Welsh once and for all, and during the spring of 1402 Hotspur returned to North Wales to oversee a strengthening of all royal castles for the monarch.

Glyndŵr, however, had switched his base and was now active in Mid Wales and he attacked several castles belonging to Edmund Mortimer, the Earl of March. Mortimer was not prepared to tolerate these losses and called for the local nobility to rally their levies and to assemble at Ludlow. Once the army was mustered, Mortimer marched from Ludlow with an army of knights and their retainers, probably some 500 strong in cavalry; with them were 1,000 archers and 1,000 spearmen or billmen as well. The one strange thing which no-one had spotted (as Mortimer's army was being assembled in the castle) is that when the nobles had called in their levies from their own lands, the town of Ludlow had suddenly become inundated with lots of Welsh archers, each noble seeming to assume that they belonged to some other lord or knight. Owain Glyndŵr had shown himself to be a master tactician but in the Pilleth campaign he pulled off one of the most perfect infiltrations in the history of warfare; his Welsh archers had been recruited, armed, fed and paid so that they could march with the English into another Welsh trap. Glyndŵr marched to Pilleth, prayed at the church and then laid his plans, for he knew by the use of his spies that Mortimer was on the march west into Wales. As ever, the Welsh army would have consisted of a mixture of spearmen and bowmen, but also, given the recent victory at Ruthin, Glyndŵr's men would have had more armour and also better basic equipment than at any time since the rebellion had begun. This meant that Glyndŵr's personal retinue, his own men at arms, would have been getting stronger too so that the army, as it grew, would be able to take on stronger English forces that were sent against them, and so it proved at Pilleth.

Glyndŵr had somewhere between 1,200 and 1,500 men, as he seems to have gathered all of his mobile raiding forces together in the centre of Wales for this encounter. Most of the Welsh raiding parties seem to have been recorded at around 400 men, so allowing for those that were continually flocking to his cause Glyndŵr may well have had 1,500 men. In addition, he had several hundred archers masquerading as part of Mortimer's force on the way to him. With plenty of time to deploy, Glyndŵr chose the top of the steep slope of Bryn Glas at Pilleth and it can still be seen today as a perfect site to fight a defensive battle; in fact, so steep is the hillside that one might question the stupidity of anyone attacking up it! All of his armoured men were placed in the centre of his line, with his main units of archers on either side; the church was well below the Welshmen, to the front left of Glyndŵr's line. Behind the church was a deep, stream-cut valley, densely wooded, a few hundred yards on the left side as Glyndŵr looked down the Bryn Glas slope; in this camouflaged gulley, all of the Welsh skirmishers, spearmen and javelinmen hid. The other key point about Glyndŵr's site was that both he and all of his men in their three locations could see the whole of Mortimer's army as it slowly marched up the valley towards them. Glyndŵr wisely kept most of his men concealed just behind the crest, invisible to the English host approaching the site.

When Mortimer's balanced army arrived at the foot of the hill, Glyndŵr sent down the slope a few hundred lightly clad archers in order to goad the English into attacking; these archers shot at the English men at arms as they prepared to attack. As the bowmen shot at the English, Glyndŵr and some more of his men stepped over the crest at the top of the hill and began to goad the English below. The nobles of Mortimer's army were so fixated on catching the rebel leader who now plainly stood high above them on the hill that the heavily armoured

Above left: Bryn Glas or Pilleth Hill seen from Mortimer's position in the valley. The trees mark the mass grave of the fallen.

Above right: Pilleth, looking down on the vale where Glyndŵr's archers baited Mortimer's knights.

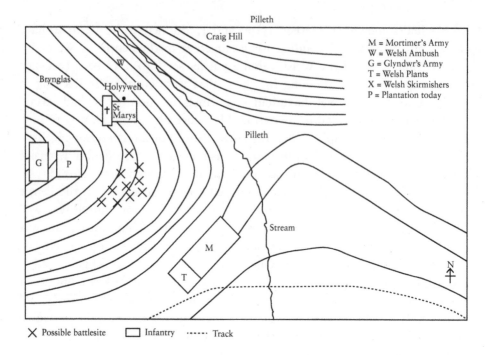

Pilleth

Craig Hill

M = Mortimer's Army
W = Welsh Ambush
G = Glyndŵr's Army
T = Welsh Plants
X = Welsh Skirmishers
P = Plantation today

Brynglas

Holyywell

W

St Marys

Pilleth

G   P

Stream

M

T

N

X Possible battlesite   ☐ Infantry   ······ Track

English started scrambling up the steep slope to get at the now fleeing bowmen and the chanting Welsh above. The slope of Bryn Glas is a hard hike in light clothing; in armour, the men would have been hard pressed to make it without pausing for breath, and so it proved. The hill is so steep that neither side could have used any mounted men; as the English knights were dismounted for their assault uphill, no doubt Glyndŵr's were too, ready for the charge down it. On the left flank of his army, Mortimer placed the Welsh archers; on his right he placed his own archers together with the English archer levies; the spearmen he placed behind his knights, who having paused once for breath began to advance again. Both armies would have shot their arrows at each other as the armies came too close to each other, the Welsh archers on the English left flank presumably shooting too wide or too low to cause casualties among their kith and kin. The English could not have charged; they were still only advancing up the steep slope when the Welsh did charge. At the same time as the whole Welsh line came crashing into the English troops, the Welsh archers on their left flank would have swivelled ninety degrees to the right and shot a murderous volley at close range into the flank of the English spearmen and knights. With the English line fully engaged from the impact of the crashing charge down the slope, Glyndŵr's hidden men emerged to take the English army in the right flank. Mortimer's army was now being attacked from three sides and and the tactics that Glyndŵr employed made up for the disparity in numbers of around 600 men, maybe more. The Welsh annihilated the English army to the extent that some knights and their entire male families present were wiped out; just two nobles, Mortimer and Clanvowe, were taken prisoner. There has always been talk of atrocities performed after the battle on the English corpses. If this is true, the women, while stripping the bodies of every useful item upon it, took the time to cut off all of the penises and insert them into the mouth of each body; the noses were also cut off and inserted between the buttocks of the same corpse. Thomas Capgrave, a chronicler at the time of the battle, records the event and Shakespeare mentions it in Westmorland's speech in Act 1 Scene 1 of *King Henry IV Part II*: 'Upon whose corpse there was much misuse, such beastly shameless transformation, by those Welshwomen done, as may not be without shame retold or spoke of.' The atrocities are not easy to understand from today's standpoint; to the Welsh women, who had been raped both physically and mentally by the English in the past, it was extracted revenge.

The basic site of the hill today has changed a little since the battle but the slope is still steep and it is covered with bracken and scrub. There is a small plantation of Wellingtonia trees halfway up the slope and this marks the main area of the mass grave into which most of the bodies went after the battle; very few were collected by their families after the carnage of a truly bloody day for the English army.

There is now a small group of houses at the base of the hill itself, but there is a small car park for visitors to the site and St Mary's Church has a small museum inside. A small spring next to the church still trickles into a holy well from which the soldiers would have drunk upon the day.

As with Grey, Glyndŵr offered King Henry IV the chance to pay for Mortimer's life but the king refused; he was prepared to pay up for his friend Grey, but not for Mortimer. This is because Mortimer, by direct lineage, had a better claim to the throne than Henry IV himself. With Glyndŵr's fame spreading, French and Breton mercenaries now started to join the Welsh army

The church of St Mary at Pilleth.

The hidden valley behind Pilleth church from where the Welsh attacked Mortimer's right flank.

and French ships began attacking English ships; with the Hundred Years War still ongoing, the French were happy to start a war on a third front; with Scotland already threatening the north and now Wales to the west, Henry simply did not have enough resources to fight all three wars and the French hoped it would help to get the English to concede in France and bring the long war to an end.

Henry IV now gathered his third great army and this time decided North Wales would be circumnavigated in the search for Glyndŵr, so in August the king and his army headed into Wales. The king found nothing, and in his fury his army destroyed Llanrwst, killing everyone they could find and stealing everything they could carry or drive before them. On the return journey, even the king must have begun to question whether Glyndŵr was a magician, for it snowed in September and then it rained like it would never stop; once more, the royal army was hit by floods and found the rivers almost impossible to cross, but in September good news at last reached the king, but not from Wales.

At the battle of Homildon Hill, Hotspur had won a resounding victory over the Scots with the capture of over 100 nobles, thirty of whom were French, the rest of Scottish lineage; this crushing victory had ended one of Henry IV's three wars in a day and it had not only freed up English troops for Wales but it had removed a potential ally for Glyndŵr as well. As the campaigning season was over for another year, matters at court turned to the ransoms that Glyndŵr was demanding. Clanvowe was released and so was Grey, for £6,000, but there was still a £4,000 balance to be paid so Grey's son had to replace him in captivity. Hotspur and a few other nobles asked for the money to be paid so that Mortimer could be freed, but the king refused and added insult to injury by taking all of Hotspur's noble prisoners for himself and pocketing all of the ransom money; there were no thanks or reward for Hotspur for bringing the Scots to their knees! Instead, in November 1402, Hotspur was sent back to

Wales to bolster defences and to negotiate with or capture Glyndŵr. Hotspur did negotiate and it is most likely that Mortimer was also present, for shortly after the negotiations and seeing the situation at Henry IV's court, Mortimer changed sides and, in an accord with Glyndŵr, married Catrin, one of Glyndŵr's daughters; it is said there was genuine affection between them. Mortimer then wrote to all of his friends and neighbours, telling them of his reason for siding with Glyndŵr, which included the fact that Richard II had been the rightful king, and that if Richard was dead, Mortimer himself was next in line. He also agreed that Glyndŵr should be prince of his own Kingdom of Wales. No doubt some sympathised and joined Mortimer, but others faithful to the Lancastrians would side with King Henry IV.

The year of 1403 opened with a succession of campaigns across Wales as Glyndŵr swept across the southern half of the country and everywhere people flocked to his call; tens of castles (including Cardiff and Carmarthen) and manors either fell to attack or sided with the Welsh cause. Students from universities across the land left their studies and returned home to join the uprising, and even Welsh workers in towns and cities well away from Wales gave up their posts and made their way home; Welsh archers left their employ in English retinues to fight for freedom. It was a mass exodus to the west. Everything was going Glyndŵr's way until the young Prince Henry of Monmouth joined his father the king in preparing for war. Prince Henry, who was just shy of being sixteen, was an experienced soldier; he gathered together, with the help of his father and some of his own funds, a force of 4 barons, 20 knights, 500 men at arms and 2,500 archers. With his new force, Prince Henry took the war to Glyndŵr, burning his homes at Glyndyfrdwy and Sycharth, and further taxes were demanded of the Welsh to fund the ongoing war to crush the rebellion. Even hardened English supporters like Henry Don of Kidwelly now went over to Glyndŵr's side because they could see that the king's policy was not designed to let Wales live and prosper, Henry IV wanted Wales to be a sweat house for the English to grow fat on its labour and use its men in his wars. This is why Glyndŵr's army had reached around 8,000 men by June 1403.

On 10 July, Hotspur raised his standard at Chester and declared himself a rebel against King Henry IV. All of the accusations now flew from Hotspur's lips as he accused Henry IV of killing Richard II, ruling without calling Parliament, and taxing the clergy without the consent of Parliament. As Hotspur raised his army, the king left his intended route to Scotland and turned his army west to deal with Hotspur. Glyndŵr was unable to bring his army to aid Hotspur as the crossing of the Severn at Shrewsbury was blocked by some of Prince Henry's forces, which allowed Henry IV to meet Hotspur a few miles north of Shrewsbury, at the place now known as Battlefield. The armies were very evenly matched, with between 12,000 and 15,000 men each, and they were similarly armed: archers and billmen for the most part, with the knights and

Above left: Kidwelly Castle's strong battlements and towers survived when the town was destroyed.

Above right: The moat and outer wall of Beaumaris Castle, Anglesey.

men at arms in the centre. Both sides would have had small contingents of crossbowmen, swordsmen and pikemen to bolster their forces. The battle was fought on 21 July 1403 and was one of the bloodiest days' fighting ever seen in Britain. The massed ranks of archers caused many casualties on both sides, so that one report likened the bodies on the field to fallen apples after an autumn gale; it was this storm of feathered death that reputedly inspired Henry V to win at Agincourt just twelve years later. But Agincourt lay in the future and Henry V was still the Prince Henry of Monmouth, the young Prince Hal, at this point. After almost a day of fighting, Henry IV was eventually victorious; Hotspur was killed along with some 6–7,000 others, casualties being roughly even on both sides. Prince Henry took an arrow to the face, which damaged his cheek, mouth and tongue, and despite the wound, the more painful extraction and the risk of infection he lived, though he was incapacitated for as long as eighteen months. The rest of 1403 saw a repeat of earlier strategies, starting in September, when King Henry IV now called in levies from thirty-five shires to mount yet another expedition, his fourth, into Wales, which again proved nothing more than a way of reinforcing the castles still held by the English and an excuse to steal from anyone they could. The Welsh continued in their strategy to besiege and take castles, and in this they were aided by French mercenaries who were experienced in the craft of constructing siege machines; as Henry once more left Wales before the winter weather could take hold, the Welsh continued their sieges, showing to the English just how hardy they were. Warfare was now constant and continued throughout 1404, when Beaumaris, Harlech and Aberystwyth castles all fell to the Welsh. Glyndŵr then switched from a military strategy to a political one and called a *Cynulliad* (Gathering) at Machynlleth, where he announced his vision for Wales, with universities, a parliament and a separate Church. While at Machynlleth he was crowned Prince of Wales and on 14 July a formal treaty was signed between Wales and France, and more aid would come from France to aid the Welsh cause. There was, however, one weakness in Glyndŵr's plan: he still did not control all of the castles and he had no navy with which to ship supplies to the castles he did hold. Therefore, he had to rely on French ships to supply arms and to harass English ships bringing supplies to their coastal strongholds; the French attacked Dartmouth and the coastal ports on the south coast of England to draw English troops away from Wales.

The Welsh suffered a minor setback when in the summer a raiding force was destroyed at Campstone Hill, somewhere near Offa's Dyke in south-east Wales, by the Earl of Warwick acting on Prince Henry's orders. A fifth royal expedition was staged in the autumn of 1404 and this relieved the siege of Coity Castle, and again the garrisons en route were restrengthened for the coming year.

The year 1405 would be the high water mark for Glyndŵr; there were very few people in Wales who were not behind him, and from early in the year French troops began to arrive to strengthen the Welsh army; the incessant campaigning by the Welsh and the counter-campaigning by the English continued unabated. The English, however, using troops and ships from Ireland, landed a large force on Anglesey with the intention of retaking Beaumaris and using the island as a base to begin a war with Glyndŵr on two fronts. Meanwhile, Glyndŵr was now so strong that he held a second parliament at Harlech in July, the castle now being his capital and home, before marching south with his Welsh army of 10,000 men to meet the French troops who had been landing in ports along the South Wales coast. The French army was one for fighting in the fields,

Above left: Shrewsbury battlefield and the church built by Henry IV in honour of his victory.

Above right: Dartmouth Castle, a town in Devon attacked by the French to help the Welsh under Glyndŵr.

with the knights used to charging across open fields supported by the French infantry, who were armed with crossbows; neither type of solider was suitable for guerrilla warfare in the mountains and woods of Wales. The French nobility had even brought their destriers with them, horses trained for war, but some had died in the crossing from France. Given the situation and rumours reaching Glyndŵr's ears of further rebellions in England, the commanders took the decision that the combined French and Welsh force would take an enormous step forward and invade England. The allied army, which was around 8,000 strong, marched north-east from South Wales before reaching, sacking and burning Worcester. They then followed the valley of the River Teme until Henry IV's army was found to be closing in on them, the king having around 8,000 men also. The allies took up a position on Woodbury Hill, where an Iron Age hillfort provided some shelter and some rudimentary defence. The English army took up a defensive position on Abberley Hill; there was a shallow valley approximately a mile wide between the two hills, where today the village of Great Witley sits.

There is much confusion as to what happened next and no source is clear; some seem to indicate that there was a complete standoff for a week, after which the allies retired to Wales as they had run out of food and were not prepared to risk everything on a battle. Another version states that two armies engaged in a week of jousts and chivalric combat before going their separate ways. French chroniclers state that the English nerve broke and the army retreated to Worcester, but once inside the massive defences of the city there was nothing the allies could do but retreat to Wales (Brough). Certainly, the English chroniclers are never very good at telling us when they were worsted by the French; in the Hundred Years War, for instance, the English are taught

Woodbury Hill above the Teme Valley, home to the Franco-Welsh army.

Abberley Hill, wooded and to the left of Great Witley Valley, where the great stand-off of 1405 happened.

about the tremendous victories of Crecy and Agincourt but not the humiliating defeats at the Battle of La Brossinière or at the Battle of Jargeau. Brough makes the point that if the French did succeed with Welsh help in chasing the English into the safety of the City of Worcester, this was the furthest penetration by any French army since the Norman Conquest and certainly the furthest a free Welsh army ever reached into England. Slowly, the French made their way back to the coast; many of the nobles left immediately for France, while most of the fighting infantry stayed on. The worst thing to happen for the Welsh was that Charles VI of France withdrew his support as he looked to make peace with England. However it came about, the English had succeeded in holding back the Welsh tide and once the tide started retreating, it continued to slowly slip away. Tudor (Owain's brother) was killed sometime in 1405 and any Welsh soldiers that were caught were executed in front of Welsh castles to show the defenders what was coming to them. Even the abbot of a Cistercian monastery at Llantarnam was killed for attending to the wounded at the Battle of Usk, which was a defeat for the Welsh forces.

The English, as their slow advance continued in Anglesey, decided to try a more modern tactic to defeat the Welsh by enforcing an economic blockade. Prince Henry used the castles that the English held to stifle all local trade, the castles themselves being supplied once more by the sea now that the French threat was reduced. Gradually, this financial squeeze began to work and some lords repledged themselves to King Henry IV. War continued but the Welsh were losing the initiative; it was not on the battlefield that the English defeated the Welsh but economically. Slowly, the English gained the upper hand, capturing the whole of Anglesey by November 1406, which gave them a secure base from which to supply and increase their armies. Slowly, one by one, the castles held by the Welsh fell; they had fallen into the trap of fighting the English way at the start of the rebellion; staying cooped up in a castle when outnumbered only led to one result and had the Welsh remained free, as an army on the move, then they could have kept the war going almost indefinitely. When they chose to fight from a castle, they had to place around that castle the infrastructure necessary to generate income and so create the economic stability that the country would need to be independent. Glyndŵr did not have the time to build that infrastructure and it would have only come about quickly if lords such as Hotspur or Mortimer could have given Glyndŵr the time necessary to build within Wales the financial independence she would need to be a completely separate country. With the tide now running against him, Glyndŵr again appealed for French help but none was forthcoming and the man who had been on the verge of becoming the King of Wales had now lost almost everything, save the undying love and devotion of his people.

The death throes of Glyndŵr's rebellion would be long and extremely costly in lives. Aberystwyth held out against the English siege army from May 1407 until November 1408, despite the English using primitive cannons against the walls. The siege of Harlech had also begun in May 1407, but it would not surrender until February 1409, when the garrison was out of food. Glyndŵr's wife, Margaret, two of his daughters (including Catrin) and four grandchildren were all taken to the Tower in London, where over the next six years they would all die; Edmund Mortimer, Catrin's husband, died in the last assault on the castle.

The torment that gripped Glyndŵr seems to have galvanised him into a quest for revenge against all of the English he could lay his hands on. He still had a small band of loyal fighters with him and this force was joined by some French and Scots soldiers also loyal to the Prince of Wales. This group of ruthless fighters now swept from the northern coast of Wales right the way through to Shrewsbury, burning Oswestry on the way and Welshpool on the way back. Somehow, Glyndŵr remained free and unharmed, but the majority of his men who were not already captured or dead were now killed or wounded in this death or glory campaign. Being either leaders of his guerrilla bands or male relations to Glyndŵr, or both, all of these men that were now captured were summarily executed in the gruesome way that traitors were dealt with, their heads being displayed on the walls of Shrewsbury and Chester as a warning to other rebels. Despite the loss of almost everything and with a price on his head, Glyndŵr managed to stay hidden for the rest of his life. There were flashes of guerrilla activity in 1412 and 1414, but the power and influence which he held in 1405–6 would never be repeated. No-one knows when or where Owain Glyndŵr died; the most common assessment is February 1416, having rejected pardons in the previous year from the new King Henry V, who had inherited the throne from his father when Henry IV died in March 1413. Henry V won his great victory at Agincourt in 1415, having learned in the rebellious wars of the 1400s the way to use the longbow to great effect; it was Welsh archers who formed a large part of that 'English' Agincourt army. Brough also raises an interesting point relating to the death of two English nobles and the possibility that they were assassinated by Welsh bowmen during the Battle of Agincourt. Dafydd Gam and Edward, Duke of York, both of whom had campaigned and committed atrocities in Wales, were killed in the battle. We know that Welsh revenge could be taken very slowly and at Agincourt, as well as the Welsh archers on the English side, there were mercenary Welsh fighting for the French. In the confusion and chaos of a bloody melee fought in mud and rain, it might have been easy for a lightly clad archer to slip a blade in-between the armour of a former enemy and let him fall 'gloriously', appearing to die bravely for his country, while a hidden smile passed a Welshman's lips.

By the time of Agincourt, 25 October 1415, full English rule had returned to Wales but the country was devastated, as were many of the border towns like Oswestry and Welshpool, and Welsh trade and markets were no more; as late as the 1490s, towns had not recovered sufficiently to pay their dues to the Exchequer. A new government body was established in 1472 for the administration of Wales; the Council of Wales and the Marches was administered from Ludlow Castle and would continue to be so until the Glorious Rebellion of 1688, which overthrew the Catholic James II, and led to the establishment of the modern kingdom of Britain. Ludlow would grow and develop over the next 200 years into an important and prosperous trading centre, built upon the important administrative role it had to play in dealing with Welsh affairs. Its fine castle is one of the most interesting in Britain and every year different festivals are held there and in the town environs to commemorate literature, theatre and music. Every November a Medieval Fayre is held, with a variety of traditional and modern foods and crafts, where everyone dresses in costume and it is easy to imagine how the castle must have looked at its height in the 1500s.

Conclusion

When Owain Glyndŵr was driven reluctantly into rebellion, it was for a cause that was of his own making, because his cause was justice – simple, honest, common sense justice – no more or less than any of us in a civilised society would expect today. The problem was that Glyndŵr did not live in a time of justice; it was partial justice, where the idiosyncrasy of one man, a local lord or the monarch, could choose whether men lived or died, and anyone who was not totally straight found it impossible to get justice. Glyndŵr was wronged and with no redress under the law, two wrongs had to make a right and it

Above left: An isolated valley in the Berwyn Mountains was home for Owain Glyndŵr and his men.

Above right: Louise and Emma beside Owain Glyndŵr's monument in Corwen.

was either accept death or die trying to change things for the betterment of all. Because he was known to be fair, seen to be fair and behaved fairly (until all was lost at the end, when he sought death but did not find it), he was ahead of his time. Parliaments; equality throughout the realm of Wales; commercial trade; recognition by the Pope, by France and Scotland; here was a master of both military and political strategy. One can understand why the people said that he would return some day: it was because people needed to believe that his kind would return, even if in another guise; they had to believe that there would be something better than their oppressed lives under a foreign power. Today, some people crave total independence and use Glyndŵr as a symbol of that independence. Glyndŵr's way, although right for its time, saw many thousands of people die, many in horrible circumstances, something he would not have wanted when he first set out to teach the thieving Grey a lesson. Today, as a United Kingdom, we have a common strength and individual identity, the devolved parliaments give local autonomy in the things that matter the most to local people. If the people of any of our four nations, all of which are bonded together by the brutal wars of the past, look at the situation in many other parts of the world, even in Europe, would any of us really be better off now by being alone?

Following the end of Glyndŵr's rebellion, there would be no battles fought in Wales until the English Civil War broke out in 1642, although many armies marched through the Principality on their way to fight in the Wars of the Roses. That is not to say that Welshmen were not fighting either; Welsh troops fought in the Hundred Years War until it finally came to an end in 1453, but by then the Wars of Roses had begun. Many Welshmen fought for the causes of both York and Lancaster, but it would be the Tudors who would finally triumph in 1485 at Bosworth Field, when Richard III was defeated and Henry Tudor took the crown and the title of Henry VII – Henry Tudor was the great grandson of Maredudd ap Tudor, who had aided, fought and died for Owain Glyndŵr, his noble cousin. The lasting power of Owain Glyndŵr can be summed up in one thing: he was never abandoned by his people and wherever he hid he was never betrayed, even though there was, for over a decade, a reward on his head.

Ludlow Castle seen from the west, the view Welshmen had when approaching the town.

CHAPTER 10

The Great Rebellion 1642–60

The English Civil War

The long period of peace within the borders of Wales continued from 1415 until the war that would divide the whole of Britain in the 1640s and 50s. The causes of the war are numerous and have commanded whole books of their own. Like all civil wars, there was a mixture of issues, all of which revolved around the finances of the kingdom, the religion of the kingdom and who should rule the country, king or Parliament? All three of these things conspired together to explode into rebellion when Parliament and the king refused to negotiate with one another with any degree of assurity or intent. Both were demonstrative and intransigent and as neither side would compromise, open war was the result.

Many terms have been coined for the war between Charles I and his parliament, the most misleading is the English Civil War. Firstly, there was not one, but a whole series of civil wars, and secondly, although the majority of these military campaigns raged across England, there was also fighting in Ireland, Wales, Scotland and even in some of the colonies between those who sided with the king or Parliament. There were in fact three separate 'British Civil Wars', punctuated at times by periods of peace. The first civil war was the most destructive; it lasted from August 1642 to August 1646, involving hundreds of sieges and skirmishes and more than fifteen major engagements. The second civil war lasted from March to August 1648, and was more a series of isolated uprisings than a full-blown war. The third civil war lasted from June 1650 to September 1651 and came about as a direct result of Parliament's actions after the end of the second civil war. Firstly, Parliament had reneged on its promise to reform the English Church into the Scottish Presbyterian system and secondly, they executed King Charles I, who was also the King of Scotland. The Scots had fought alongside Parliament to 'release the King from his evil counsellors', not to have him murdered. So on hearing the news that Charles I had been executed, there was disbelief and outrage in Scotland, and therefore Prince Charles was proclaimed Charles II in Edinburgh on 5 February 1649. The first attempt at restoring Charles II to the throne met with disaster at the Battle of Dunbar on 3 September 1650. But despite this defeat, the Scots remained undaunted and gathered their forces for an invasion of England, which took place in the summer of 1651. The Scottish and Royalist army eventually reached Worcester, where it was soundly beaten by Oliver Cromwell on 3 September 1651. Charles's dream of obtaining the throne was gone but at least, after nine years of almost continual warfare, Worcester turned out to be the last military action of the civil wars. Given how many people were killed and that as soon as the wars were over the Parliamentarians fell out among themselves, thereby committing many of the acts which they had earlier condemned Charles and his 'evil' ministers for, it would seem that a more appropriate term for this period of British History would be 'The Great Rebellion'. However, for ease of reference we will stay with the more common title for these wars, the English Civil War.

Armies During the English Civil War

The infantry, or foot, element would generally (there are always exceptions) make up around 75 per cent of the combatants in a Civil War army. These men would be formed into regiments, each in theory consisting of 1,200 men, 800 of whom were armed with muskets and the other 400 with pikes. The pikeman was the more heavily armoured and had for bodily protection a buff coat or a metal back and breastplate (the cuirass, which we mentioned in conjunction with plate mail), sometimes both. In addition, many would have had a metal helmet, the commonest of which was called a morion. The pike, as we know, was a very long spear, anything up to 18 feet in length, and carried by men who generally had some body protection. The musketeers were vulnerable to attack, especially from enemy horsemen, while they went through the slow and cumbersome system of loading and firing while rotating their ranks. The pikemen, therefore, acted as protection for their musketeers by keeping the enemy horsemen from engaging with them as cavalry would not charge home against the densely formed pike ranks. The pikemen could stand behind the musketeers and still reach out past them to engage any enemy horse that came too close and threatened the musketeers. However, the role of the pikeman was not only a defensive one; when the time came to charge, the pikemen would raise the pikes to their shoulders and, levelling the blade out in front of them, advance to 'push-of-pike', aiming their points at the faces of the enemy.

The musketeer at best had a buff coat for protection, but often would be in just his shirt and doublet; if they were lucky, they might all have a uniform coat colour. Such was the nature of the English Civil War that very few regiments ever reached their theoretical number and some regiments had as few as

Above left: A regiment marches towards the enemy, pikemen in the centre. (Susanne Atkin)

Above right: Musketeers give fire with a full volley. (Susanne Atkin)

400 men. The role of the musketeer was to shoot as many of the enemy as possible, softening them up before the pikemen advanced and drove the enemy from the field. The musketeers would be formed up in many ranks, possibly as many as ten. They would then advance and fire, while the line that had just discharged their muskets would retire to the rear, slowly reloading their musket as they advanced through the files, ready to fire again. Thus, in theory a never-ending series of volleys could be discharged at the enemy, one rank (or line) after another. The reason for this cumbersome system of firing was the appalling inaccuracy of these muzzle-loaded, smoothbore weapons; the only effective way to hurt your enemy was to bring a lot of firepower to bear upon them at a range of 100 yards or less. It would not take long for the musketeers to discharge all of their shot, as generally they only had enough ammunition and powder for twelve shots, normally carried in a bandolier worn across the shoulder and chest and commonly known as the 'Twelve Apostles'. Once all of the shot was discharged, it was common for the musketeers to join in the charge alongside their pikemen, using the hard shoulder stock of their musket as a club to try and win the day with an aggressive charge.

When war was declared, the king held few centres of industry, as Bristol, Norwich and London, the three key cities of the day, were all held by Parliament. Therefore, Royalist regiments were reliant on what equipment was stored in the personal homes of the king's supporters. When the war began in earnest, the majority of men within the Royalist regiments were armed solely with pikes and some of the rear ranks had to be content with cudgels or even farm implements. Gradually, due to victories in the field and the eventual capture of Bristol in August 1643, the king was able to equip his foot with better weapons, and interestingly it was the musket that was adopted by the infantry rather than the pike. Indeed, by the time of Naseby, 14 June 1645, the

Royalist foot regiments were almost entirely armed with muskets, indicating that the days of the now cumbersome and slow pike blocks were numbered. In contrast, the Parliamentarians, by gaining control of London at the outset of the war, had a ready-made army of foot, namely the London trained band regiments that were designed for the defence of the capital, the only force approaching a standing army in England and Wales. The army of Parliament, under the command of the Earl of Essex, was able to use the armouries that supplied these trained bands and equip the Parliamentarian regiments in the proper manner of the time, with the correct proportions of musket to pike, a ratio of 2:1. However, despite the proven successes that Montrose and the later Royalist armies had had in using a far higher ratio of muskets to pike, when the New Model Army was formed under Thomas Fairfax in 1645, he chose to stick with the drill books of the day and kept the ratio of two musketeers to each pikeman.

Artillery at this time was not the sophisticated cannon that fired a shell and destroyed men and buildings alike. All of these cannon were muzzle-loading and relied on a team of people working together to ensure that they could be operated effectively and safely. Starting from scratch, in order to be able to fire a cannon, one first had to clean the inside of the barrel with a wet sponge, after which a young boy, the 'powder monkey' as they were called, would place his finger over the touch hole to ensure that there was no chance of a stray spark getting into the barrel while the cannon was being loaded. A drying rag was then used to remove any excess damp and then the naked gunpowder would be ladled into the gun barrel, followed by a piece of wadding to keep it in place. The appropriately sized solid iron cannon ball would then be loaded by simply letting it run down the barrel, and finally a wad of earth and grass

Above left: Cannon, musket and pistol balls from the English Civil War, part of the author's collection.

Above right: An English Civil War-era light field cannon being loaded while musketeers skirmish in the background.

or an old cloth would be rammed down the barrel to keep the ball in place (in case the cannon had to be swivelled round or point downhill), and also to provide compression for the explosion. With the cannon loaded, the powder monkey would step aside and the master of the gun would then pour some loose gunpowder onto the touch hole. Ignition was provided by the same method as that used by musketeers, but the lighted cord was attached to a linstock (a 6-foot pole with attachments to hold the chord in place). The master gunner would then light the cannon, literally at arm's length, by placing the smouldering cord onto the touch hole. These steps would be followed for every type of artillery piece, whether it was a light fawcon that shot a 2.5 lb ball, or a culverin that could shoot a 19 lb ball for around a mile. The heavier guns of 12 lb and above would be used during sieges to cause destruction to the walls of the town or castle and the defenders sheltering behind them. All of these solid cannon balls did damage through the violence of their passage, smashing into the ranks of a regiment and knocking men down like skittles. At close quarters, the cannon would be loaded with bags of small cannon balls or even musket balls and this 'grape shot' would be used at a range of 100 yards or less, causing many casualties with one shot as around 200 small lead balls flew into the enemy ranks. There were also a few mortars, which were large barrelled cannon that pointed upwards at an angle of around 45 degrees. The mortar was loaded the same way as a cannon but it fired a shell instead of a solid iron ball. Once primed and loaded, a fuse would be lit on top of the shell and then the touchhole would be ignited. The explosion would throw the shell high into the air so that it would come down among the enemy before exploding. The mortar could not fire a missile as far as a cannon, and so it tended to be used only in siege warfare, for throwing shells into an enemy stronghold over high walls. Although the cannon changed little between 1600 and 1800, the mortar developed into the howitzer, which was a much more effective weapon by the 1750s than these early versions.

18 September 1644 Montgomery – Powys

The small town of Montgomery developed as a place of strategic importance for two very simple reasons: there was an important ford nearby across the River Severn and Roman roads connected to the ford, making those roads the arterial routes of their day. This was not an ordinary small ford that one still sees on narrow roads in the rural part of the country today – this was one of the few places that the mighty River Severn could be crossed when the river was not in spate. There are few places once she has reached a mature stage that England and Wales's longest river can be forded. The ford at Rhydwhyman sits roughly halfway between Newtown and Welshpool. Some time out of mind, in the early days of human movement, this ford became a meeting point; as tribes developed, it would have come under the dominion of a chieftain and then as warfare followed it became a strategic crossing point – whoever controlled the ford had influence over other tribes. Such was the importance of the crossing that the Ffridd Faldwyn hillfort was built to guard it. Some centuries later, this was joined by a large Roman fort, Levobrinta, which was constructed in the mid-2nd century and was occupied until the Romans left Britain. After the Norman Conquest this was followed by a motte and bailey which is now known as Hen Domen, built between 1071 and 1074 on the orders of Roger de Montgomery, who was the Earl of Shrewsbury, probably to try and keep order in the area as the Welsh had allied with the Saxon Edric the Wild to destroy Shrewsbury in 1069. Finally, a strong stone castle was started in 1223, a mile further south-east than Hen Domen and much higher up the hills; set on a rock promontory, it was an imposing position. Even today, when the once-majestic fortress is in ruins, Montgomery castle is still an impressive stronghold, dominating the town and lands below it.

Prelude to Battle

Almost from the moment that Charles raised his standard at Nottingham in August 1642 until the battle we are about to examine in September 1644, a steady stream of recruits marched down the Severn Valley from Wales to fight for the king, with many Welsh regiments becoming the mainstay of Charles's Royalist army. Obviously, with time that stream slowed as 'war weariness' and a shortage in general of men who were willing to fight took hold. There were some long and at times bitter sieges in Wales during the English Civil Wars but

The ruins of Montgomery Castle give a clue as to its original size and strength.

very few battles. With most of Wales being strongly for King Charles I and far removed from most Parliamentary forces, the Princedom was comparatively trouble free for the first two years of the war.

At the time of the civil war, Montgomery Castle was a key link in the Royalist supply chain. Convoys of troops from Ireland and both troops and supplies from Wales, including cotton, butter, cheese and cattle, would regularly pass on the road that runs alongside the River Severn, just a few miles away from the protection of the castle. These supplies were vital for the garrison of Shrewsbury, one of the Royalists' key strongholds. As Wales had long been the nursery for many of the king's infantry regiments, it was natural that eventually Parliament would turn its attention to this part of the kingdom. The reason Wales was the last area on Parliament's list was simply its location. Much of the Parliamentarian support was in the Home Counties and East Anglia, as far away from Wales as it is possible to get. Taking any decisive action against Wales was extremely difficult as it meant marching an army across the breadth of Britain and through territory in the south and West Midlands, which was Royalist in sympathy. As the Parliamentarian armies began to triumph in the east, it fell to local Parliamentarians to begin the action against Wales to see if they could make an impression without any help from London.

The local Parliamentarian generals were Sir Thomas Middleton and his brother-in-law, Colonel Thomas Mytton. Middleton was exiled from his home in Chirk Castle, Clwyd, very early in the war when the Royalists under Robert Ellice captured the castle in his absence. He was therefore happy to accept a commission from Parliament to become responsible for all the military action on their behalf in North Wales. Mytton was from Halston, an estate outside of Oswestry, and he established the first Parliamentary garrison in Shropshire when he captured Wem in 1643. Mytton then went on to capture Ellesmere and the vitally important town of Oswestry; this gave the Parliamentarians a garrison en route to the Severn Valley and a supply line towards Wales. Buoyed by their success, Middleton and Mytton began to increase their patrols south from Oswestry towards Welshpool and Shrewsbury, keeping a watchful eye for convoys of arms or recruits. In late August 1644 Middelton and Mytton led 500 horse in a dawn raid on Welshpool in Montgomeryshire (now Powys), where they routed a detachment of Prince Rupert's Royalist cavalry under the command of Sir Thomas Dallison before plundering the town.

Prince Rupert himself was on his way to Cornwall to confer with the king, who had been pursuing into Cornwall the Earl of Essex, who was commanding Parliament's second-largest army. Rupert had left the garrison at Montgomery to protect the area, but unfortunately for the Royalists, the garrison commander at Montgomery Castle was a rather reluctant Royalist, Lord Edward Herbert. Lord Herbert was a man of the 'Arts', more a gent than a general, who counted Ben Jonson among his friends; his brother, the Reverend George Herbert, was a skilled poet. Following his elevation to the peerage in 1629, Lord Herbert became something of a recluse, choosing to remain at home with his beloved books and work on his own future publications than attend social gatherings or Parliamentary matters in London. This, coupled with a deterioration in his own health, may have led Lord Herbert's interest in military matters and the civil war to lapse and it is likely that this *laissez-faire* attitude may have also spread to the rest of the garrison. This lapse in Lord Herbert's attention to the defence of the area under his protection would not have been helped by two years without any real military threat. Often the twists of fate are cruel and no sooner had Prince Rupert departed than the Parliamentarians unexpectedly captured a Royalist supply train with a large quantity of gunpowder on its way through Newtown, thus depriving the Shrewsbury and Chester garrisons of some much-needed supplies. No doubt buoyant with their two recent successes, Middleton and Mytton advanced on Montgomery; it may have been just a reconnaissance patrol or they may have had news of the apathy that exuded from Montgomery, but with their 800 men they decided to trust to luck and push on against the isolated castle.

According to John Speed's 1610 drawing of Montgomery, the town was surrounded by a ditch and palisade, but it is not known what state of repair these old-fashioned defences were in at the time of the battle and it is doubtful whether the roads were defended as only one of the four roads that enter the town, the road from Newtown, is shown as passing through a defensive gateway. Given that Middleton's troops appear to have met no resistance in entering the town, it is safe to assume that the defences of the town were in such poor repair that no effort was put in to either repairing them or defending them. Incredibly, this apathy also seems to have spread to the garrison of the castle, as Middleton went on to capture the old defences outside the inhabited parts of the castle without even disturbing the garrison; clearly there was no watch posted and no defensive artillery ready for action. Immediately, Middleton began negotiations with Lord Herbert for the surrender of the castle. Lord Herbert was a man of considerable words and he cleverly managed to negotiate a 36-hour period for the garrison to consider the terms offered by Middleton. Middleton agreed, but a proportion of the garrison had to be sent from the castle as a guarantee. Lord Herbert agreed to this and his defenders were reduced accordingly to the agreed maximum of twenty-four; the rest were sent away, presumably to spread word of events. Middleton, confident of success, decided to store the newly acquired powder from Newtown within the castle grounds.

However, before the night was out Middleton became nervous, he realised that 36 hours was actually a long time to be outside an enemy fortress in the middle of hostile country and he decided to break his own terms and sent a scaling party to attack the castle gate. After climbing the rock-face upon which the castle sits, the Parliamentarian troops managed to force the gates and overpower the guards. Some of the defenders climbed over the castle walls to escape while others begged for mercy as Middleton threatened to blow up the gates. Lord Herbert saw that he was in no position to bargain and so he surrendered on the understanding that he and his family, his servants and all of his personal belongings would be unmolested and then he handed his fortress over to Parliament. Montgomery Castle sits in an enviable position on a rocky outcrop, towering hundreds of feet above the town below. The only route by which to approach the castle is along the narrow neck of the rock outcrop so it should have been be a very easy castle to defend; through a lack of interest and a lack of basic military routine, the Royalists had let one of their strongest castles fall without a shot being fired in its defence.

Mytton took over the role of garrison commander and at once set about fortifying the outer defences of the castle so as to avoid the previous night's events recurring with him and his 500 men, most of whom were taken from Middleton's regiment. Middleton meanwhile took the rest of the force, some 300 cavalry, on a foraging expedition for supplies for the new garrison. News of the loss of the supply train and the capture of Montgomery Castle reached Shrewsbury within hours and Sir Michael Ernley, the area commander for Shropshire, gathered together a relief force, which set out from Shrewsbury as soon as it was mustered. Ernley's cavalry arrived to find Middleton's men scattered in foraging groups; these were quickly chased off and, along with Middleton himself, fled north to Welshpool before carrying on to Oswestry to regroup. Having assessed his situation, Middleton pushed on into Cheshire and managed to enlist the aid of Sir John Meldrum, Sir William Brereton and Sir William Fairfax to come to the relief of what was now the Parliamentary garrison of Montgomery Castle.

Ffridd Faldwyn hillfort, seen from Caerhowel.

Mytton, having been temporarily abandoned by Middleton, now found himself besieged by a large Royalist force, which had swelled to almost 5,000 troops with the arrival of the experienced regiments of Lord Byron's army. On 7 September, the Royalist infantry began digging trenches and earthworks around and above the castle in a concerted effort to regain the stronghold as quickly as possible. Meanwhile, Middleton's relief column had been placed under the command of the experienced Sir John Meldrum and his force of around 3,000 men reached the outskirts of Montgomery on 17 September, so that the castle had been withstanding the siege for ten days. Byron took up an excellent position, high above the castle on Ffridd Faldwyn Hill (B on the map on p. 265), which gave him a clear view of the siege unfolding below him and allowed him to monitor all the approach roads to the town. Having seen the approach of Meldrum's men from the north, Byron gave orders for all of his men to be brought back to the town and he deployed them on the high ground around the town. Meldrum retained his men in readiness of an assault and, having approached from the north, positioned his army in the fields on the eastern side of 'Salt Bridge', a little over a mile from the town. Protecting this bridge ensured that the Parliamentarians had a means of escape should one be required, while the River Camlad would protect their rear. Also, Offa's Dyke ran to the east of their position and it is most likely that Meldrum would have at least patrolled this to ensure no attack came from that direction, which led to Chirbury and Shrewsbury.

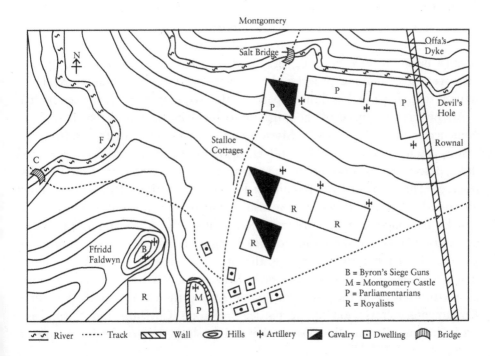

Montgomery

Salt Bridge

Offa's Dyke

N

Devil's Hole

F

Stalloe Cottages

Rownal

C

R

R

R

R

R

Ffridd Faldwyn

B

R

M

P

B = Byron's Siege Guns
M = Montgomery Castle
P = Parliamentarians
R = Royalists

River ⌇ Track ······ Wall ▧ Hills ◉ Artillery ✛ Cavalry ◼ Dwelling ▣ Bridge ▥

Unlike so many of our earlier battles, there are eyewitness reports for Montgomery but they are both tempered with elements of propaganda. The night of 17 September passed without incident and on the morning of the 18th, Meldrum, seeing no movement from the Royalist troops stationed on the hills above, decided to send 500 of his cavalry in search of more provisions. Byron, from his vantage point, saw some of the Parliamentary horse leaving their camp and, sensing that the moment was right to strike, Byron assembled his men and marched down through the town. The Royalists' army would have attacked almost due north from Montgomery, heading towards the defensive position that Meldrum had adopted the night before. Given that Meldrum's force was at least 2,000 less than Byron's, especially since he had reduced his cavalry by sending 500 men foraging, it is most likely that Meldrum would have stayed in his defensive overnight location. Using his considerable experience, Meldrum would have occupied Offa's Dyke to his left with his infantry and defended the vital crossing of the Camlad, Salt Bridge, with his cavalry on his right. In the centre would have been the rest of his infantry and any light cannon that the army had with them. This would have made a formidable defensive position but gamely, the Royalists came on at full pelt. Meldrum said in his later account of the battle that the Royalist cavalry under Colonel Marcus Trevor charged into the Parliamentary horse 'with great courage, resolving to breake through our Forces and make themselves Masters of a Bridge we had gained the night before, which would have cut-off our retreat'. [*Archaeologia Cambrenesis* consolidated edition *The Castle of Montgomery*, undated, p. 29] Clearly this is Salt Bridge, confirming where Meldrum's cavalry had been deployed and indicating that both sides grasped the importance of controlling the bridge. In this battle, Sir William Fairfax was mortally wounded and the Parliamentarian cavalry began to give ground. Against the Parliamentarian infantry, Byron's men were also making progress, but Brererton's Cheshire infantry regiment refused to give ground and the impetus of the Royalist charge had been halted.

At this crucial phase of the battle, two incidents occurred which were to influence the outcome. Firstly, Mytton and his 500 men surged out from the castle, assaulted the Royalists still engaged in the siege and having routed them, descended the steep hill to the town and attacked the rear of the Royalist reserves. This panicked the remaining Royalists; a furious Trevor maintained afterwards that the Royalist 'Lancashire Horse ran without a blow being struck'. [*Archaeologia Cambrenesis* 1846 edition pp. 37–8 and 1849 edition pp. 237–8] Secondly, the Parliamentary foraging party now returned, bringing 500 cavalry back into the fray as the infantry were locked in their titanic struggle along the whole line of battle. With cries of woe from the Royalists as Mytton fell upon their rear and panic among the cavalry as the returning Parliamentary horse joined the battle, Brereton's Cheshire 'Lions' suddenly broke through Byron's line. From what only a short time earlier had seemed a certain victory, the Royalists collapsed to a humiliating defeat, but unlike most battles of the period this was not a short and bloody affair but a long and bloody one; Parliament was told that the battle lasted for a total of 8 hours.

Byron's army was completely destroyed; as few as 100 infantry made it back to the safety of Shrewsbury, though some fled west, presumably never to return to their regiments. At least 500 were killed, and perhaps as many as 1,500 were taken prisoner. The cavalry had been scattered to the four winds. Crucially, all the baggage, cannon, supplies and weapons were lost. The Parliamentarians lost only forty men, with another sixty wounded, according to Brereton, but given that the Royalists had the upper hand, particularly in the initial cavalry melee for Salt Bridge, these losses seem unduly low casualty figures for an 8-hour battle which had gone against them for most of the day; no doubt, propaganda played no small part in all of the general's reports that came out about this battle. Sir William Fairfax died the next day as a result of the dozen wounds he had received in the battle. A Major Fitz-Simons was the only other notable casualty for the Parliamentarian forces.

In 1982 the author was fortunate enough to visit the excavations at Montgomery Castle and was able to confer with the then current Senior Archaeologist for Wales. The author was shown over 250 musket and pistol balls that had been discovered, together with coins and rings from the civil war period, some in mint condition. The majority of the projectiles were found close to the southern walls of the castle and as there had been no shots from the Parliamentarian troops when they captured the castle, this indicates that this shot was from Royalist troops concentrating their firing around the gateway of the castle, which Mytton had reinforced. From a military aspect, there were two important finds outside the castle. Firstly, evidence emerged that earthworks had been dug, separate to those of the original hillfort Ffridd Faldwyn, which were on the same hill west of the castle and consistent with a seventeenth-

The low ridge halfway between Salt Bridge and Montogmery town, a possible site for the battle.

Caerhowel Bridge over the River Severn, an alternative place to Salt Bridge that the Parliamentarians may have defended.

century artillery battery; this is presumably where the Royalist cannon would have been set up to bombard the castle. This was Byron's great vantage point (B on the map on p. 265), from which many of the troops' movements around the area could have been seen. At this site, a series of small wooden blocks used for the production of musket balls were also found, together with an actual row of cast musket balls lying where they had been set to cool after casting more than 350 years ago. During the excavations, ponds, ditches and other damp drainage areas around the town were dredged. In one of these a complete lobster-pot helmet, normally worn by cavalrymen, emerged from the mud; upon closer examination, the helmet was found to still contain the skull of its original owner, the victim seeming to have had his head cleanly severed from his neck during the battle.

There is much conjecture about where the battle was fought. Some historians believe the battle to have been fought on the Montgomery side of the wooden bridge that stood at Caerhowel (C on the map on p. 265). If that was so then none of the Parliamentarian garrison would have been able to have seen any of the action at all as the Royalist-held Ffridd Faldwyn is directly in between; this means that Mytton's garrison would not have known when to leave the castle and join in to complete the Royalist defeat. Secondly, the bridge at Caerhowel was not the only means of crossing the Severn. The ford at Rhydwhyman (F on the map on p. 265), just a couple of miles north along the river, provided an alternative crossing and the Parliamentarian force was not sufficient to form a frontage to defend both river crossings and no commander would split his force into two separate divisions, each one then only a quarter of the enemy's strength. In addition, the whole point of Meldrum's force was to relieve the castle; with the castle surrounded, unless the relief force came from the north it could not be seen, which was a vital consideration for a trapped army defending itself against superior numbers besieging it. Furthermore, some of the

Royalists made it back to Shrewsbury, which means that they would have had to pass back through the garrison's ranks and back past the castle, a scenario which simply does not fit with a fleeing force. However, the generally accepted site of the area around Salt Bridge is clearly visible to all parties from the castle and from Ffridd Faldwyn.

A second possibility is that the battle was fought alongside the road to Chirbury, possibly in the vicinity of the county boundary bridge; this is close enough to the castle of Montgomery for the armies to have seen each other and to have been aware of the events as they unfolded. However, the river going east is not an obstacle as such and defending a bridge over it would not be of such vital importance. If one couples with that the fact that some of the ground is completely unsuitable for either cavalry or infantry warfare, neither side is likely to have accepted or offered battle there. The final possibility is that the battle was fought half-way between Salt Bridge and the town, on the saddle or low ridge of ground that runs from Stalloe cottages to Rownal. This is possibly the position that the Parliamentarian army took upon its arrival, but this is so close to the Royalist batteries on Ffridd Faldwyn that it would have been an unwelcome place to camp. So it is unlikely that they would have made a camp there and stayed overnight when they could have been repeatedly shot at from the Royalist artillery positions without being able to reply due to the height of the former upon the hill. If this was the site of the battle then the Parliamentarians would have been much further away from the River Camlad and they would not have been defending the bridge. As the terrain is much wider there and not so easy to defend, this would have allowed a Royalist cavalry manoeuvre to place themselves between the Parliamentarians and the River Camlad, so the ridge is not really a viable position.

Given all of the evidence, the author maintains that the battle was fought on the flat ground to the south of the River Camlad. The cavalry battle ebbed and flowed on the right wing of Meldrum's army as they vied for control of Salt Bridge, while east of the bridge the infantry held the advancing Royalists long enough to allow his foraging cavalry to return and Mytton to launch his rear attack from the castle. Given these events coming at different times of the day and with the distance involved from Ffridd Faldwyn and the castle to the battlesite, one can see how some hours would pass, giving us the long duration of the battle. With the arrival of the reinforcements, Meldrum was then able to leave his defended position and commence his own counter-attack and the Royalists, engaged on three sides, crumbled into submission. The battle, then, would have been fought in a square formed by the following points: Stalloe Cottages; Salt Bridge; Devils Hole (is this name perhaps a reference to severe fighting that took place here?); and at Rownal. The Royalists would have advanced past Stalloe Cottages, charging steadily downhill to the

The meandering Camlad runs to Salt Bridge, top left; the banks are 6 feet deep to the surface of the water.

The flat meadow between Devil's Hole and Salt Bridge; the River Camlad runs along the base of the distant hill.

Looking from Salt Bridge towards Devil's Hole and Offa's Dyke, which is the tree line across the middle of the picture.

Parliamentarians, who occupied the two sides of the square formed by the three points of Salt Bridge, Devils Hole and Rownal.

Conclusion

It is very rare that a single action can determine the outcome of a whole war, yet the events of Montgomery in the summer of 1644 were to prove an absolute disaster for the king. The escalating series of events that had begun with the simple loss of a convoy of ammunition did in itself lead to the loss of Montgomery Castle. The loss of this garrison resulted in the experienced field army of Byron being drawn out as a relief force, fighting a battle in which it was totally destroyed. Byron's field army of 5,000 men would have been invaluable in the Midlands campaign the following summer, especially at Naseby in June 1645, because that battle was very closely fought and at one point looked like being a Royalist victory; if so, then those extra 5,000 men of Byron's could have made all the difference. After the loss of Montgomery Castle, the stream of recruits which had flowed from Wales to the Royalist-held towns of the west was lost, and the strength of the Royalist regiments declined. The final blow was that the route which passes Montgomery in the Severn Valley could no longer be used by the supply convoys carrying food, powder and clothing to the Royalist armies and garrisons in the west of England. The effects of the loss of Montgomery were far more devastating than any other military action of its size in the whole war.

There were many sieges during the civil war in Wales, especially towards the end of the wars, when it was clear that the Royalist cause was lost and only the most resilient castles were holding out. There were several small civil war battles in Wales and these were as follows. At Newcastle Emlyn in Carmarthenshire on 23 April 1645, the Royalist Lieutenant-General Gerard surprised and defeated Colonel Laugharne's Parliamentarians, who were besieging the Royalist garrison there; the Parliamentarians were routed with over 500 killed or captured. Colonel Laugharne was to get his revenge a short time later, when with a force of 200 horse, 550 foot, and 150 men from a Parliamentarian naval squadron he waited for the advancing Royalists under Stradling and Egerton, who had more than double Laugharne's force. The ensuing Battle of Colby Moor was fought on the evening of 1 August 1645, when, as the Royalists deployed, Laugharne sent his cavalry to attack, supported by his musketeers. After an hour of combat the Royalists broke and were routed, having lost around 150 men killed, a further 700 being rounded up as prisoners; Laugharne's losses are not known. This was effectively the end of the First English Civil War in Wales, but not an end to fighting as the Parliamentarian forces now fell out among themselves, as the Royalist General Sir Jacob Astley had prophesied that they would.

In April 1648, Parliamentarian troops in Wales rebelled and declared for the king. The rank and file of the army had not been paid for a long time and they now feared that with the king captured and about to stand trial, their arrears would never be paid. Colonel Poyer, the Governor of Pembroke Castle, led the initial revolt but he was later joined by the now Major-General Laugharne who had fought so gamely for the Parliamentarian cause. A detachment of around 3,000 men from the New Model Army was sent under Colonel Horton with orders to re-secure South Wales for Parliament and if necessary to crush the rebels completely. Horton's force consisted of around 1,000 foot and 2,000 horse and dragoons, and he billeted them in and around the west of St Fagans Laugharne led around 8,000 men to meet Horton's advance but most of his men were regiments were of foot and he had only 500 horse in total. Early on 8 May 1648, Laugharne attacked with 500 men to try and surprise Horton's men but the Parliamentarians were ready and this initial attack was easily routed by a charge from some of Horton's cavalry. This bought the Parliamentarians time and they now deployed north-west of the village. The terrain was crossed by high hedges and it was difficult for the infantry to manoeuvre, but this suited Horton's dragoons and Okey's men forced the Royalists back while some of Horton's cavalry managed to get behind the Royalist flank, charge and break the Royalist army. Reports of 200 dead and 3,000 taken prisoner show the enormity of the Royalist defeat; Horton's killed and wounded are not known. This was the end of serious fighting in Wales as the last few garrisons surrendered.

Following the execution of King Charles I on 30 January 1649 there were further Royalist risings with the aid of the Scots against the Parliamentarian rule of Oliver Cromwell but the Lord Protector would go on to rule England until 1658, and his son until 1660 and the restoration of Charles II. Neither these events nor the subsequent rebellions of Monmouth and the Jacobites would really touch Wales at all. Welsh people were involved, Welsh regiments were in the now British Army, but having endured centuries of incessant warfare and brutal civil war at that, Wales was finally at peace. The final military action in Wales was one of the most bizarre in the military history of the United Kingdom and it took place at the western extremity of Wales.

CHAPTER 11

The Last Invasion of Britain

24 February 1797 Fishguard – Pembrokeshire

On 16 February 1797, a small fleet of four French ships left Brest under the command of Commodore Castagnier with orders to sail into either the Bristol Channel or the Dee Estuary. Aboard the four ships were 1,400 men under General Tate, a mercenary Irish-American officer who had been court-martialled in the United States for submitting false accounts for his regiment and was just the man, it seemed, to lead a small army of bandits and cut-throats, most of whom had been convicts. Tate's brief was to land and cause as much confusion, disturbance and terror as possible around either Bristol or Chester, depending on where they landed. The idea was for this isolated force to distract British forces from the French assistance which was being given to the Irish rebels who looking to break away from British rule. Instead of picking an important port at which to cause their mayhem, the French ships anchored off one of the remotest and least populated areas of southern Britain, between St David's and Fishguard. At this time the defence of Britain fell upon the 'Fencibles'. These were small units of local volunteers who were responsible for patrolling the coast, freeing up the regular troops to be active, particularly on the Continent or, at this time, in Ireland. Fishguard at this time was guarded by two units of Fencibles and three Royal Artillery invalids who manned the 'Old Fort' guarding the harbour.

All of the French ships anchored off Carregwastad Point on 22 February, ready to unload their cargo of men together with a great quantity of arms, ammunition and powder, but there were no provisions. The story that a French ship had been seen off from Fishguard harbour by blanks fired from the Old Fort cannon appears to have been a fictitious event, added to the story in a book of the 1890s. Under cover of darkness, the French ships lowered their ships' boats on to the water and the French force rowed their stores ashore and scaled the cliffs, regrouping at the top near Trehowel, where earthworks and several local springs made it a natural base. This invasion force consisted of

The French landing, captured in the Fishguard 200th anniversary tapestry in the Fishguard Library Museum.

just one full-strength regiment, the Legion Noire; whether the name came from their brown uniforms or their criminal backgrounds is not clear, maybe it befits both elements. Of the 1,400 men landed, only 600 were regular troops but this included some Grenadiers, the rest were irregulars. The French command, having established a base in the farmhouse at Trehowel, proceeded to cook supper, telling their men to live off the land, as was normal for the French on campaign. The discipline of the irregulars immediately broke down totally and they left the camp to not only find food but also to steal anything they could from the local people, which even included the plate from the church at Llanwnda. The local Welsh population were not going to stand idly by while their homes, goods, food and potentially their livelihoods were taken from them. Without any general signal or anyone issuing any orders, the people simply armed themselves and set to against the French irregulars, who were searching the headland in large groups, as one would expect from troops who had orders to make a nuisance of themselves and spread terror among the populace. The Welsh were now unofficial Fencibles as hundreds of them, armed with pitchforks and pikes as well as the occasional musket, took matters into their own hands to defend both their property and their country. There were some skirmishes across the headland and there were some casualties on both sides; somewhere between twenty and thirty of the French were killed and six Welshmen also died. The French were scattered all over the headland like an ill-disciplined mob so that there was no co-ordination to their foraging or any plans for what to do when they had eaten. While this skirmishing was happening along the cliff-tops, the French ships below were making sail and soon departed for France, leaving their countrymen to fend for themselves.

Around early afternoon, Lord Cawdor arrived in Fishguard to take charge of the defence of the town together with some of the local militias, who had been mobilised as news of the French invasion spread along the coast. Somewhere in the region of 700 men had marched or ridden to the town as fast as they could. There were the Cardigan Militia and the Fencibles from Newport and Pembroke and mounted men were provided by the Castlemartin yeomanry, who looked the part in their smart blue coats and were a mounted unit of around fifty men. In addition, two naval guns were also dragged to the assembly which took place in the main square, though the majority of the militia were posted on the approaches to the town as guards. The French morale had dropped a little with the departure of the ships and that morale dropped further when they could see several hundred regular British troops in their fine red coats and tall black shakos advancing along the cliffs across the bay on the cliffs above Fishguard. These fine red-coated soldiers were in fact Welsh women of the area who were attired in their traditional clothing of red shawls and black bonnets, but the illusions suited Lord Cawdor's purpose.

Cawdor took charge in the building which is now the Royal Oak Inn on Fishguard square. Once Cawdor had assessed the situation, he decided to attack before it got dark that evening and organised his men to attack the French position, which was reported to be on the hills above Goodwick. Cawdor led around 600 men as far as Trefwrgi Lane and then realised that it was going to be too dark to do anything that evening and retreated back to Fishguard. Unbeknown to Cawdor, the Grenadiers of the Legion Noire had lined the hedges atop that lane, and had the militia advanced much further they would have been shot to pieces at close range and in the confines of the narrow lane they would have suffered heavy casualties; as it was, they had been saved by the onset of night, but luck was to play an ever greater part before midnight. Many of the French were now the worse for wear, having partaken of copious amounts of port and poultry, which appears to have been off or not cooked properly; the greater part of the French were now ill and incapacitated. They were so demoralised that by the late evening of 23 September, Tate was being asked by his fellow officers to negotiate a ceasefire and so he sent two junior officers into the town under a flag of truce.

In the interim, Cawdor had returned to the Royal Oak in order to make his final preparations for the day ahead and was still involved in those plans when

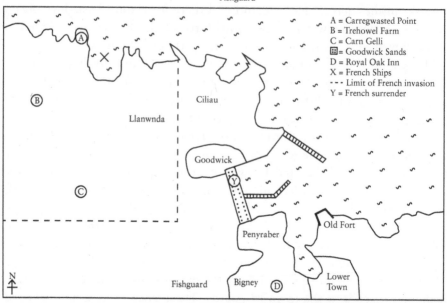

The old harbour at Fishguard.

The Old Fort at Fishguard.

Fishguard town lies on top of the cliffs.

Royal Oak Inn at the centre of Fishguard, which Cawdor made his headquarters.

news came that Tate wished to negotiate a ceasefire. Cawdor received the two officers but not knowing the reason for this change in the French position, he was not prepared to show his weakness by accepting the offer from Tate of just a ceasefire. Instead, Cawdor advised the Frenchmen that he would only be prepared to accept an unconditional surrender at ten the next morning. After due preparation, the Welsh volunteers were down on the beach by eight, while around the cliffs upon every vantage point the local people stood waiting, still armed with their improvised weapons, the ladies of the town still in their traditional red shawls. There were some further negotiations between Cawdor and Tate but Cawdor stood firm and eventually, in the early afternoon of 24 February, the drums of the Legion Noire could be heard as the Frenchmen descended the hill towards the shore. The regiment marched into Goodwick, the little village below Fishguard, where they surrendered on the beach known as Goodwick Sands. Excepting those that had been killed, the French surrendered to a man, so almost 1,400 were now prisoners and were marched to Haverfordwest before being shipped, eventually, back to France. One local lady, a Jemima Nicholas, reputedly singlehandedly rounded up a dozen French soldiers just with her pitchfork when she found them skulking in her fields. Alone, she 'persuaded' them to return to Fishguard, where they were imprisoned inside St Mary's church.

The British Navy intercepted the French ships that had bought the Legion Noire to Wales and successfully captured two of the ships, one of which was renamed HMS *Fisgard* in honour of the victory. The invasion, although a minor one, had been dealt with by the local people and officially by the volunteer forces and no doubt valuable lessons were learnt and shared among the army as the reports filtered through the chain of command. It also showed how if the French had been serious about an invasion and had sent a larger army in a series of small fleets so as not to draw undue attention to a possible invasion then a serious amount of damage could have been done. As it was, the stupidity of the French soldiers in eating poorly and drinking profusely made the job of the militia force that much easier.

The part played by the volunteers was also recognised when, in 1853, on the verge of the Crimean War, Lord Palmerston conferred upon the Pembroke Yeomanry the battle honour 'Fishguard'. This regiment therefore has the unique honour of being the only regiment in the British Army, regular or territorial, that bears a battle honour for an engagement on British soil, and it was also the first battle honour to be awarded to a volunteer unit. Fishguard is one of the places in Wales where a battle was fought and where the local people have ensured that its importance will be preserved so that both local people and visitors can see for themselves what happened just over 200 years ago. There is a small museum in the local library, which houses the unique 200th anniversary tapestry, which tells in embroidery the events of February 1797. There is ample parking at all the sites connected with the battle around the town, as well as up at the 'old fort'

Goodwick Sands, where the Légion Noire filed in to surrender.

and on Goodwick Sands, where the French surrendered. There are information boards and signs at all the sites to inform people as to what happened where they are currently standing. The areas around the headland where the French camped are less easily found, and due to the narrowness of the country lanes parking places can be found but are limited, but Carregwastad Point where the French landed can be reached and the bay seen from the coastal path.

Conclusion

From the way that the people around Fishguard reacted to being invaded, one can see that the same spirit of defiance and the ability to rise and defend themselves against a common enemy was still in the hearts of the people, where it had been for over 1,000 years. They did not wait for the official defence to arrive: they took matters into their own hands, a spirit that would be rekindled when the next major threat of invasion came in 1940. Fishguard is a strange military encounter as the ability of the French to fight was totally undermined by their own ill disciple and lack of professionalism, which led to their incapacity, in some cases through their drunkenness and in others through illness. Meanwhile, the amateur local levies showed a resolve and steadfastness in the face of being heavily outnumbered by what should have been a ruthless enemy. The invasion tested the resolve of the Welsh people at a time when rebellion had occurred in America in 1776, and again in France in 1789. Rebellion had also broken out just across the sea in Ireland and was happening even while the action at Fishguard was taking place. The reason for the lack of desire for a revolution in Britain is that she had had her own series of revolutions in the seventeenth century and now she was past those dark days of bitter civil war which were still gripping other nations. The prosperity of Britain was founded on an ever-growing empire, and Wales was not a colony but a part of that empire, and Welsh people were helping to forge that empire. So when Welsh people compared themselves to the people in other nations as they heard tales of the revolutions in both France and Ireland, they would look to their own lot and be proud that their land had been stable at this point in time for over fifty years. More importantly, she would remain stable and her people were ultimately prepared to die for that stability.

The Wisdom of an Ancient

The history of the Welsh people has been one of endurance, descended as they are, since the time of birth of Jesus Christ at the first millennium, as the people nearest to being true Britons. Most probably the oldest Christian people in the world, and emanating perhaps from the Trojans of ancient history, the Welsh in the Dark Ages sat three to a shared meal out of respect for the Holy Trinity; they shared with strangers whatever they had, their food, their clothes, even their beds. Throughout the military invasions from 47 to 1421, the history of Wales is a pattern repeated over and over again where the Welsh people were always fighting to save their lands and their identity from outside control and interference. It is neither the fighting spirit nor the military strategy and tactics of their generals that led to the Welsh being defeated; time and again, the Welsh out-thought their invaders and beat them despite being outnumbered. When the Welsh fought from a position of strength, not in numbers but in the use of the terrain and the weather, they were very difficult to defeat. When they tried to fight in the manner of their opponents, they lost; it was when they stuck to their ways of fighting that they triumphed. Ultimately, like so many conflicts in the distant past, it was not military might that told in the end but economic wealth. It was not the armies that defeated the Welsh but the financial power of Rome, and later England, to build and maintain the centres (forts and castles respectively) that dominated the way of life of the people. The Welsh people could not save their lands from being occupied but through their language and their customs they did preserve their identity while at the same time they were part of what ultimately became the strongest nation on the planet: they were an integral part of Great Britain. Gerald of Wales summed up the tenacity of the Welsh people at the end of his *Descriptio Cambriae*, quoting an old man of Pencader who prophesied on Wales to King Henry II as follows:

> This nation, O King, may now, as in former times, be harassed, and in a great measure weakened and destroyed by your and other powers, and it will also

prevail by its laudable exertions, but it can never be totally subdued through the wrath of man, unless the wrath of God shall concur. Nor do I think that any other nation than this of Wales, nor any other language, whatever may hereafter come to pass, shall on the day of severe examination before the Supreme Judge, answer for this corner of the earth.

The Densest Battlesites in Wales

The Welsh border is, by its very name, the place where the Celtic and Roman, Saxon and Briton, Welsh and English armies and, to a certain extent, cultures clashed. Welshpool was classed as the most important town in Wales in early medieval times and the reason was its location, for it was where routes east–west and north–south met and crossed each other. The mighty River Severn was fordable and whatever your commercial business was then Offa's Dyke was a dry route to travel along the border, touting your wares. If, as a general, you wanted to invade Wales then the Severn Valley took you into the centre of the country. Due to its geographical position, Welshpool has by chance become one of the most fought around towns in Britain and there are five battlesites within a 10-mile radius of the town which have been covered in detail within this book. In addition, there are some smaller battles which could be included within the ten-mile catchment, such as that at Welshpool in 1644, which have only been mentioned in passing but would bring the total up even higher, as the map below illustrates.

Future of Welsh Battlesites

All battles have an importance, some more so than others. Fishguard is a unique battle, though it was actually a series of running skirmishes as there was not a full-blown 'battle' as such. Yet the actual invasion attempt makes the site one of the most important places in British, as well as Welsh, history because it was the last time any foreign force managed to land successfully on the British mainland. In this book I could have listed all of the hundreds of battles fought within the boundaries of Wales, but many are the names of sites which can no longer be discerned, names that were first recorded centuries after the event from ancient tales, with very little evidence to provide their location let alone any details as to how many men took part and how the battle was actually fought. Even when battles that I have included, such as Montgomery and Orwein Bridge, have some contemporary source information, it does not mean that the battlesite is easy to find; only when one walks across the potential sites does an examination with a military eye bring into perspective a tangible

Battles around Welshpool

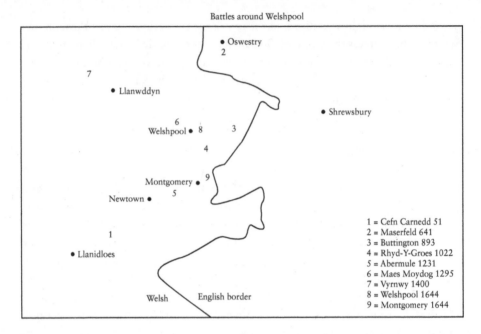

1 = Cefn Carnedd 51
2 = Maserfeld 641
3 = Buttington 893
4 = Rhyd-Y-Groes 1022
5 = Abermule 1231
6 = Maes Moydog 1295
7 = Vyrnwy 1400
8 = Welshpool 1644
9 = Montgomery 1644

location as to where the armies may have deployed or moved. Where there is an element of doubt I have given my interpretation, and the reasons behind that interpretation, and I hope that the reader will understand if they visit the site why I may have gone with one location over another. In the case of a battlesite like Pilleth, the site and the movements are much easier to interpret, especially as the land has changed so little over the last 600 years. I have included twenty-four of the most important Welsh battles in this book and I hope that the reader will agree that in the majority of cases many of them were lost, and not all for the same reasons. I hope that I have now brought these fascinating episodes of Welsh history to life for the reader; with the relevant maps and the very latest photographs, the information is as accurate as can be at the time of going to print. I am optimistic that the significance of these sites will not be as 'lost' in the future and that this may lead to more recognition for the struggles that created the nation which is an integral part of the United Kingdom today, but still with its own wonderful and cherished identity. In time I hope that some of these Welsh battlesites will come to have the same attention as Bosworth (1485) and Shrewsbury (1403), Killiecrankie (1689) and Culloden (1746) do for England and Scotland respectively and at the very least they will all have some commemorative plaque and some information signboards as to their importance, as Crogen, Pilleth and Orwein Bridge currently do.

Bibliography

As the reader will appreciate, the information available on this period varies greatly; some of the later battles are documented in great detail and yet different historians still put different interpretations upon those details and come up with a different scenario for where an army was deployed or in some cases a different axis, deciding that the battle was fought east–west and not north–south. I have based my interpretation of these battles not only on all of the written material available, both original material and the latter-day interpretations, but also on two other important things. The first is the site evidence, where a visit and an examination of the relevant topography allows me to see for myself where the relevant action was most likely to have taken place, allowing of course for urbanisation or industrialisation such as quarrying or mining where applicable. The second thing is to use my knowledge of how the army would have fought. What was its composition at that time? Was it missile armed troops who kept their distance and caused casualties through shooting or were they armed and armoured for getting into close contact and wearing down their enemy by brute force? So all that information has been blended with the information gleaned from the sources below to arrive at the accounts you have read. I have not listed specific websites where one has been used to try and confirm some minor detail unless they are particularly relevant to the text and then, for example, a BBC site may be listed. Finally, there are what I term the local 'traditions', which are often quoted on local history and village websites as gospel, but there are simply so many similar 'stories' for some battles and the problem encountered on many of them is the lack of a reference for their source data, and therefore it is impossible to quote them. However, local knowledge is sometimes fascinating when one is on a battlesite; for instance, when a retired farmer can tell you where a battle was fought or where the original track of a Roman road went across their land, having been trodden for time out of mind; they had no direct source material that they could refer to, it was simply handed down to them from their fathers and from their forefathers before them with the 'it has always been said that,' and the 'so you know the dead, they were buried over there!' Sometimes such information is priceless.

Select Bibliography

Alcock, L., *Arthur's Britain,* The Penguin Press, 1971.
Ashe, G., L. Alcock, C. A. R. Radford and P. Ratz, *The Quest for Arthur's Britain,* Book Club Associates, 1972.
Ashe, G., *A Traveller's Guide to Arthurian Britain,* Gothic Image Publications, 1997.

Barber, C., *In Search of Owain Glyndwr*, Blorenge Books, new edition, 2004.

Barker, P., *Army Lists Book One – 3000 BC–75 AD*, Wargames Research Group, 1981.

Barker, P., *Army Lists Book Two – 55 BC–1000 AD*, Wargames Research Group, 1982.

Barker, P., *Army Lists Book Three, Armies Originating after 1000 AD*, Wargames Research Group, 1982.

Bartlett, C., *English Longbowman 1330–1515*, Osprey Publishing, 1995.

Bennett, M., *Campaigns of the Norman Conquest*, Osprey Publishing Ltd, 2001.

Blake, S. and S. Lloyd, *The Keys to Avalon*, Rider, 2003.

Bradbury, J., *Medieval Warfare*, Routledge, 2004.

Brooks, R., *Cassell's Battlefields of Britain and Ireland*, Weidenfeld & Nicholson, 2005.

Brough, G. J., *Glyn Dwr's War*, Wales Books Glyndwr Publishing, 2002.

Burne, A. H., *The Battlefields of England*, Greenhill Books, 1996.

Call to Arms, *Re-enacting Directory 2004/5*, Beta Print, 2004.

Caradoc of Llancarvan, *Brut Y Tywysogion: Or, The Chronicle of the Princes*, Edited by John Willliams, Longdon, Green Longman & Roberts, 1860.

Carter, G., *Outlines of English History*, Wardlock, 1984.

Castleton, R., *King Arthur*, Routledge, 2000.

Cunliffe, B., *Iron Age Communities in Britain*, Book Club Associates, 1975.

Davis, P. R., *The Forgotten Castles of Wales*, Logaston Press, 2011.

Denny, N. and J. Filmer-Sankey, *The Bayeux Tapestry: The Norman Conquest 1066*, Collins, 1994.

Durham, K., *Viking Longship*, New Vanguard 47, Osprey Publishing Ltd, 2002.

Fairbairn, N., *A Traveller's Guide to the Battlefields of Britain*, Evans Brothers, 1983.

Falkus, M. and J. Gillingham, *Historical Atlas of Britain*, Book Club Associates, 1981.

Forte, A., R. Oram and F. Pederson, *Viking Empires*, Cambridge University Press, 2005.

Fossier, R., *The Middle Ages, The Cambridge Illustrated History I 350–950*, Cambridge University Press, 1989.

Fox, A., *South West England 3,500 BC–AD 600*, David & Charles, 1973.

Frere, S., *Britannia*, Book Club Associates, 1987.

Froud, C., *Imperial Warfare Army Lists 130 BC–471 AD, The Third Book of Hosts*, Colin Froud, 1994.

Froud, C., *Dark Age Warfare Army Lists 475–1000 AD, The Fourth Book of Hosts*, Colin Froud, 1998.

Froud, C., *Medieval Warfare Army Lists 1300 AD–1500 AD, The Sixth Book of Hosts*, Colin Froud, 1999.

Funcken, L. and F., *Arms and Uniforms: Ancient Egypt to the 18th Century*, Wardlock, 1972.

Gater, D., *The Battles of Wales*, Gwasg Garreg Gwalch, 1991.

Gidlow, C., *The Reign of Arthur*, Sutton Publishing Ltd, 2004.

Gilbert, A., A. Wilson and B. Blackett, *The Holy Kingdom*, Bantam Press, 1998.

Gildas, *On the Ruin of Britain*, Translated by J. A. Giles, Serenity Publishers, 2009.

Graham-Campbell, J. and D. Kidd, *The Vikings*, Book Club Associates, 1980.

Gravett, C., *Hastings 1066*, Campaign 13, Osprey Publishing Ltd, 1992.

Gravett, C., *Norman Knight 950–1204*, Warrior 1, Osprey Publishing Ltd, 1993.

Gravett, C., *The Castles of Edward I, 1277–1307*, Fortress 64, Osprey Publishing Ltd, 2007.

Gregory, D., *Wales Before 1536, A Guide*, Gwasg Garreg Gwalch.

Griffith, P., *The Viking Art of War*, Greenhill Books, 1995.

Guest, K. and D., *British Battles*, Harper Collins, 1996.

Gummere, F., *Beowulf*, The Harvard Classics, Volume 49, Collier & Son, 1910.

Hackett, M., *As Told in the Great Hall, A Wargamer's Guide to Dark Age Britain*, Amberley Publishing, 2013.

Hackett, M., *Lost Battlefields of Britain*, Sutton Publishing Ltd, 2005.

Hallam, Dr E., *The Plantagenet Chronicles*, Book Club Associates, 1986.

Harrison, I., *British Battles*, Harper Collins, 2002.

Harrison, M., *Anglo-Saxon Thegn 449–1066 AD*, Warrior 5, Osprey Publishing Ltd, 1993.

Harrison, M., *Viking Hersir, 793–1066 AD*, Warrior 3, Osprey Publishing Ltd, 1993.

Haywood, J., *The Atlas of Past Times*, Sandcastle Books, 2006.

Head, V., *Hereward*, Alan Sutton Publishing Ltd, 1995.

Heath, I., *Armies of the Dark Ages*, Wargames Research Group, 1980.

Heath, I., *The Vikings*, Elite 3, Osprey Publishing Ltd, 1985.

Herm, R., *The Celts*, Book Club Associates, 1976.

Higham, N. J., *The Death of Anglo-Saxon England*, Sutton Publishing Ltd, 1997.

Hinde, T., *The Doomsday Book, England's Heritage Then and Now*, Century Hutchinson Limited, 1985.

Hobbes, N., *Essential Militaria*, Atlantic Books, 2003.

Holmes, M., *King Arthur: A Military History*, Blandford, 1996.

Hooper, N. and M. Bennett, *Cambridge Illustrated Atlas of Warfare in the Middle Ages 768–1487*, Cambridge University Press, 1996.

Horspool, D., *The English Rebel*, Viking/Penguin Group, 2009.

Howe, G. M., *Man, Environment and Disease in Britain*, Harper & Row Inc., 1972.

Humble, R., *The Saxon Kings*, Book Club Associates, 1983.

Jackson, R., *Dark Age Britain: What to See and Where*, Book Club Associates, 1984.

Johnson, S., *Later Roman Britain*, Book Club Associates, 1980.

Keys, D., *Catastrophe*, Book Club Associates, 1999.

Kightly, C., *A Mirror of Medieval Wales*, CADW, 1988.

Kightly, C., *Folk Heroes of Britain*, Thames & Hudson Ltd, 1982.

Kinross, J., *Discovering Battlefields of England and Scotland*, Shire, 2004.

Kinross, J., *Walking and Exploring the Battlefields of Britain*, David & Charles, 1988.

Konstam, A., *The Forts of Celtic Britain*, Fortress 50, Osprey Publishing Ltd, 2006.

Konstam, A., *British Forts in the Age of Arthur*, Fortress 80, Osprey Publishing Ltd, 2008.

Konstam, A., *Historical Atlas of the Celtic World*, Mercury Books, 2003.

Laing, L., *Celtic Britain*, Book Club Associates, 1979.

Laing, L. and J. Laing, *Anglo-Saxon England*, Routledge & Kegan Paul, 1979.

Laing, L. and J. Laing, *Medieval Britain*, Book Club Associates, 1996.

Laing, L. and J. Laing, *The Origins of Britain*, Book Club Associates, 1980.

Lavelle, R., *Fortifications in Wessex c. 800–1066*, Fortress 14, Osprey Publishing Ltd, 2003.

Lawson, M. K., *The Battle of Hastings 1066*, Tempus Publishing Ltd, 2002.

Leahy, K. and R. Bland, *The Staffordshire Hoard*, British Museum Press, 2009.

Le Goff, J., *The Medieval World*, Parkgate Books Limited, 1997.

Lindsay, J., *The Normans and Their World*, Purnell Book Services Ltd, 1977.

Loades, M., *The Longbow*, Osprey Publishing, 2013.

Lloyd, D. M. and E. M. Lloyd, *A Book of Wales*, Collins, 1954.

Lloyd, J. E., *A History of Wales, From the Norman Conquest to the Edwardian Conquest*, Barnes & Noble Books, 2002.

Low, S. J. and F. S. Pulling, *The Dictionary of English History*, Cassell & Co., 1911.

Main, L., *In the Footsteps of King Arthur*, Western Mail & Echo Ltd, 1995.

Marren, P., *Grampian Battlefields*, Aberdeen University Press, 1990.

Marsden, J., *Northanhymbre Saga*, Book Club Associates, 1992.

Morris, R. M., *Gerald of Wales*, University of Wales Press, 1987.

McLynn, F., *1066: The Year of the Three Battles*, Book Club Associates, 1999.

Nennius, *Historia Brittonum*, Translated by J. A. Giles, Dodo Press, no date.

Newton, P., *Gwenllian, The Welsh Warrior Princess*, Gwasg Carreg Gwalch, 2002.

Nicholson, T. R., *The Vikings*, Senate Publishing, 1999.

Nicolle, D., *Arthur and the Anglo-Saxon Wars*, Men-at-Arms 154, Osprey Publishing Ltd, 1984.

Nicolle, D., *European Medieval Tactics (1)* Elite 185, Osprey Publishing Ltd, 2011.

Nicolle, D., *European Medieval Tactics (2)* Elite 189, Osprey Publishing Ltd, 2012.

Nicolle, D., *Medieval Warfare Source Book*, Brockhampton Press, 1999.

Nicolle, D., *The Age of Charlemagne*, Men-at-Arms 150, Osprey Publishing Ltd, 1984.

Nicolle, D., *The Normans*, Elite 3, Osprey Publishing Ltd, 1987.

Norman, A. V. B. and D. Pottinger, *English Weapons & Warfare 449–1060*, Arms & Armour Press, 1979.

Norris, J., *Gunpowder Artillery 1600–1700*, The Crowood Press, 2005.

Oman, Sir C., *The Art of War in the Middle Ages Volume One: 378–1278 A.D.*, Greenhill Books, 1991.

Philips, G. and M. Keatman, *King Arthur: The True Story*, Century, 1992.

Rayner, M., *English Battlefields*, Tempus Publishing Ltd, 2004.

Reid, H., *Arthur the Dragon King*, Headline Book Publishing, 2001.

Richards, J., *Blood of the Vikings*, Hodder & Stoughton, 2001.

Richardson, J., *The Local Historian's Encyclopaedia*, Historical Publications Ltd, 1986.

Ritchie, A., *Picts*, Edinburgh Stationery Office, 1989.

Rothero, C., *The Scottish and Welsh Wars 1250–1400*, Osprey Men At Arms Series No. 151, 1984.

Rowley, T., *The Welsh Border*, The History Press, 2010.

Rudgley, R., *Barbarians: Secrets of the Dark Ages*, Channel 4 Books, 2002.

Smurthwaite, D., *Battlefields of Britain: The Complete Illustrated Guide*, Mermaid Books, 1984.

Snyder, C., *An Age of Tyrants, Britain and the Britons A.D. 400–600*, Sutton Publishing, 1998.

Stanford, S. C., *The Archaeology of the Welsh Marches*, S. C. Stanford, 1991.

Sutherland, E., *In Search of the Picts*, Constable, 1994.

Tacitus, *The Annals of Imperial Rome*, Book Club Associates, 1990, 1993 revised edition.

Taylor, Dr A. J., *The King's Works in Wales 1277–1330*, HMSO 1974.

Thomas, W. V., *Wales – A History*, Michael Joseph Limited, 1985.

Turvey, R., *Owain Gwynedd, Prince of the Welsh*, Y Lofla Cf, 2013.

Wagner, P., *Pictish Warrior AD 297–841*, Warrior 50, Osprey Publishing Ltd, 2002.

Walker, I., *Harold: The Last Anglo-Saxon King*, Sutton Publishing Ltd, 1997.

Warner, P., *Famous Welsh Battles*, Fontana Collins, 1980.

Watson, M., *Shropshire: An Archaeological Guide*, Shropshire Books, 2002.

Williams, Revd J., *Annales Cambriae*, Longdon, Green Longman & Roberts, 1860.

Williamson, D., *Kings and Queens of Britain*, Webb & Bower, 1991.

Whitelock, D., *The Anglo-Saxon Chronicle*, Eyre & Spottiswode, 1961.

Wise, T., *Saxon, Viking and Norman*, Men-at-Arms 85, Osprey Publishing Ltd, 1979.

Wood, E., *Collins Field Guide to Archaeology in Britain*, Collins, 1972.

Wood, M., *In Search of the Dark Ages*, BBC, 1981.

Index